EDUCATIONAL ENTREPRENEURSHIP TODAY

THE EDUCATIONAL INNOVATIONS SERIES

The Educational Innovations series explores a wide range of current school reform efforts. Individual volumes examine entrepreneurial efforts and unorthodox approaches, highlighting reforms that have met with success and strategies that have attracted widespread attention. The series aims to disrupt the status quo and inject new ideas into contemporary education debates.

Series edited by Frederick M. Hess

Other books in this series:

The Strategic Management of Charter Schools
by Peter Frumkin, Bruno V. Manno, and Nell Edgington

Customized Schooling
Edited by Frederick M. Hess and Bruno V. Manno

Bringing School Reform to Scale
by Heather Zavadsky

What Next?
Edited by Mary Cullinane and Frederick M. Hess

Between Public and Private
Edited by Katrina E. Bulkley, Jeffrey R. Henig, and Henry M. Levin

Stretching the School Dollar
Edited by Frederick M. Hess and Eric Osberg

School Turnarounds: The Essential Role of Districts
by Heather Zavadsky

Stretching the Higher Education Dollar
Edited by Andrew P. Kelly and Kevin Carey

Cage-Busting Leadership
by Frederick M. Hess

Teacher Quality 2.0: Toward a New Era in Education Reform
Edited by Frederick M. Hess and Michael Q. McShane

Reinventing Financial Aid: Charting a New Course to College Affordability
Edited by Andrew P. Kelly and Sara Goldrick-Rab

The Cage-Busting Teacher
by Frederick M. Hess

Failing Our Brightest Kids: The Global Challenge of Educating High-Ability Students
by Chester E. Finn, Jr. and Brandon L. Wright

The New Education Philanthropy: Politics, Policy, and Reform
Edited by Frederick M. Hess and Jeffrey R. Henig

EDUCATIONAL ENTREPRENEURSHIP TODAY

FREDERICK M. HESS
MICHAEL Q. MCSHANE

Editors

Harvard Education Press
Cambridge, Massachusetts

Library of Congress Control Number 2015955162

Paperback ISBN 978-1-61250-927-3
Library Edition ISBN 978-1-61250-928-0

Published by Harvard Education Press,
an imprint of the Harvard Education Publishing Group

Harvard Education Press
8 Story Street
Cambridge, MA 02138

Cover Design: Ciano Design
Cover Photo: Willie B. Thomas/DigitalVision/Getty Images
The typefaces used in this book are Minion Pro and Myriad Pro

Contents

Introduction   1
    Frederick M. Hess and Michael Q. McShane

1   From Generation to Generation   11
    Fifteen Years of Education Entrepreneurship
    Stacey Childress

2   Carrots, Sticks, and Sermons   35
    How Policy Shapes Educational Entrepreneurship
    Ashley Jochim

3   Tailwinds and Headwinds   53
    Unleashing Entrepreneurial Energy to Transform Education
    John Bailey

4   Barbarians at the Gate?   77
    How Venture Finance Could Support Radical K–12 Innovation
    Dmitri Mehlhorn

5   The View from Abroad   95
    Does American Education Suffer from a Deficit of Innovation?
    Marc S. Tucker

6   But Does It Work?   105
    Evaluating the Fruits of Entrepreneurship
    Jon Fullerton

7   A Matter of Practice   125
    Entrepreneurship in Teaching and Learning
    Elizabeth City

8   **Go Small or Go Home**   143
    Innovation in Schooling
        Matt Candler

9   **Transparency, Authenticity, Civility**   157
    The Prerequisites to Sustainable Entrepreneurship in Education
        John Katzman and Jillian Youngblood

10 **Ten for the Next Ten**   177
    Lessons for the Next Decade
        Ross Baird and Daniel Lautzenheiser

Conclusion: 197
    Entrepreneurship and American Education
        Frederick M. Hess and Michael Q. McShane

Notes   209

Acknowledgments   227

About the Editors   229

About the Contributors   231

Index   237

Introduction

Frederick M. Hess and Michael Q. McShane

THE PAST DECADE OF EDUCATIONAL ENTREPRENEURSHIP

In recent years, high-profile entrepreneurs have helped bring educational entrepreneurship into the national spotlight. Salman Khan was feted on the cover of the November 2012 issue of *Forbes* with the headline "The $1 Trillion Opportunity."[1] His Khan Academy began as a YouTube channel where he taught lessons on everything from mathematics to history to finance. With financial support from the Bill and Melinda Gates Foundation, Google, and several business magnates, Khan was able to build out exercises and a complete learning dashboard to guide students through courses on a wide variety of topics.

And Salman Khan is just one part of the story. In the past decade, both the number of students in charter schools and the number of charter schools themselves have more than doubled, to more than 2 million students in more than 7,000 schools. In 2006, there were 46 KIPP charter schools serving 9,000 kids; in 2016, more than 160 KIPP schools were serving more than 60,000 students. In 2006, Teach For America (TFA) had 5,000 corps members and generated $65 million in operating revenue. In 2016, TFA had over 10,000 corps members teaching over 750,000 students, and was generating more than $300 million in annual revenue. In 2006, the ClassDojo behavior management application was five years away from being created. By 2016, it was being used by more than 35 million parents, students, and teachers. Clever, a login management app founded in 2012 by a trio of twenty-five-year-olds, is now used in one in five schools in the United States.

Other entrepreneurs have failed, many quite publicly. InBloom, a student data warehouse that started with $100 million in funding from the Gates Foundation and the Carnegie Corporation of New York, was scuttled in late 2014 after outcry from student data privacy advocates. About the same time, ConnectEDU went bankrupt, leaving open questions about the status of performance data for 20 million students. The Los Angeles Unified School District's $1 billion contract with Apple—intended to provide iPads to all district students—ended with a federal grand jury subpoenaing procurement records. In short, it hasn't all been roses.

But much of today's educational entrepreneurship is more prosaic than these high-profile successes or failures. Dude Solutions offers SchoolDude, a technology platform for school leaders to automate key tasks like setting up a single calendar, routing work requests to custodial staff or security personnel, and for facilities managers to process inventories of repair parts and cleaning supplies. There is nothing particularly eye-popping about any of this, but it can save a lot of time and money. Investors recognized this and invested $100 million in 2014 to support the venture.[2]

On a much smaller scale is Enriched Schools, a venture designed to help schools find and place substitute teachers, launched in 2012.[3] Founder Andre Feigler reports that the average student in New Orleans spent one year of K–12 schooling in the care of substitute teachers, time that was often effectually wasted due to the quality of the substitute teaching pool. Feigler saw an opportunity to provide a higher-quality pool of substitutes, one that featured more training and individuals with particular skills (including musicians, artists, or poets). Feigler's venture is now widely used by charter schools in New Orleans and is seeking to start up in other cities.

The technology infrastructure available to entrepreneurs has evolved dramatically over the past decade. In 2006, nobody had ever seen an iPhone or an iPad. State-of-the-art education technology was entirely a question of laptop computers and Internet access, and digital textbooks were still regarded as a flight of fancy rather than a practical consideration. Meanwhile, when it came to public policy, no state was using value-added scores to evaluate teachers, the School Improvement Grant program did not exist, and no one had yet imagined the Race to the Top or the Common Core.

The world of educational entrepreneurship has changed—*a lot*—in the past decade. This change has altered things for students, teachers, schools, and entrepreneurs, and the contributors to this volume seek to make sense of how entrepreneurship works today.

WHAT EXACTLY IS AN "ENTREPRENEUR"?

Entrepreneurship is a notoriously slippery concept. Jean-Baptiste Say, the French economist who coined the term two centuries ago, held that an entrepreneur "shifts economic resources out of an area of lower and into an area of higher productivity and greater yield."[4] For our purposes, educational entrepreneurship is understood as *risk-taking behavior intended to boost school productivity or offer new services in a manner that makes a lasting difference for students.*

Entrepreneurs need the opportunity to devise new solutions, the inclination to act, the skills to execute, and the means to turn their handiwork into a lasting venture. Entrepreneurs can exist inside or outside big organizations—but their need for freedom to rethink and reimagine means that they're much more likely to be found outside than in. Our focus is on how they fit in the world of schooling and what it takes to encourage entrepreneurship that delivers more of what we find socially valuable—and less of what we don't.

When the topic of educational entrepreneurship arises, there's a tendency to focus on a handful of entrepreneurial personalities and either celebrate them as heroes or condemn them as enemies of public education. We're interested in the realities of entrepreneurship—in the obstacles, bottlenecks, policy context, lessons learned, and how to think about the value and impact of this kind of behavior. We hope to help readers make sense of educational entrepreneurship today. In the chapters to come, the contributors tackle questions like:

- How do we assess the impact of entrepreneurship on schooling?
- How have policies like the Common Core, charter schooling, Race to the Top, and No Child Left Behind changed the landscape of entrepreneurship?
- How have the politics around "school reform" affected the work of entrepreneurs?
- What role does technology play in fostering entrepreneurship?
- How do entrepreneurs navigate the complex bureaucracies of school districts?
- How do venture capital and other financial considerations shape educational entrepreneurship?

These are the kinds of questions that benefit from careful inquiry, whatever one's feelings about educational entrepreneurship.

WHAT'S THE VALUE OF EDUCATIONAL ENTREPRENEURSHIP?

Educational entrepreneurship isn't everyone's cup of tea. It involves startups, for-profit ventures, major foundations, disruptive changes, and plenty of failed efforts—all of which have attracted criticism. The concerns are fair, even if some of the specific attacks may not be.

But it's also important to keep in mind the underlying rationale for educational entrepreneurship. The entrepreneurial premise is that American education is in need of transformative improvement, and it's easier to promote that kind of change by launching new ventures than by wrestling with the constraints and conventions of established systems. Inventing and launching new solutions inside an old organization is difficult because there are entrenched routines and hierarchies. In new organizations, things can be arranged to support the new model. New ventures can be single-minded in their pursuit of new approaches to learning and teaching and can hire and adopt technology with that in mind. Big, established organizations— whether they are school systems, testing companies, or state departments of education—already have personnel and technology in place.

The promise of entrepreneurship is not about business plans, technological gizmos, or impressive jargon. It's that entrepreneurs tackle stubborn problems with fresh thinking, devise new models and modes of delivery, and then expect to be accountable for the actual results of their various innovations. Unlike the traditional world of K–12, where reform tends to be driven by innovators and advocates telling school systems what else they should be doing—their direct involvement is mostly a matter of consulting and cheerleading—entrepreneurs put themselves and their ideas directly on the line.

If American education were in terrific shape, and the big challenge was to fine-tune the workings of elegant K–12 machinery, it would be more difficult to make the case for entrepreneurship. But there's widespread agreement—even among those who disagree on the methods—that we need more engaging school models, better career and technical education, improved models of teacher preparation, new ways of learning online, and much else. However talented and well-meaning the staff in existing systems are, they have a lot of thickets to fight through in order to reimagine delivery—and limited incentives to do so. That's where entrepreneurship comes in.

THE ENTREPRENEURIAL IMPULSE VERSUS SYSTEM REFORM

American K–12 education is a massive enterprise. It involves more than fifty million students and more than three million teachers, and spends more than $700 billion a year. Public school enrollment in the United States exceeds the *combined* populations of Canada, Finland, Norway, Sweden, and Singapore. Even after a quarter-century of steady growth, charter schools still educate barely 5 percent of the nation's students. Even with hundreds of millions of dollars devoted to scaling a small number of high-quality charter organizations, providers have thus far made only the tiniest dent on the national education landscape. Frustrated by that slow pace, many reformers express an affinity for "system" approaches that will drive improvement more rapidly.

As Marc Tucker, president of the National Center on Education and the Economy, thoughtfully explains in chapter 5, the entrepreneurial impulse and system reform proceed from very different views about the most promising paths to school improvement. System reformers see alignment and coordination as key, understand that careful planning is essential to manage the many elements of a sprawling educational system, and believe that this kind of approach is the only way to ensure that "best practices" are widely utilized and properly adopted.

Those who embrace entrepreneurship see things differently. The entrepreneurial impulse appeals to those distrustful of grand solutions, those who doubt that system reformers can effectively manage all the moving parts, and those who fear that grand system reforms will fail to deliver and also stymie promising alternatives. Entrepreneurs believe that efforts to impose best practices on large, preexisting bureaucratic organizations tends to disappoint—that it is new ventures with a tightly focused sense of mission that are most likely to apply best practices well and to develop new ones.

The appeal of educational entrepreneurship depends in large part on how one thinks about the promise of system reform. This good-faith, thoughtful disagreement about how best to serve students can get too easily get lost amid heated public debates or brushed aside by those who insist that system solutions and the entrepreneurial impulse are wholly compatible. Funders, policymakers, and advocates frequently seek to wish this tension away by offering up homilies about "experimentation" and "innovation" and explaining that the goal is simply to use those entrepreneurial efforts to inform system solutions. There's a lot to that and it's certainly possible for the two to work in tandem.

It is also the case, however, that system reform and the entrepreneurial impulse ultimately reflect two different ways to think about school improvement. That means there are times when decisions around accountability, regulation, school funding, and much else will either reflect the dictates of system reform *or* of entrepreneurship. As the contributors will make clear in the chapters ahead, there are times when it has to be one or the other. When we don't think about the whys and hows of entrepreneurship, it can be easy to make decisions that unintentionally squelch entrepreneurial improvement.

THE FORCES SHAPING ENTREPRENEURSHIP

Observing that entrepreneurial activity *can* make a big difference is not to say that it *will*. The impact of entrepreneurship depends on a lot more than the entrepreneurs themselves. A number of forces shape the kinds of ventures that entrepreneurs launch, the nature of their development, and their prospects for success. After all, entrepreneurs succeed only if there's an appetite for what they're offering, if they have a chance to prove their worth, and if they can access the resources they need to have a chance. For instance, even if entrepreneurs have a plan to develop phenomenal programs for teaching Mandarin or civics, they need schools or parents to be interested—or else they won't make it very far.

Three topics in particular—incentives, politics, and money—will come up repeatedly over the course of this volume.

Incentives

It matters a lot what schools or parents are willing to pay for. Entrepreneurs will only create the things that they are encouraged and rewarded for creating. An overwhelming focus on reading and math performance has tended to reward certain kinds of solutions, while a web of state and federal regulations has tended to discourage entrepreneurial ventures from offering innovative approaches to special education or challenging entrenched textbook and assessment companies.

Politics

Low-performing schools and systems are where reformers, policymakers, and community members are most inclined to demand something different—and, consequently, where entrepreneurs are most likely to find openings. This means that entrepreneurs are disproportionately serving the nation's most vulnerable students, which has led to extraordinary tensions in cities like New Orleans and Newark. How entrepreneurs manage those tensions and how they go about serving broader populations are critical in understanding the impact and viability of the entrepreneurial sector.

Money

Entrepreneurs need resources in order to succeed. Yet the vast majority of K–12 spending in the United States flows to school districts, with the majority of that $700 billion per year going to compensation for district employees.[5] Those dollars that are paid to vendors typically flow through complex, bureaucratic procurement systems—giving a big advantage to giant companies that have the manpower and expertise to negotiate the system. This also means that there is precious little funding available for new ventures seeking to develop unproven models. This challenge has created a major role for foundations and given them outsized influence over the direction of entrepreneurial activity. Where and how future ventures will find funding determines the shape of the sector.

ENTREPRENEURSHIP IS A MIND-SET, NOT A BADGE

Here's the irony of entrepreneurship: every big, frustrating corporate bureaucracy was, once upon a time, an entrepreneurial venture. Every big, frustrating public bureaucracy was once a small, scrappy agency. Over time, as organizations thrive, they begin to change, morphing from entrepreneurial upstarts to entrenched members of the status quo.

Once organizations become part of the established order, the messiness of the entrepreneurial impulse can start to feel unnecessary and distracting. The insurgent retailer or tech firm that wants room to run in its early years will eventually view the noisy, free-for-all of unfettered competition not as a spur, but as a nuisance. This is the circle of entrepreneurial life. It means that embracing the entrepreneurial impulse is not a question of celebrating particular ventures—especially those of yesterday's successful entrepreneurs—but of paying attention to the conditions that allow tomorrow's entrepreneurial problem-solvers to emerge.

This tension is on full display in charter schooling. After a quarter-century, high-performing charter schools and the foundations that support them think they've cracked the code of best practices. Meanwhile, lots of charters have floundered, complicating things for the sector in terms of public relations and politics. Thus, there's an understandable tendency in the charter establishment to view a lot of the messiness and failures of brand-new start-ups as bad news, and to instead focus primarily on growing the established, successful charters.

Those who think this way are certainly not *wrong*. It's normal enough and perfectly reasonable to want to close the door behind you once you've entered the club—to make sure the riff-raff doesn't squeeze in. There is, however, a failure to recognize just how this kind of mind-set can stymie the emergence of schools that might be pioneering models for using talent and technology in fundamentally different and more productive ways. After all, today's high-performing charter schools tend to look remarkably like their district counterparts—just with improved recruiting, longer hours, heightened discipline, and strong cultures. The next frontier is to seek the emergence of schools that more fundamentally reimagine teaching and learning. (There's also a failure to acknowledge how closely this tack mirrors the way school districts tried to close the door on today's high-performing charter schools ten or twenty years ago.)

In any event, the goal of this book is to understand educational entrepreneurship today, how it works, and how it might help promote great teaching and learning. The intent is decidedly not to celebrate entrepreneurs, much less to throw laurels at any particular venture.

THE BOOK FROM HERE

Taken together, the contributors offer a rich, multifaceted look at educational entrepreneurship today. They offer hard-learned lessons, lay out the strengths and weaknesses of the entrepreneurial imperative when it comes to schooling, and provide concrete advice on what it will take if schooling is to reap more benefits from entrepreneurial activity.

Stacey Childress, CEO of NewSchools Venture Fund, kicks things off in chapter 1 by taking stock of the last decade of educational entrepreneurship and framing the major trends that have shaped today's entrepreneurial environment. From the public impulse driving young social entrepreneurs in the wake of September 11 to the pipeline of talent that organizations like Teach for America have created, she walks through the human capital, financial, and social drivers of the skyrocketing entrepreneurial sector. In chapter 2, Ashley Jochim of the University of Washington's Center on Reinventing Public Education maps the policy landscape, looks at how the Obama-era reforms regarding charter schooling, the Common Core, teacher evaluation, and school accountability have both encouraged and stymied educational entrepreneurship. All of these reforms have focused a great deal of attention on the performance on standardized reading and math exams, which have both aided entrepreneurs by creating a common measuring stick by which ventures can be evaluated and compared and at the same time thwarted entrepreneurs whose schools or tools don't fit neatly into a box that can be judged by test scores. In chapter 3, John Bailey, vice president of policy and executive director of Digital Learning Now!, talks about the complex relationship of technology and education, and how it's distinct from the role of technology in other sectors.

In chapter 4, Dmitri Mehlhorn, a partner with the venture capital firm Vidinovo, talks money, addressing the role of venture capital and why so little of that kind of investment flows into K–12. He highlights how the world of venture capital operates under fundamentally different assumptions than our education system traditionally has. Many funded ventures fail, but those ventures that have succeeded have transformed industries and the lives of the consumers who use them. While it is impractical and frankly unwise to try and design a school system that features the disruption and churn of the venture capital ecosystem, some of the lessons learned around innovation and risk taking can apply to education reform. Marc Tucker, president and CEO of the National Center on Education and the Economy, offers up a critical perspective on the whole question of educational entrepreneurship in chapter 5, cautioning that the entrepreneurial impulse, whatever its surface appeal, is more likely to hinder educational improvement than to hasten it. In chapter 6, Jon Fullerton, director of the Center for Education Policy Research at Harvard University, asks the crucial but slippery question, "How do we know if entrepreneurial ventures are actually helping?" He argues that we are not nearly as close as we think we might be in finding the ultimate measure of success: *fit*. How well does a particular school or particular app or particular teacher work for a particular student? The more tools we create, the more important that measure becomes. In chapter 7, Harvard University's Elizabeth City explores how entrepreneurship can play out in schools and classrooms. Most importantly, she echoes much of the macro-level conversation about the forces that drive entrepreneurialism and how they play out in classrooms across the country. Great teachers "fail forward" and encourage their students to do so as well, trying new things, experimenting with new systems, and learning when things don't turn out as planned. Entrepreneurial ventures that hope to improve the day-to-day lives of students and teachers need to foster this kind of behavior, not thwart it.

Chapters 8 through 10 feature tales from on the ground. In chapter 8, Matt Candler, founder and CEO of New Orleans's 4.0 schools discusses lessons learned and the merits of "tiny schools." He urges those interested in promoting educational entrepreneurship and innovation to think about making many small bets instead of a few large ones, as we simply don't know what is going to succeed and what is going to fail. In chapter 9, John Katzman, founder of Princeton Review, 2U, and Noodle and Jillian Youngblood of Noodle sketch a new model of the education venture, a dual-bottom-line "E Corp," designed to both make money and serve the broader community. And in chapter 10, Ross Baird, founder of Village Capital, and Daniel Lautzenheiser of the Boston Consulting Group write about ten lessons they've learned about education entrepreneurship and how it will transform the next decade.

Ultimately, much contemporary debate about educational entrepreneurship tends to miss the point. The measuring stick that matters—namely, *is this good for kids?*—often gets lost amid the heated rhetoric. The most important thing about successful entrepreneurs is that they are solving problems that others haven't solved before, from the best use of school facilities to ways to link children learning a new language to tutors across the globe. This volume is an attempt to better understand when and why that happens, the price of success, and what it would take to create a world in which dynamic problem-solving is the norm. We close the volume by returning to these key themes, highlighting points of tension, and considering what the entrepreneurial impulse ultimately means for education. With that, let's get started.

From Generation to Generation

Fifteen Years of Education Entrepreneurship

Stacey Childress

O ver the last twenty-five years, education entrepreneurs have launched and scaled organizations focused on improving the K–12 public education system in the United States. After a decade of bold but relatively small efforts, entrepreneurial activity heated up around the new millennium and accelerated for the next fifteen years. Private schools and charities that work with children have been around since America's earliest days, but the activities over this period have been distinctive. The new entrepreneurs work *outside* the public school bureaucracy while aiming to improve the results *inside* it.

As chief executive officer of NewSchools Venture Fund, I am part of a team that distributes philanthropic grants to entrepreneurial schools and to organizations that build tools and services to support such schools. We also make seed-stage equity investments in for-profit education technology companies through our affiliate, NewSchools Capital. Before joining NewSchools, I spent four years at the Gates Foundation leading the K–12 next-generation learning team. Over that time, we granted more than $200 million to innovative schools and to the tools and conditions they needed to be successful. I joined Gates from the faculty of Harvard Business School, where I had the privilege of writing and teaching about education entrepreneurship for several years. These experiences have given me a front-row seat to the phenomenon for fifteen years, observing and trying to make sense of the entrepreneurial activity discussed in this chapter.

What have education entrepreneurs been up to in the United States since the turn of the century? Though their efforts are varied and widespread, the majority of entrepreneurial activity has taken place in three broad categories—schools, tools, and people. This includes creating charter schools, developing tools and services to support students and teachers, and preparing teachers and leaders for the education system. This chapter provides a brief background of the nature of education entrepreneurs and entrepreneurship, then describes and analyzes each category before highlighting the opportunities that exist today given the work of education entrepreneurs over the last fifteen years.

WHO ARE EDUCATION ENTREPRENEURS?

The vast majority of people who have become education entrepreneurs share a number of attributes. They are young—most start their first organization in their twenties and early thirties. They are well-educated, usually having attended an elite university for undergraduate or graduate studies, often both. They are analytical, are market- and business-minded, and exhibit missionary zeal for the problem they are trying to solve and their particular solution or theory of change for fixing it.

The first notable education entrepreneur in this tradition is Wendy Kopp, who started Teach For America (TFA) as she was graduating from Princeton in 1989. TFA places high-performing college graduates as a corps of teachers in high-needs schools for two-year assignments. School districts agree to hire some number of corps members each year and pay their salaries as they would any new teacher. Twenty-five years later, in 2014, more than fifty thousand young people applied for approximately five thousand teaching spots. By then, TFA had reached more than six hundred thousand K–12 students, most of whom were low-income, and had more than thirty-seven thousand alumni who had spent at least two years in a classroom.[1]

This alumni network has proven to be an important driver of education entrepreneurship. In a 2011 study, education scholars Monica Higgins and Frederick M. Hess found that of the forty-nine top education reform organizations launched since 1989, 15 percent were founded by TFA alumni.[2] The drop-off between TFA and the next-largest pipelines was dramatic: only 4 percent of founders came from significantly larger and older organizations like the public school systems in Chicago, Newark, and San Francisco; the US Department of Education; and McKinsey & Company. Higgins and Hess concluded that TFA was "punching above its weight" in spawning entrepreneurs.

For instance, in 1994 Mike Feinberg and Dave Levin launched the Knowledge Is Power Program (KIPP) after serving together as TFA corps members in Houston. For five years, they each ran a single school, one in Houston and one in New York City, but in 2000 they began growing into a national nonprofit organization. Today there are 162 KIPP schools in twenty states, making KIPP the largest charter school network in the country, nonprofit or for-profit.

WHY DID EDUCATION ENTREPRENEURSHIP ACCELERATE?

Around the year 2000, a critical mass of entrepreneurial talent began launching charter management organizations, working on human capital challenges, and creating technology solutions. Like TFA and KIPP, many of these organizations are nonprofits—organizations such as Aspire Public Schools, New Leaders, TNTP, and Khan Academy—but there are plenty of for-profit, especially in education technology. Notable for-profits include pioneers Wireless Generation (now called Amplify) and Schoolnet, and more recently Newsela, LearnZillion, BrightBytes, and Schoolzilla.[3] Though they do a range of things, education entrepreneurs often share a common cause: reducing the achievement gaps between low-income and more affluent students, as well as between US students and those in higher-performing countries.

Four factors combined to accelerate entrepreneurial activity around the turn of the century:

Bipartisan support for policy initiatives focused on closing the achievement gap. The policy design of the federal No Child Left Behind (NCLB) law in 2001 and its subsequent implementation serve as a prime example of political alignment. NCLB was championed by both President George W. Bush and Senator Ted Kennedy and included carrots (money) and sticks (consequences) that were favorable to entrepreneurs working to improve outcomes for low-income and minority students. This bipartisan theme extended to the states, where Republican and Democratic governors alike supported statewide exams for math and reading, stronger accountability, and school choice—all components of an entrepreneur-friendly education sector.

Pioneers showing the way to scale. A number of entrepreneurial organizations such as TFA and KIPP had developed replicable programs and business models by 2000, inspiring others to create organizations that could be scaled. Entrepreneurs began to launch with scale in mind, including nonprofits such as Aspire Public Schools and New Leaders for New Schools and for-profits like Wireless Generation, Schoolnet, and National Heritage Academies.

New sources of capital. In the late 1990s and early 2000s, a number of successful business entrepreneurs began to focus their giving on supporting education entrepreneurs. These include the Fisher family, who began supporting KIPP in 1996 and then broadened their giving to other education entrepreneurs in 2000, as well as the Walton family, who established the Walton Family Fse foundation began giving to education in 1992 and became more deeply committed to seeding and scaling charter schools in the early 2000s. Other high-net-worth families interested in education launched new foundations at the turn of the century, such as Eli and Edythe Broad (1999), Michael and Susan Dell (1999), and Bill and Melinda Gates (2000). These new philanthropists were entrepreneurs themselves who had created their wealth by reshaping entire industries with their companies (the Gap; Wal-Mart; KB Homes and SunAmerica; Dell; and Microsoft). They brought to their education philanthropy a bias toward entrepreneurs and innovative operating models that could achieve massive scale. They also understood capital markets and were willing to channel some of their giving through value-added investment funds such as NewSchools Venture Fund and Charter School Growth Fund. These new donors collectively brought around $600 million of new money annually into K–12 education philanthropy.

General rise in interest in social entrepreneurship. After the terrorist attacks of September 11, 2001, many young people craved work with meaning and were often drawn to public service careers. I saw this with my own graduate students in the years following the attacks. Four years later, Hurricane Katrina accelerated this interest, especially in regard to education entrepreneurship. In 2009, *Newsweek* reported on the general trend:

> Like other historical events, 9/11 was a pivotal moment for this generation, clarifying for some their life's mission and purpose. Indeed, a recent survey of college students found that they include the government and groups like the Peace Corps and Teach for America among the top 10 places they'd like to work. Before 9/11, for-profit corporations dominated students' top choices.[4]

Together, these factors deepened the commitment of the pioneering entrepreneurs of the 1990s and attracted a growing number of young people into the sector as founders and senior leaders of entrepreneurial organizations, helping to accelerate their creation and growth over the last fifteen years.

WHAT IS EDUCATION ENTREPRENEURSHIP?

John Doerr, a legendary Silicon Valley venture capitalist and founding member of the NewSchools Venture Fund board, is fond of saying, "Entrepreneurs do more than anyone thought possible with less than anyone thought possible."[5] Doerr possesses a very people-centric view of entrepreneurship. This is in keeping with a rule of thumb in the venture world; though we often say we bet on people and ideas, we are actually betting on people *with* ideas. Our assessment of the team is usually the most important consideration in funding a start-up. Venture investors know ideas will shift over time and the business model might have to change more than once before finding a sweet spot. But the founding team has to make those choices and have the smarts, drive, and risk-bearing mind-set to see it through, or not. In other words, it's all about the people.

Howard Stevenson, a Harvard Business School professor whose scholarship focuses on entrepreneurship, has a slightly different view. He says that entrepreneurship is better described as an activity rather than a type of person or company—the "pursuit of opportunity without regard to the resources currently controlled."[6] This definition is in contrast to administrative behavior, which entails managing for the best possible result within existing resources and constraints. Entrepreneurial behavior is, at its core, identifying an opportunity to create value and then making it happen by mobilizing the necessary resources along the way.

Social entrepreneurs are a particular breed. The late Greg Dees, who held faculty appointments in the business schools at Harvard, Stanford, and Duke, spent his career studying them. Dees asserted that a social entrepreneurs' first priority is the mission at the heart of their enterprise, whether they choose to organize as a nonprofit or for-profit. Just as Joseph Schumpeter called entrepreneurs "change agents of economies," these entrepreneurs are change agents in the social sector. Dees created a useful description that blends personal motives with organizational activities, asserting that social entrepreneurs typically:

- Adopt a mission to create and sustain social value (not just private value)

- Recognize and pursue new opportunities to serve that mission
- Engage in a process of continuous innovation, adaptation, and learning
- Act boldly without being limited by resources currently in hand
- Exhibit heightened accountability to the constituencies served and outcomes created[7]

How should we think about social entrepreneurs working in K–12 education in the United States? Kim Smith and Julie Peterson's 2006 overview of the efforts of education entrepreneurs still hold a decade later. They wrote that in a general sense, entrepreneurs develop a vision and recruit others to it, start new organizations, and believe they can change the way things are done. More specifically, they defined education entrepreneurs as:

> . . . visionary thinkers who create new for-profit or nonprofit organizations from scratch that redefine our sense of what is possible. These organizations stand separate and independent from existing institutions like public school districts and teachers colleges; as such, they and the entrepreneurs who start them have the potential to spark more rapid, dramatic change than might otherwise be created by status quo organizations.[8]

Like all entrepreneurs, those working in education have a higher tolerance for risk than professionals working in the existing system—they are willing to try and fail and be held directly accountable for their choices and actions. Education entrepreneurs are also willing to break the established rules if they see a better way to create results. This combined risk-bearing and rule-breaking mind-set can lead to new models that shift beliefs about what is possible, and new policies and arrangements that allow their breakthroughs to create change in the larger system.

As noted, though education entrepreneurs pursue a variety of opportunities, they tend to focus on three areas—schools, tools, and people. Below, I analyze and discuss each area in depth.

CREATING AND DEVELOPING NEW SCHOOLS

In 1991, Minnesota passed the nation's first charter school law and then opened the first charter the following year. States continued to pass laws authorizing charter schools throughout the 1990s, but rapid growth didn't begin until 2000. In fact, student enrollment in charter schools doubled three times between 2000 and 2014. By 2014, 6,440 charter schools served 2.5 million students, or about 5 percent of public school students in the United States.[9]

For most of the first decade of charter school entrepreneurship, local groups used the laws to open up stand-alone schools in their communities to provide either more flexibility for principals and teachers to create school environments they preferred, or more choice for families by creating an alternative to the nearby district school.

Then, beginning in the late 1990s, a group of school operators, funders, and thought leaders began focusing on "market share" to effect system-wide change. This shift was based on the theory that if charter schools in a given city served around 20 percent of the market (as defined by total public school students), it would create a tipping point for better performance in the local district overall. Those running the school district would have to copy what the charters were doing or create better approaches in order to retain their students and continue to receive sufficient public funding to keep their operations afloat. Figure 1.1 shows the thirty-two cities that had the 20 percent market threshold by 2014.

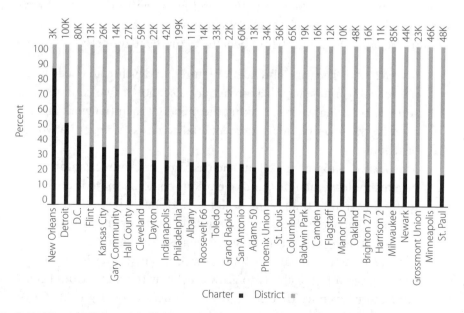

FIGURE 1.1   Cities with Charter Market Share At or Above 20 Percent
Source: National Alliance for Public Charter Schools.

The growth of charter schools and the increasing number of cities with significant market share was driven by four factors:

- *Rise of multisite networks* known as education management organizations (EMOs) and charter management organizations (CMOs)
- *Development of a more organized capital market* for charter creation and growth
- *Charter authorizers focused on scale* and, in some states, on quality
- *State takeovers* and other alternative governance structures in distressed districts such as New Orleans, Detroit, and Philadelphia

The first two factors, driven primarily by entrepreneurs rather than policymakers, are described in detail below.

The Rise of Multisite School Networks

Beginning in the mid-1990s, entrepreneurs established systems or networks of charter schools. Some were launched and managed by a single entity, others were more loosely affiliated but shared a brand and instructional approach. In 2000, less than 1 percent of all charter schools were part of a multi-unit network; by 2008, that figure had risen to 24 percent, and stood at 40 percent by 2014.[10] Between 2008 and 2014, networks opened new schools at a much faster rate than single-site operators.

Entrepreneurs saw a number of benefits to multisite models:

- *Instructional:* The time and talent required to develop an effective teaching and learning approach for a school or two could be spread across many sites, making the most of the initial work and creating the potential for consistent quality across a bigger network of schools.
- *Managerial:* Support functions such as human resources, information technology, facilities, and operations could be shared across many sites, rather than being designed and staffed by individual schools. Teacher and leader professional development, partnerships, and fundraising could also be shared across the network.
- *Financial:* Instructional and managerial efficiencies would lead to cost savings, and the ability to grow quickly with quality would generate more revenue. This would result in operating margins that would decrease dependence on philanthropy for nonprofit operators and allow for-profit operators to generate returns for their investors.

In the for-profit segment, a crop of entrepreneurs launched EMOs that managed district schools under contract and launched and ran charter schools. The business case for multisite, for-profit school operators relied on realizing the three benefits described above.

In the mid- to late 1990s, pioneering EMOs such as Edison Schools (now Edison Learning), Advantage Schools, and Beacon Education Management (which merged with Chancellor Academies to become Chancellor Beacon Academies in 2002) established the business model still largely followed by for-profit school operators: running public schools as a contractor to local school districts or securing authorization to start public charter schools. Edison, Advantage, and Chancellor Beacon were ultimately unsuccessful, since their capital structures required them to grow early and rapidly to meet their investors' financial expectations. Unlike the nonprofit KIPP network, which waited five years before growing beyond its initial two successful schools, the first wave of for-profit EMOs sought scale immediately in order to spread corporate fixed costs across many schools, which at best were low-margin businesses. This led to far-flung, unwieldy geographic footprints for the operators before they had established a reliable set of practices and processes for achieving strong student outcomes. This quality and scale challenge, along with the inherent political challenges of privatizing public-sector jobs and aiming to generate a profit by spending less per pupil than they received from states and districts, resulted in the demise of the first wave EMOs.

A second generation of EMOs learned from these missteps, and a few have proven more durable. They worked out effective instructional models before expanding, and they managed the pace of growth and selection of new markets more deliberately. They also focused mostly on charter schools rather than contracting with districts to operate schools, thereby avoiding some of the political challenges of their predecessors. Among these are National Heritage Academies (NHA) and Charter Schools USA (CSUSA), the two largest for-profit charter operators in the United States. CSUSA (founded in 1998) operates seventy schools in seven states, and NHA (founded in 1995) runs eighty-two schools in nine states. While their aggregate numbers might appear large, for-profit operators still only serve 12 percent of all charter students and less than 1 percent of all public school students.[11]

The nonprofit charter market is larger, more visible, and remains a focus of attention and energy for education entrepreneurs. Charter management organizations (CMOs) are the fastest-growing segment of the overall charter market, gaining 10 percent of market share between 2008 and 2014 by accelerating their growth rate even as growth slowed in the nonprofit single-site and for-profit operator segments.

How did the nonprofit CMO model get started? Don Shalvey, a successful district superintendent in California, founded Aspire Public Schools in 1998 and opened its first school in 1999. He and his cofounders intended to create a multi-school network from the start. Beginning in 2001, Aspire began opening multiple schools each year, so that by 2014, it was running thirty-seven schools in California and Memphis, Tennessee.

Uncommon Schools, an East Coast CMO, took a different approach. Its first school, North Star, opened in Newark in 1997, but remained the only school until 2005, when expansion began under the newly formed Uncommon Schools brand. Through a mix of new school openings and existing high-performing charter schools joining the network, Uncommon Schools grew to forty-two schools in three northeastern states by 2015.

As mentioned earlier in this chapter, the largest network is nonprofit KIPP, which at 162 schools in 2014 was about twice the size of the largest for-profit chain. KIPP has yet another approach to growth, which is to recruit future KIPP school leaders, give them a year of support for school design and launch planning, and then allow them to open new schools under the KIPP brand in regional clusters around the country. The national organization doesn't "own and operate" schools; it supports local and regional entrepreneurs who do.

Emergence of a Capital Market

An organized capital market has helped fuel the charter school sector's growth. Beginning in 1999, NewSchools Venture Fund (NewSchools) helped seed the start up of many schools that became CMOs. Between 1999 and 2014, NewSchools made $175 million in grants to spur the creation of 442 new charter schools that serve 171,261 students.

In 2005, a small group of large donors backed the creation of the Charter School Growth Fund (CSGF) to support the rapid growth of the most successful charter networks. Between 2005 and 2014, CSGF donated $185 million to help its portfolio of forty-eight high-performing CMOs grow from serving around 50,000 students to 160,000 students. Along with supporting CSGF, a few large foundations such as Walton, Dell, and Broad funded the growth of CMOs either directly or through regional intermediaries.

Did Growth in Market Share Lead to Improved Citywide Performance?
The market share theory of change for charters predicts that as the number of charter schools grows in a city, its district schools will improve as well, raising a city's overall performance. In March 2015, a new CREDO (Center for Research on Education Outcomes) study found that black, Hispanic, and low-income students fare much better in urban charter schools than comparable students in non-charters. For example, low-income black students experience the equivalent of nearly three additional months of learning in math and two in reading. Hispanic English language learners experience the equivalent of nearly four months in both subjects.[12] But what, if anything, do we know about the correlation between charter market share and overall performance improvement in a city? In cities such as New Orleans, Washington, DC, and Boston, sustained growth in charter market share is associated with a rise in overall student performance. But cities such as Detroit, Cleveland, and Philadelphia exhibit no such relationship. (See figure 1.2.)

A review of the local context in various cities suggests that at least three of the following five conditions must be in place for significant growth in charter market share to translate into an overall lift in citywide performance.[13]

- *High-quality authorizer:* Cities need a charter authorizer that can recognize quality and maintain a high bar for entry into the system. This helps limit the number of low-quality charters and build credibility for the sector.
- *High performance:* The charter sector as a whole in a city must be high performing in order to create meaningful pressure for change on the system.
- *Empowered, aligned governance:* School boards are often unwilling or unable to make significant change, but district leaders must be empowered to take action in a relatively short time frame. Mayoral control or state takeover mechanisms can help and have supported a combination of market share growth and other factors to help drive improvement. But these governance arrangements are certainly no guarantee, as the struggles in Detroit and Philadelphia illustrate.
- *Effective, stable district leadership:* Superintendents and their teams must be competent and willing to implement meaningful reforms and to manage a healthy and productive tension with the local charter sector. Rapid turnover remains a major challenge in many cities and makes sustained progress challenging.

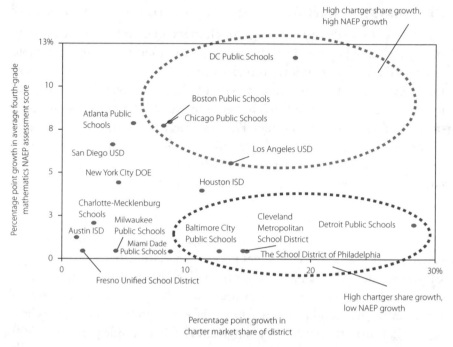

FIGURE 1.2   Growth In Fourth-Grade Mathematics NAEP* Scores (2003–2013) Versus Growth in Market Share (2006–2013) by TUDA** City

Note: Beginning in 2000 results for charter schools are excluded from the TUDA results if they are not included in the school district's Adequate Yearly Progress (AYP) report to the US Department of Education.

* National Assessment of Educational Progress.

** Trial Urban District Assessments.

Source: National Center for Education Statistics; National Alliance for Public Charter Schools.

- *Serious consequences for low performance:* Cities must show they are willing to take action against persistently low performing schools through aggressive turnaround programs or closure. And they must be willing to do it consistently in district schools as well as charters.

ATTRACTING, DEVELOPING, AND SUPPORTING PEOPLE

In the US public school system, 80 percent of all spending is related to people costs—salaries, benefits, and so forth. At the school level, salaries and benefits account for more than 90 percent of spending, so it's not surprising that a significant amount of entrepreneurial activity in K–12 education is targeted at improving the performance of the teachers and leaders. By increasing, the performance of individual educators, schools could generate much better results at the same costs.

This combination of challenge and opportunity attracted the attention of education entrepreneurs from their earliest days, but in the late 1990s and throughout the 2000s, four factors contributed to an acceleration of entrepreneurship focused on human capital.[14]

Policy. In 2001, NCLB federalized the idea of a highly effective teacher, but left it to states to define the term and hold districts accountable for meeting it. For all the inherent flaws and unintended consequences of the mandate, the provision gave new importance to what researchers had long known—teachers matter more for student learning than any other in-school factor. Later, Race to the Top (RTTT) included requirements about teacher evaluation that spurred action in the states, and the adoption of the Common Core State Standards (CCSS) shed light on a gap between the professional practice of most teachers and the level of instruction required to help students meet the new expectations.

Data creation and reporting. Statewide math and reading exams and the associated data they generated gave researchers and policymakers much more information about how students were doing and how this correlated with various teacher characteristics (prep program, years of experience, college major, master's degrees, etc.). This allowed for new analyses of macro trends about teachers across a state or district and gave administrators data to use for strategic questions related to hiring, assignments, differential pay, and a host of other issues.

Research. In 1998, Stanford economist Eric Hanushek and coauthors used publicly available data to quantify the contribution of effective teachers to student learning. The study showed that past performance is a better indicator of future performance than any other factor.[15] One implication of this finding was that it was possible to distinguish between the effectiveness of individual teachers. In a later study, Hanushek and coauthors showed the significant effects on students who have low-performing or high-performing teachers multiple years in a row.[16] Then in 2006, Rob Gordon, Tom Kane, and Doug Staiger published a paper through the Brookings Institution that found no correlation between various preparation paths and teacher performance. Some teachers were high performers and others were low performers, but whether someone attended a traditional teacher prep program or received alternative or emergency certification or went on to earn a master's degree was of no predictive value when it came to effectiveness.[17] The Brookings paper called into serious question the widely held policy assumption that attending an ed school and later completing advanced degrees were contributors to improved performance.

Advocacy. Organizations like the Education Trust and TNTP (formerly The New Teacher Project) turned the wealth of data and academic research into easy-to-understand narratives about a number of issues, including: the importance of teachers; the dearth of rigorous approaches to evaluating their performance; a culture that prioritized treating everyone the same and resulted in all teachers being rated effective or highly effective, even in districts where vast majorities of students were failing to meet minimum standards; and the disproportionate assignment of low-performing teachers to high-needs schools.

These factors mingled to increase attention from state and federal politicians and policymakers along with philanthropists, which in turn attracted entrepreneurs. In general, entrepreneurs focused on improving the quality and preparation of teachers and leaders basically fall into two broad categories: pipeline builders or direct support providers.

Pipeline Builders

As noted at the beginning of this chapter, Wendy Kopp's original aim for Teach For America was to recruit a corps of high-performing college graduates who would teach for two years in high-needs schools. But TFA has become much more than a teacher corps; it's a valuable pipeline. TFA alumni are teachers, but they are also school leaders, district administrators, and state education chiefs. They start education organizations and populate the management ranks of philanthropic foundations and policy shops.

As TFA experienced success, new pipeline builders began to emerge in the late 1990s and accelerated throughout the 2000s. TNTP launched in 1997 to attract professionals from other sectors into teaching, though their focus and activities broadened over time into consulting and knowledge sharing. The Boston Teacher Residency launched in 2003 to better attract and prepare a diverse pool of candidates to teach in Boston Public Schools. Inspired by the medical model of professional preparation, entrepreneurs in a number of cities followed suit over the next decade. Rather than allowing teaching candidates to self-select into teacher credential programs at local colleges and then enter urban classrooms with only coursework and a short student teaching requirement, highly selective residency models attract college graduates and place them for a full year "in residence" at a school with a mentor teacher, along with coursework that usually qualifies them for a master's degree at a local university. As a signal that residency models had become an established alternate pipeline into teaching, Urban Teacher Residencies United (UTRU) launched as a membership organization to help residency programs learn from each other and advocate for shared priorities.

Entrepreneurs were focused on developing leadership pipelines as well. New Leaders launched in 2000 to build a new cadre of school leaders focused on eliminating the achievement gap. Every year, aspiring principals in fifteen cities receive high-quality preparation and support; during its fifteen years the organization has developed 1,600 leaders for schools serving 325,000 students. The Broad Residency launched in 2002 and has groomed 150 leaders from business, policy, and nonprofit backgrounds to take on senior roles in district and charter networks. In early 2015, the Residency was accredited and can now grant master's degrees in education leadership. Broad has also prepared nontraditional superintendents as an alternative to university prep programs and has built a strong alumni network.

Direct Support Providers

On the district support side, a number of organizations launched to compete directly with existing professional development providers in order to increase the capacity of teachers and leaders in districts and charter school networks. More recently, entrepreneurs have launched technology ventures around the need to more effectively connect feedback from teacher evaluation and feedback to professional learning. Examples include companies such as BloomBoard (2010) and nonprofits such as Teaching Channel (2011). It remains unclear if technology-centric models such as these will be able build sustainable professional development businesses. Two illustrative examples of promising programs with potential for scale are the New Teacher Center (NTC) and Relay Graduate School of Education.

NTC was created as part of the University of Santa Cruz in 1997 to focus on improving the induction of new teachers in schools districts. In 2009, NTC became an independent nonprofit under the leadership of Ellen Moir. This coincided with the increased focus on teacher quality from big foundations and the federal government, which resulted in policy changes and increased funding. When NTC began generating data about the increased effectiveness of new teachers who had gone through its induction program as compared with those who had not, demand for its services grew. As a result, NTC has created a tech-enabled version of its program. The organization generates nearly 60 percent of its operating revenue from paying customers and supplements the rest of its costs with philanthropy.

In 2007, Relay launched as a partnership of three northeastern charter school networks: Achievement First, KIPP, and Uncommon Schools. Dissatisfied with the quality of their teaching candidates, these networks decided to prepare their own candidates in coordination with each other. Originally a partnership with Hunter College called Teacher U, Relay now serves teachers from other charters and districts and is intensely focused on tracking and sharing data that demonstrates its graduates' superior performance in achieving results for students. In 2011, the state of New York accredited Relay as an independent college of education, making it the first new institution to get accredited in more than eighty years. Today it operates campuses in five cities across the country and delivers its content around the world through a partnership with online provider Coursera. It also advocates for evaluating the effectiveness of education schools based at least partly on the performance of the students served by the teachers it prepares.

In fact, teacher preparation is shaping up to be a next frontier for entrepreneurs. Growing attention from federal and state policymakers and newly available capital from large philanthropic sources such as the Schusterman and Gates foundations are attracting attention from entrepreneurs looking to break the lock that universities have on preparing teachers.

DEVELOPING AND SCALING NEW TOOLS

In addition to creating new schools and preparing higher-performing teachers and leaders, education entrepreneurs have pursued opportunities to develop better tools and services for students, teachers, and administrators. Just as the market for schools is deeply shaped by the political and regulatory environment at the city, state, and federal levels, so too is the market for instructional materials, assessments, and data platforms.

The combined spending for basal and supplemental materials, instructional software, assessment, and tech hardware segments is around $19 billion annually. Though this is a lot of money in absolute terms, it only accounts for around 3 percent of the total annual spending in K–12 public education. If these budgets were zeroed out—no future spending on servers, data systems, laptops or tablets, instructional software, digital and printed assessments, interactive whiteboards, textbooks or any book at all— and every penny was reallocated to other K–12 spending, there would be enough extra money to run the entire system for only six additional days in a 180-day school year. It's an astonishingly small amount in light of the provocative headlines from the education press and bloggers about private interests in education and union leader talking points about the corporate takeover of public education.

Even so, entrepreneurs flocked to education technology between 2010 and 2014 following a market contraction in the previous decade, as displayed in figure 1.3. In 2009, there were seventeen investments in K–12 companies totaling approximately $91 million; in 2014 there were eighty-five, totaling $643 million. This represents a five-year compound annual growth rate of 48 percent, compared with 19 percent for total US venture capital.[18] In 2014, K–12 ed tech investing surpassed the level of capital flows it had attracted in 2000, at the height of the Internet boom.

Five factors contributed to the growth from 2010 to 2014:

Broader technology trends. Throughout the 2000s, technology devices became cheaper and easier to use, concurrent with a general growth in web services and mobile applications. Even as systemic inequalities in social

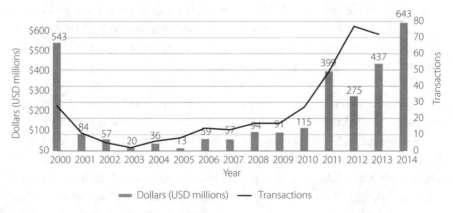

FIGURE 1.3   K–12 Education Technology Investment Dollars and Transactions, 2000–2014

Source: CBInsights 2014; GSV Advisors; NewSchools.

outcomes such as educational attainment and family income remained stable, sophisticated consumer technologies caught on and crossed socioeconomic boundaries.

Education industry dynamics. The market for print and digital instructional materials and assessments totals approximately $10 billion. The market overall grew very slowly between 2009 and 2014, while the ed tech market boomed. There were also significant shifts in purchasing from print to digital resources, and from "basal" (mostly textbooks) to supplemental materials. In fact, at about 8 percent annual growth from 2011 to 2014, digital supplemental instructional materials were the fastest-growing segment in the industry.

High-profile "exits" that generated significant returns for entrepreneurs and investors. News Corp bought Wireless Generation (WGen) in 2010, and Pearson purchased Schoolnet in 2011.[19] The companies sold for a premium, equal to between six and seven times revenue. Each had two things their acquirers wanted: (1) data collection, analysis, and reporting products and platforms that teachers and administrators used and liked, and (2) entrepreneurial, visionary leaders and talented product development teams.

These acquisitions had a profound effect on the imaginations of ed tech entrepreneurs. In 2007, WGen CEO Larry Berger coauthored "Slow Entry, Distant Exit," an influential paper about how industry dynamics made it hard to build an ed tech company.[20] But in November 2010, Berger and his cofounders were able to sell 90 percent of their company to News Corp at a $390 million valuation. Suddenly, it seemed possible to build a company focused on creating educational value *and* generate significant financial returns for the founders and investors.

New capital sources. In 2011, NewSchools Venture Fund allocated $1 million in unrestricted dollars to launch a seed fund to make equity investments in early stage ed tech companies. The Seed Fund eventually attracted capital from individual philanthropists and a few foundations, including Gates and Dell. Three years later, it had invested approximately $10 million in thirty-eight companies. Its companies have raised more than $160 million in additional capital and reached more than sixty million students. In the same time period, two new K–12 focused venture funds, Rethink and Owl Ventures, launched. Both invest in companies after the seed stage after some of the early risk has been reduced. A number of prominent venture capital firms also began investing during this period, including KleinerPerkins Caulfield & Byers, Bessemer Venture Partners, Accel Partners, and Google Ventures.

Government actions. Between 2000 and 2009, NCLB, Reading First, and the State Longitudinal Data Systems initiative sparked activity in segments such as tutoring services, early grade reading materials, and data storage and management. From late 2009 through 2014, additional state and federal initiatives created opportunities and challenges for entrepreneurs:

- The widespread adoption of Common Core State Standards (more than forty states) created more of a national market for math and reading content, in contrast to the fifty individual state markets that existed previously. Mass adoption of CCSS also created a "moment in time" in which school and district leaders in the adopting states were looking for new content and assessments in line with the new standards.
- Race to the Top's awards for Instructional Improvement Systems (IIS), totaling around $500 million, required state education departments to create statewide systems for delivering content and assessments and collecting and reporting performance data. Because this initiative happened concurrently with CCSS, it created new demand in many states for platforms that could manage content, assessments, and data to personalize learning for students.
- State and federal programs like CCSS, RTTT, and the Partnership for Assessment of Readiness for College and Careers and Smarter Balanced Assessment Consortia (groups of states who had adopted CCSS and agreed to work together on developing aligned, shared assessments) slowed down the market for content, assessments, and platforms in some ways. They extended already long sales cycles for state and district data and assessment platforms by at least two years while buyers tried to figure out the implications of CCSS and the assessment consortia on the architecture and functionality of their statewide IIS platforms. And once states accepted tens of millions of federal dollars for things they had always funded themselves, federal compliance rules came into play. This exacerbated the inherent risk-aversion and "box-checking" request for proposal processes in state education offices and school districts by adding federal

sanctions to the list of risks they already faced in their procurement processes. As a result, few entrepreneurial companies secured business through these mechanisms; rather, the largest entrenched companies such as Pearson, secured large contracts from multiple states and the assessment consortia.

Though these factors created a mix of positive and negative incentives, on balance they added up to new opportunities for entrepreneurs. Between 2010 and 2014, investors poured money into companies that developed product and business model innovations in response to the market dynamics. Below are just three examples of the many types of innovation that took place in that timeframe:

"Users before institutions" business models.   In an effort to reach teachers and students directly and avoid complicated procurement processes for as long as possible, a number of entrepreneurs pursued new approaches to sales and distribution. One version is bottom-up—targeting individual teachers who adopt the product, which then often spreads to groups of their fellow teachers and sometimes schoolwide with the goal being full district adoption. These are usually "freemium" models where teachers pay nothing for basic access and a small amount for additional features such as classroom dashboards and reports; school- or districtwide packages come with a licensing fee. Growing companies that have taken this approach include Newsela, eSpark, LightSail, DreamBox, and ST Math.

Another version of this business model generates revenue from other partners in order to keep the product free to schools and districts. Examples of companies who grew with this approach are Clever, a data integration solution, and Edmodo, a classroom management platform; both charged vendors for access to their products so that teachers, schools, and districts could use them at no charge. (Edmodo has recently switched to more of a freemium model.) And of course, nonprofit Khan Academy is free to its twelve million monthly users, but generates revenue from corporate partnerships and philanthropy.

Teachers as creators and decision makers.   On the premise that no one knows teaching like teachers, some entrepreneurs have developed products around the instructional expertise of teachers. LearnZillion uses "Dream Team" teachers every year to create CCSS-aligned video lessons available to teachers everywhere. Nearpod gives every teacher the tools to create and share lessons with students and other teachers. Teachers Pay Teachers is a platform through which teachers sell lessons and instructional resources they create to peers. A number of top-selling teachers have grossed over $1 million in sales through the platform. Class Wallet is a secure application that allows schools, districts, or donors to allocate money to specific teachers to purchase resources for their classrooms.

Speed, flexibility, and quality within stalled market segments. With the temporary slowdown caused by CSSS adoption and the assessment consortia structure, teachers and schools were hungry for formative assessment resources that were affordable and more consistent with the expectations of CCSS. Because the large existing vendors had few incentives to fundamentally change their existing products and were mostly focused on the large state-level opportunities, a number of entrepreneurial providers such as Mastery Connect, TenMarks, i-Ready, and Khan Academy 2.0 gave teachers and schools access to lighter-touch, frequent formative assessments while the traditional markets were stalled. All four of these companies built growing businesses as a result.

WHERE MIGHT ENTREPRENEURS HEAD NEXT?

Education entrepreneurship has flourished since the dawn of the new millennium and created measurable impact for young people. But entrepreneurs are people who look at problems and see opportunities, and some of the problems that motivate them today are rooted in the limitations of the last two decades of education reform. Opportunities abound for education entrepreneurs willing to bear risk and break rules. Below is a sketch of four of the many opportunities on the horizon.

Entrepreneurs are beginning to focus on expanding the definition of student success beyond test scores. Over the last fifteen years, high-performing charters showed that when students have the support they need to reach high expectations, they reach them. This is true across race, ethnicity, and income levels. However, this performance proof point has come at a cost. In the vast majority of instances, these schools narrowed their focus to the demands of the accountability system and prioritized scores on state reading and math exams as the measure of success. But even some of the highest-performing schools on these metrics are disappointed with their students' college reme-diation, persistence, and completion rates. Some are creating mechanisms to follow their students into college to continue the structured support that helped them do well enough on state tests and college entrance exams. But this will be impossible for most schools to afford or put into practice.

A few pioneers are now attempting to create schools designed to help stu-dents develop the competencies, agency and identity they need for long-term success.[21] Rather than trying to squeeze even more out of schools that were designed to prepare students for the industrial age, these entrepreneurs are rethinking the use of time, talent, and technology to create schools that meet students where they are and prepare them for success in an ever-changing world. Summit Public Schools, Achievement First's greenfield school, and Montessori For All are a few examples of the many schools innovating in this way. Over the next five years, there will be hundreds more.

Along with redesigned schools, there are opportunities for entrepreneurs to create research-based tools and interventions that help students develop the factors associated with the competencies, agency and identity necessary for success. These include things like enhanced knowledge and skills, mind-sets, self-regulation and values.[22] The field will also need ways to diagnose and gauge progress in ways that are reliable yet flexible.

The expanded definition of success is appealing to school districts as well. Entre-preneurs have opportunities to create service organizations that can help smooth the way for district school redesign and implementation. Early exam-ples of this are New Classrooms, Summit Basecamp, and Transcend Learn-ing. Many service providers will be needed to meet the growing demand of communities and districts for schools that help every student reach an expanded definition of success.

The market for digital content, assessments, and platforms still has significant gaps that constrain the ability of schools, teachers, and students to take full advantage of the power of technology. Ed tech entrepreneurs who make the effort to understand these gaps and the needs of teachers and students will find significant opportunities. Three such gaps are: rigorous, interactive science courseware aligned with the Next Generation Science Standards, especially for middle grades; effective applications to support learning for upper-grade English language learners, and platforms affording compe-tency-based pathways that can integrate content and assessments from multiple providers and help teachers support the personalized learning paths of every student.

The progress in New Orleans and Washington, DC over the last decade is very promising. Though the education systems of these cities have some differences, a common attribute is a coordinated entrepreneurial community. New Schools for New Orleans played a critical role in incubating new schools, attracting and supporting human capital entrepreneurs, being a connector for national philanthropy, and advocating for policies that helped create more good schools and fewer low-performing ones. In Washington, the DC Schools Fund and CityBridge have collaborated to provide similar citywide coordination. Given the conditions necessary for charter school growth to influence citywide performance mentioned earlier in this chapter, local and regional intermediary organizations like this (called "harbormasters") might be critical to the next decade of entrepreneurship in specific geographic regions.

However, the mere presence of a well-intended intermediary isn't enough. If they are to truly replicate the success of places like New Orleans and Washington, DC, these organizations must have leaders and teams who understand school quality, policy, politics, entrepreneurship, philanthropy, community engagement, and much more, *plus* have the credibility and gravitas to get things done. It's a tall order. Education Cities is a national nonprofit focused on helping strengthen the capacity and effectiveness of these types of local and regional intermediaries, but it remains to be seen if the model will live up to its potential beyond New Orleans and DC.

CONCLUSION

Education entrepreneurs have had significant impact on students and learning since the turn of the century. Millions of students have access to better schools, tools, and teachers due to their efforts. It is an immense achievement. But we have a long way to go before every family has at least one great school in their neighborhood. In April 2015, Achievement First, a high-performing East Coast charter network, received lottery applications from twenty-one thousand families for its one thousand New York City seats. Schools around the country have similar wait lists. Families are hungry for better options, and they deserve them. We also have a long way to go before every student has the preparation and support it takes to be truly free to live the lives they choose, not restricted to a limited set of options because of the narrow focus of their schools. There are massive gaps between the aspirations our young people have for themselves, their families and their communities and what our education system currently delivers.

Therein lie the most exciting opportunities for education entrepreneurs. Just as the previous generation brought a risk-bearing and rule-breaking mind-set to the challenges they began tackling fifteen years ago, motivated entrepreneurs are emerging to meet the needs of this new era. And increasingly, the new entrepreneurs are more heterogeneous in background, race and ethnicity, and geography, bringing with them more shared experiences with the students and communities they aim to serve. In 2030, it will be fascinating to look back on another fifteen years of education entrepreneurship and assess who led the way, the progress they made, and what challenges remain.

Carrots, Sticks, and Sermons

How Policy Shapes Educational Entrepreneurship

Ashley Jochim

Public policy profoundly shapes the prospects for entrepreneurship in education. Government is the single largest purchaser of services in the education sector, injecting billions of dollars each year into schools, professional development, curriculum, and assessments. Federal, state, and local governments regulate who can deliver services, how services can and cannot be provided, and in what ways service providers are held accountable.

This chapter begins by considering how different kinds of policy tools—*carrots*, *sticks*, and *sermons*—shape entrepreneurship. It then considers how changes to the post–NCLB policy landscape, including Common Core, charter schools, teacher evaluation, and test-based accountability, have influenced the opportunities and obstacles entrepreneurs face, including their access to resources, demand for their services, and oversight of their work. It concludes with recommendations about how public policy can more effectively harness the power of entrepreneurship to solve public education's most pressing challenges.

HOW POLICY SHAPES ENTREPRENEURSHIP

> "Public policy almost always attempts to get people to do things that they might not otherwise do; or it enables people to do things that they might not have done otherwise."
>
> —Anne Schneider and Helen Ingram, 1990[1]

First, some definitions. *Public policy* is the result of government actions (and inactions) intended to shape the behavior of public and private actors.[2] It can take many forms, including laws, regulations, court decisions, and programs. *Entrepreneurship* is any activity related to the development of new organizations, methods, or products that challenge or improve existing ways of doing business.[3] Entrepreneurship can create benefits for private actors (as when firms profit from a new product or service) and the public at large (as when a new product or service serves the public interest).

Public policy shapes entrepreneurship in three ways: (1) incentivizing action through grants or subsidies; (2) prescribing action through regulation; and (3) encouraging action by providing information. Colloquially, these different approaches to shaping individual and organizational behavior are known as *carrots* (incentives), *sticks* (regulations), and *sermons* (information).

Perhaps the most traditional means of shaping entrepreneurship is through regulation. Regulation affects entrepreneurs by requiring certain processes to be followed. In the public sector, regulations limit the kinds of individuals who can become teachers, how students may be assigned to schools, the number of students allowed to be served by a single teacher, the types of curriculum that can be used, and the length of the school day and year. These rules about how schools are organized and staffed can open or close opportunities for entrepreneurs looking to employ new methods of instruction (e.g., competency-based learning), make use of untapped labor pools (e.g., local artists or museum staff to provide enrichment), or make trade-offs between people and technology (e.g., by using resources dedicated to hiring a teacher to instead purchase software and instructional aides). While regulation typically imposes costs on entrepreneurs, it can also open opportunities. Common instructional standards, for example, can lower barriers to entry to entrepreneurs and expand potential markets for their offerings.

Regulation also dictates how and what kinds of services districts and state education agencies demand from the private sector, thereby shaping the prospects for entrepreneurship by nonprofit and for-profit organizations. For example, a byzantine procurement process within a district central office can make it impossible for smaller firms to offer products and services to districts; rules meant to prevent collusion between educators, district staff, and for-profit firms often mean that entrepreneurs cannot have access to the consumers that would enable them to tailor their products to better meet the needs of educators and schools.[4]

Government can also affect entrepreneurship by incentivizing desired behaviors. Providing grants, subsidies, and other resources encourages public and private entities to engage in preferred activities. For example, the Obama administration's Race to the Top (RTTT) program offered states the possibility of securing millions in grant dollars in return for passing favored policies around teacher evaluation and Common Core standards.

Like regulation, incentives can open or shut off opportunities for entrepreneurs. In the case of RTTT, the grant program was a boon to those entrepreneurs providing Common Core–aligned professional development and curriculum, enabling them to vastly expand their market base as states rushed to adopt the standards. It was less promising to providers of alternative materials and supports.

Public policy can also work by persuading individuals to act. Unlike regulation or incentives, persuasion is not coercive and its effectiveness relies entirely on the voluntary actions of target groups. It includes marketing campaigns (e.g., the "Just Say No" campaign against drug use), reports that provide recommended actions (e.g., *A Nation at Risk*), or policies that seek to improve information available to individuals or organizations (e.g., quality ratings). Among the most significant uses of information as a policy instrument in education is the effort by government agencies to create report cards that provide information to families on school performance. Report cards do not directly require or incentivize actions but they do influence school and parent behavior.

THE POLICY LANDSCAPE AND ITS IMPLICATIONS FOR ENTREPRENEURSHIP IN K–12

The last decade has brought a number of changes to the policy landscape that shaped the prospects for entrepreneurship in education. This section considers how four prominent reforms—Common Core, charter schools, teacher evaluation, and post-NCLB accountability—have impacted the opportunities and constraints entrepreneurs face.

Common Core State Standards

In 2009, the National Governors Association and the Council of Chief State School Officers launched an effort to develop common standards in English and mathematics to ensure that "all students, regardless of where they live, are graduating high-school prepared for college, career, and life."[5] By 2011, one year after the standards had officially been released, forty-five states plus the District of Columbia had signed on.

Common Core, like all education standards, aims to shape what teachers teach and students learn. Its impacts on entrepreneurs stem from regulations that shape the market for instructional materials and assessments and investments in technology and professional development to support implementation. Because Common Core provides a content framework that is shared across a diverse group of states and millions of schools, its impacts on the landscape have been much larger than previous iterations of standards-based reforms.

The market for instructional materials (textbooks, but also supplementary materials like lesson plans, workbooks, and supporting software) has long been dominated by the "big three" publishers—Pearson, McGraw-Hill, and Houghton Mifflin—which together control 85 percent of the $3.2 billion K–12 market and are struggling to adapt to the growing use of digitally based content.[6] Early evidence from the field suggests Common Core has enabled new providers to gain a foothold in the market by lowering barriers to entry and improving marketability for instructional content providers, who will no longer have to tailor their products to fifty states' different standards.[7]

A report from the Center on Education Policy in 2014 suggests that fewer than four in ten districts reported using curriculum materials produced by for-profits and about half reported relying on for-profits for professional development.[8] Nonprofits, arguably smaller and less established in the provision of instructional content, were providing curriculum content for 14 percent of districts and professional development for 35 percent of districts.[9]

In New York, an invitation by the State Education Department for new curriculum required all bidders to put their materials online for free. According to journalist Sarah Garland, the big three publishers balked, enabling four nonprofits to secure the $8 million bid.[10] Early reviews of the materials, branded EngageNY, have been positive and their reach has extended well beyond the borders of the state, with about half of all downloads coming from outside of New York State.[11]

Importantly, common standards have enabled niche nonprofits to find new audiences for their particular brand of education reform. As Garland reports, Expeditionary Learning, an organization that advocates for project-based curriculum, won contracts from Teach For America, KIPP charter schools, and the state of Delaware to train teachers in the new standards. Another nonprofit, Core Knowledge, which advocates a back-to-basics approach to reading comprehension, was one of the four groups to secure contracts from New York State to develop curriculum in English language arts.[12]

Common Core has also enabled the expansion of repositories for digital instructional materials like Share My Lesson. Since 2012, when Share My Lesson was launched by the American Federation of Teachers and TES Connect, the site has generated over three hundred thousand free teaching resources. While these repositories could exist without Common Core, their potential impact is much more significant in a world where a teacher in Utah can share instructional materials with a teacher in Maryland.

In contrast to the implications for content developers, changes to the testing landscape have thus far largely favored the largest testing companies: Pearson, McGraw-Hill, and the Educational Testing Service. While in previous years, smaller companies may have been able to compete by specializing in a given state, the reach of the new assessments have significantly expanded the scope of the work, thereby privileging the testing industry's largest players.[13]

Of course, changes in the membership composition of the two main consortia developing Common Core–aligned assessments could greatly affect the marketplace. In early 2015, eighteen states remained committed to the Smarter Balanced Assessment Consortium (SBAC).[14] Just ten states plus Washington, DC, remained in the Partnership for Assessment of Readiness for College and Careers.[15] Twenty-one other states were relying on other tests developed by other vendors.

How the new tests affect teaching and learning is a key concern. Some critics worry that the Common Core will lead to a narrowing of curriculum and limit opportunities for innovation in schools. As Robin Lake and Tricia Maas observe, charter leaders have expressed concern that the standards "could end up taking away . . . teachers' freedom to use diverse options to meet student needs by forcing schools to teach certain standards in certain grades, at certain times of the year, or eventually, by prescribing a curriculum."[16] Frederick Hess and Michael McShane note that, given the standards' increased attention to scope and sequencing of content, Common Core may prove problematic for newer school models like Carpe Diem or Summit Academies, which use competency-based learning models that enable students to progress at their own pace.[17]

Others have suggested that the new investments have done little to drive improvements in what teachers are teaching and students are learning. As education historian Larry Cuban noted, the old reasons for buying technology emphasized making schools more efficient, productive, and personalized. Now, he asserts, "the rationale for getting devices has shifted. No longer does it matter whether there is sufficient evidence to make huge expenditures on new technologies. Now what matters are the practical problems of being technologically ready for the new standards and tests in 2014–2015: getting more hardware, software, additional bandwidth, technical assistance, professional development for teachers, and time in the school day to let students practice taking tests."[18]

While it remains to be seen how the standards will affect student learning, implementation challenges and expanded political opposition have generated much uncertainty among entrepreneurs working on Common Core–aligned assessments and instructional content.[19]

Teacher Evaluation

Efforts to improve the quality of the teaching workforce are as old as public education and have varied in their focus from managing what kinds of educational experiences teachers must have before they enter the workforce, shaping the professional development of teachers already in the workforce, and most recently, refashioning how teachers are evaluated on the job to inform decisions about recruitment, retention, and development.

The Obama administration's RTTT competitive grant program and Elementary and Secondary Education Act (ESEA) flexibility waivers favored states that put in place evaluation systems that used multiple measures, including student achievement. The results of these pressures have been extensive changes to the teacher evaluation landscape. The National Council on Teacher Quality (NCTQ) reported that between 2009 and 2013, twenty-six states changed their teacher evaluation policies. By 2013, forty-one states plus the District of Columbia required student achievement to be a "significant factor" in teacher evaluations, twenty-six states differentiated levels of performance, and thirty-nine used classroom observations.[20]

Reforms to teacher evaluation shape the entrepreneurial landscape in three ways:

Generating demands for new evaluation tools and rubrics. Teacher evaluation reform has resulted in states and districts in search of evaluation models, tools, and rubrics, and billions of dollars invested in designing and implementing teacher evaluation systems. While much of the controversy over teacher evaluation has focused on the use of student achievement data, a key feature of reform efforts was the inclusion of multiple measures of effectiveness, including classroom observations and student feedback.

These investments created an opportunity for entrepreneurs to offer new evaluation tools tailored to the needs of the schools and districts that used them, but evidence suggests the reforms to date have favored only a few providers. According to the Center for Great Leaders and Teachers, twenty-three states either recommend or require the use of Charlotte Danielson's *Framework for Teaching*, while another nine use Marzano's Teacher Evaluation Model.[21] In the vast majority of other states, locally developed models dominate (e.g., the Minnesota Performance Standards for Teacher Practice), suggesting either a lack of appetite or demand for more specialty evaluation products.

The lack of innovation in evaluation tools and rubrics is problematic given important differences in what effective teaching looks like in different contexts. As discussed by Hess and McShane, the current landscape of teacher evaluation may underappreciate the kinds of skills that are important for classroom management and lesson planning in online schools or schools that rely on a blend of technology and people to guide instruction.[22] For example, the teacher evaluation tools in place at Summit Public Schools, a CMO with nine schools, rely less on high-touch observation and more on data generated from common assessments, which are tailored to tap the skills and content knowledge school leaders have identified as key to student success.[23]

Three factors may have dampened opportunities for innovation in teacher evaluation tools and rubrics. One is that teacher evaluation reform has largely been undertaken from the statehouse, resulting in systems that are prescribed and apply to all districts. According to the National Council on Teacher Quality, twelve states have a single statewide system and another ten have "presumptive models," which prescribe a method but allow districts to opt out.[24] Even states that allow districts to select from a preapproved list may inadvertently curtail innovative approaches to evaluation or evaluation models tailored to particular kinds of schools (e.g., blended learning models). Another factor is that, because it spread rapidly, teacher evaluation reform favored organizations already working in this area and those who could ramp up rapidly to provide tools and rubrics to states and districts. For example, Charlotte Danielson's *Framework for Teaching*, which is among the most widely used models for judging teacher effectiveness, was developed in 2007. A final factor is the byzantine procurement systems of many state education agencies and school districts. As discussed by Tricia Maas and Robin Lake, complicated procurement systems often favor large firms with established working relationships with education bureaucracies.[25]

Opening up opportunities for entrepreneurs providing professional development services and supports. A second way in which teacher evaluation could shape the landscape for entrepreneurs is by generating demand for professional implementation support. Reforms to teacher evaluation required investments in the design of statistical models, training for principals and other evaluators, and support for district and state education agency staff who are charged with overseeing implementation.

The Obama administration's RTTT program as well as new state appropriations to support implementation efforts injected billions of dollars into reforming teacher evaluation. A report by the American Institutes for Research and RAND found that the three studied districts spent between $6.4 million and $24.8 million to support the development and implementation of teacher evaluation.[26]

According to a 2011 review by the *Hechinger Report*, a range of nonprofit and for-profit groups are benefiting from the demand for support and the infusion of cash.[27] The American Institutes for Research and Houghton Mifflin Harcourt won large contracts from Florida to develop classroom observation methods and statistical models for grading teachers based on student achievement.[28] The New Teacher Project, the American Federation of Teachers, the Danielson Group, Mathematica Policy Research, and the National Institute for Excellence in Teaching have all had a hand in designing or supporting implementation of teacher evaluation in districts and states across the country.[29]

Changing the market for teacher preparation programs. A final impact of teacher evaluation is on the landscape for teacher preparation programs, which are dominated by traditional schools of education but also increasingly operating in a competitive environment with newer, nontraditional providers such as Teach For America and High Tech High. Teacher evaluation reform has generated new data by which different kinds of teacher preparation programs can be evaluated. Not only can evaluation data be used to identify and potentially phase out weak teacher preparation programs, but it can also be used to validate newer, nontraditional models of teacher preparation. As reported in a 2013 report by the National Council of Teacher Quality, three states—Louisiana, North Carolina, and Tennessee—have pioneered the use of teacher evaluation data to rate teacher preparation programs.[30] It remains to be seen whether these rating programs will influence consumer demand for different types of teacher preparation programs.

Charter Schools

Charter schools aim to create new regulatory spaces for entrepreneurship by providing entrepreneurs opportunities to create new schools, and indirectly, by creating demand for new services and supports traditionally provided by the district central office.

Charter schools are publicly funded but privately managed, and they enable individuals and groups with new ideas about how to organize schools—e.g., a longer school day or different curriculum—the opportunity to put their ideas into practice free from many of the regulatory constraints that limit what traditional public schools can do. In exchange for their wider freedom of action, charter schools are typically held to higher performance standards than traditional public schools and face closure if they fail to meet those standards.

In 1991, Minnesota became the first state in the nation to authorize the creation of charter schools. Since then, forty-three states plus the District of Columbia have charter laws on the books. In the 2014–2015 school year, sixty-seven hundred charter schools were operating, serving more than 2.9 million students.[31] In several urban school systems, including New Orleans, Washington, DC, Detroit, Philadelphia, Cleveland, and Indianapolis, charter schools serve a quarter or more of all public school students.[32]

One way in which charter schools have shaped entrepreneurship is by stimulating demand for services traditionally provided by the district central office. For-profit and nonprofit organizations have emerged to provide a range of services including back-office services (e.g., EdTec), professional development for teachers (e.g., BloomBoard), data management (e.g., Illuminate Education), food services (e.g., 4th Sector Solutions), substitute teachers (e.g, Enriched Schools), special education services (e.g., Seneca), and supports for at-risk students (e.g., Success Highways). While the extent of growth driven by demand from charter schools is difficult to track, there is little doubt that the expansion of the charter sector has created opportunities for new service providers to enter the market.

State policies shape the size of the charter sector. While the number of charter schools serving students has grown tremendously over the last decade, in many states growth is constrained by caps that limit the number of charter schools allowed to operate. Twenty-three states and the District of Columbia impose caps on the number of charter schools allowed.[33]

Other state policies can restrict the growth of charters by limiting the number and type of entities allowed to authorize charter schools. In seven states (Wyoming, Iowa, Virginia, Maryland, Alaska, Kansas, and Oregon), local education agencies (LEAs) are the only entities authorized to sponsor charter schools. Of course, because charter schools are in competition with district schools for students, they typically have few incentives to regularly authorize schools. While 90 percent of the nation's 1,045 authorizers are school districts, LEA-authorized schools account for just over half of the total sector. State education agencies, independent charter boards, municipal government, and nonprofits are much more likely to be large authorizers, with portfolios of ten or more schools.[34] These policies are important because a primary way in which charter schools can shape entrepreneurialism is by eliminating the monopoly over public education and creating competition that in theory can benefit families and students.

Federal, state, and local financial support for charter schools can also affect the size and quality of the sector. A report produced by the School Choice Demonstration Project at the University of Arkansas found that charter schools typically receive $3,814 less in funding than their traditional peers, a difference of 28.4 percent.[35] While this gap is substantial, significant variability was found across states: in Tennessee, charter schools and district schools received nearly equal per-pupil funding while in Louisiana, charter schools receive half as much as their peers in districts.

In addition to different per-pupil allotments, charter schools also typically lack access to capital improvement funds to support buying and/or renovating facilities. As detailed by the Charter School Facilities Initiative, the lack of capital funding means that charter schools typically have smaller facilities and lack kitchens, gymnasiums, computer labs, and other specialized instructional spaces.[36]

Increases in federal funding have helped to mitigate the effects of limits on state and local funding. The US Department of Education's Charter Schools Program provides financial support to create and scale high-quality charter schools.[37] In 2012, the program provided over $14 million in funding to support expansion efforts of large nonprofit charter management organizations like Democracy Prep and KIPP. In early 2015, the Obama administration's budget included a 48 percent increase for the charter school program, totaling over $253 million.[38]

In addition to access to facilities and funding, the regulatory environment critically shapes the ways in which charter schools can operate. When freed from typical constraints over hiring, use of time and technology, and curriculum, charter schools have an opportunity to experiment with new approaches to teaching and learning. According to the Education Commission of the States, states vary considerably in whether charter schools qualify for a waiver from most regulatory requirements.[39] In many cases, operational autonomy is constrained by requirements that charter schools participate in state teacher evaluation systems or local collective bargaining agreements, or by requirements that they negotiate with state education agencies for any needed waivers.[40]

One of the most significant changes to the regulatory environment for charter schools has been the increased focus on accountability and public oversight. The National Association of Charter School Authorizers was established in 2000 and works to disseminate best practices in charter school authorizing. In 2012, it initiated the "One Million Lives Campaign" in an effort to pressure authorizers and state policymakers to adopt best practices for authorizers.[41] One consequence of these efforts has been new policies that establish guidelines for charter authorizing and renewal, automatic closure policies for charter schools facing academic or financial mismanagement, and efforts to strengthen state oversight of authorizers. In states like Ohio and Michigan, whose large charter sectors are not as high-performing as counterparts elsewhere, legislation tightening rules on authorizers has support from both Republicans and Democrats.[42]

While the increased focus on authorizing has improved the quality of the charter sector nationwide, unintended consequences may serve to limit innovation in the sector moving forward.[43] One factor is raising barriers to entry for new operators. Applications for charters are increasingly lengthy, a trend that no doubt favors large, established CMOs to the detriment of smaller, community-based nonprofits.[44] Another is providing disincentives for risk-taking and experimentation, a key motivation for establishing charters.[45] According to 2014 data from the Center on Education Reform, the most popular educational approach among surveyed charters was college preparatory (30 percent), a 17 percent increase compared with similar data reported in 2002. Technology-based approaches were used by a small minority of surveyed charters (6 percent reported using blended learning and 2 percent were fully virtual).[46] These trends suggest that while charter schools provide educators with much more flexibility to innovate in school organization, curriculum, and talent management, they also face regulatory pressures that constrain their actions in unintended ways.

Post-NCLB Accountability

In public education, test-based accountability is a regulatory reform that aims to shift the focus from specifying what schools do to instead making schools accountable for what they achieve. In theory, the shift in focus from inputs to outputs should enable entrepreneurship by providing schools and those that support them with additional flexibility and incentives to achieve desired aims. Yet because the public objectives for K–12 education are broad and multifaceted, including such equivocal concepts as "citizenship" and "college readiness," test-based accountability has been hotly contested and had unintended negative consequences. Even when implemented well, accountability pressures can crowd out ideas and people who excel in areas that are not measured, as well as limit risk-taking and experimentation for fear of failure.

The experiences of states with NCLB offers a case in point. Because NCLB focused on raw proficiency levels, it provided an incredibly crude yardstick for judging the effectiveness of different educational programs and resulted in a variety of perverse consequences, including a weakening of state standards, narrowing of curriculum, and a focus on "bubble kids" on the cusp of meeting proficiency.[47] The law also vastly over-identified the number of failing schools, with nearly 50 percent of the nation's public schools failing to make AYP in the 2010–2011 school year.[48]

Dissatisfaction with NCLB led to a series of programs and reforms that aimed to improve accountability and provide the incentives and support to turn around low-performing schools. The administration's signature initiative came in 2009 when the US Department of Education announced a new program that used $3.5 billion from the American Recovery and Reinvestment Act (ARRA) to expand the budget of Title I School Improvement Grants (SIG) and make the award of funding competitive. The SIG program offered state education agencies and districts additional flexibility for identifying low-performing schools but made the funds contingent on implementing one of four prescribed turnaround models, including closure and staff replacement.

The program generated important opportunities for entrepreneurs working in both the public and private sectors. The influx of funding, which typically included investments of up to $2 million per year per school for up to three years, enabled the purchase of targeted supports and materials as well as provided opportunities to design innovative school models featuring expanded learning time and greater personalization.[49] Schools were also typically granted additional flexibility through regulatory waivers and freedom from typical staffing constraints.

Available research on how these funds were deployed suggests that private support providers won a significant share of dollars, including nonprofits and for-profits, new and established groups.[50] A *Denver Post* analysis found that among states that tracked funds going to outside groups, the average was 25 percent of awarded dollars. In Colorado, consultants won a 35 percent share of the $26.6 million awarded to the state between 2010 and 2012, which went to purchase instructional coaches for teachers, leadership coaches for principals, analysts to review data, and professional development for school staff.[51]

Evidence about the effectiveness of these providers is generally lacking. The aforementioned *Denver Post* review pointed to lackluster performance by the New York City–based Global Partnership Schools, which took over six schools in Pueblo, Colorado (the company also operates SIG schools in Baltimore and Bridgeport, Connecticut). A US Government Accountability Office report found "inconsistent review of contractors" and a general lack of accountability for results among districts, schools, and contractors.[52] These findings generally echo those from the larger SIG program: nearly as many schools exhibited gains as saw declines, despite the fact that they received millions in federal funds.[53]

These discouraging outcomes likely have their roots in several factors. One is that states, districts, and schools were often not well positioned to oversee contractors or the larger school improvement plan. Compliance offices in state education agencies and school districts were developed to ensure grantees and contractors submitted the right paperwork and followed other procedural requirements. They are not generally well equipped to hold grantees and contractors accountable for performance. As a testament to this fact, studies have documented the lack of oversight of the program, with few states using student achievement data to make grant renewal decisions.[54] Indeed, a 2012 Department of Education audit found that many schools did not follow through with planned efforts to expand learning time or hire new staff and neither the state nor district had followed through to approve changes to their turnaround plans.[55]

The lack of effective oversight was likely exacerbated by the speed with which the program was launched and then concluded—schools had just three years to design and implement their turnaround plans, including the expenditure of all awarded funds. According to an *Education Week* series documenting schools' experiences with the SIG program, the time crunch seriously impeded the success of the program, leaving districts with little time to make the staffing changes required by the program's approved turn-around models.

A third factor relates to specificity with which the program prescribed approved turnaround models. While all of the models were supported by research on school turnaround, the SIG program took these models to new contexts where the reality of talent pipelines for teachers and principals, school culture, and students' learning difficulties varied considerably. Many rural districts reported frustration with provisions that required replacement of teachers and principals.[56]

A final factor was the lack of attention to the need for reforms to state and district operating systems, which in many cases created barriers to engaging in effective oversight, identifying internal and external supports for schools, and implementing and sustaining different turnaround models. For example, expanding learning time was a key component of the SIG program, but many schools bumped into teacher collective bargaining agreements that limited what they could do on this front.

These challenges hold important lessons for policymakers seeking to leverage funds to stimulate entrepreneurship. For funding to be an effective shaper of entrepreneurial effort, outcomes need to be clearly specified and overseen. In the case of the SIG program, guidance was far more prescriptive on what schools should do and less prescriptive on what they needed to achieve, flipping the conventional wisdom of performance-based contracting, in which outcomes are clearly specified and means are left to decision makers who have the required skills and expertise.

POLICY AND THE FUTURE OF ENTREPRENEURSHIP

Public education in the United States remains more open to entrepreneurs than ever before. Education is more transparent and focused on results, due in no small part to reforms like teacher evaluation, Common Core, and test-based accountability. School districts no longer hold a monopoly on operating schools, and in many cities and states, charter schools are a large and growing provider of public education.

But challenges remain. Education persists as a highly regulated enterprise that is resistant to new sources of talent and ways of organizing schools. While some of these regulations are important for protecting children and taxpayers, many are artifacts of previous eras that persist due to the power of inertia and politics.

At the same time, the structures in place to oversee both public and private ventures in education remain weak. State education agencies and districts often lack the capacity to administer grants and contracts in ways that will incentivize entrepreneurialism. In the absence of good oversight, millions in public funds are spent with little to show for it.

The movement toward performance-based regulation, including teacher evaluation and test-based accountability, sought to create clear metrics for evaluating quality and incentives to drive the actions of educators and other service providers. In theory, these reforms provided a basis for moving away from prescribing inputs to instead focusing on results. Yet the changes to the reform landscape that have unfolded over the last decade have done little to address the scope of compliance responsibilities laid on administrators, principals, and teachers or to bolster the capacity of the compliance office to move towards performance-based oversight.

In the wake of the lessons emerging from the previous decade of reform, federal and state policymakers can take a variety of concrete steps that greatly shape entrepreneurs' opportunities to innovate and ultimately address some of public education's most pressing challenges. Federal, state, and local policymakers looking to encourage entrepreneurialism in public education ought to leverage their authority and unique policymaking roles to:

Reform procurement processes. In public education, government is a huge consumer of private-sector products and services. This gives government leverage to stimulate entrepreneurship through its purchasing power. Yet regulation of contracting and procurement creates unnecessary barriers to entry and limits the diffusion of innovative practices. As discussed by Tricia Maas and Robin Lake, state and local policymakers can leverage their existing investments in entrepreneurship by eliminating barriers that favor large firms and focusing procurement systems on end-users (whether they are families, principals, or teachers).[57]

Refashion the compliance office. While procurement processes keep private-sector organizations from contributing to public goods, the compliance office often works against public-sector employees seeking to try out new ideas or tweak routines. While state and district officials can and should refashion the compliance office by eliminating outdated regulatory requirements, these reforms should be coupled with efforts to improve the capacity and skill of individuals working within the compliance office.[58] Taking these steps will ensure that compliance officers are willing to help educators interested in finding ways to innovate within existing regulatory frameworks.

At the same time, it is important that efforts to reform the compliance office do not result in weakened agencies that are incapable of holding grantees and contractors accountable for outcomes. As revealed by the weaknesses in the SIG program, the solution to failures in the public sector is not simply to channel funds into the private sector. Contracting and grant-making is difficult work and requires investments in capacity building to ensure desired outcomes are achieved.

Invest in research. Federal and state policymakers devote little to education research, especially when compared with investments in other areas. While the National Institute for Health spent over $30 billion in health research in FY2014, the Institute for Education Sciences (IES) invested just $600 million. This difference is all the more remarkable given the considerable investments private companies make in health research and development.

Investing in research serves two purposes. First, it can directly produce or contribute to innovations in education. Second, investments in research can help schools and districts be smart consumers of the many products, services, and improvement strategies on offer. One notable example of an effective federal effort to invest in research is the Investing in Innovation (i3) fund. Originally created through the American Reinvestment and Recovery Act, i3 is a competitive grant program managed by the Department of Education that aims to help grantees develop and scale innovative practices that address common challenges. While many grant programs discourage partnerships with philanthropy and the private sector, i3 aimed to capitalize on collaborations across sectors. As Martin West, an associate professor of education at the Harvard Graduate School of Education, writes, i3 differed from the other competitive grant programs launched through RTTT in that it was much less prescriptive and more focused on evidence.[59] States looking for evidence about what works in their own backyards could launch similar programs to draw attention to and learn from innovation that's already happening.

Encourage transparency in reporting student outcomes. Most states have invested in longitudinal data systems that enable tracking of school performance over time and by subgroup. Yet few have worked to disseminate this information in formats that are easy to digest and understand. Federal policymakers should encourage greater transparency by requiring states to report disaggregated student outcomes in an easily digestible format. Transparency is a powerful, if underutilized, tool for government to pursue public objectives without the heavy hand of regulation. It addresses a key market failure by improving the information available to families choosing among schools. And it can provide a basis for conversations about what communities are not being well served by existing schools.

While these reforms are far less provocative than the ones that have reshaped the policy landscape over the last decade, they could have tremendous impact on entrepreneurship. Through a thoughtful mix of "carrots, sticks, and sermons," policymakers can ensure taxpayers are protected, children benefit, and public education advances in the next era.

3

Tailwinds and Headwinds

Unleashing Entrepreneurial Energy to Transform Education

John Bailey

Sailors use the terms *tailwind* and *headwind* to describe events or conditions that impact their progress. A tailwind refers to favorable conditions, when the wind is at the ship's back, propelling it forward at a faster pace. A headwind blows against the ship under way; this creates a condition that slows forward progress and makes the journey more difficult. While often used to describe certain economic conditions, the terms can also help categorize broad trends facing education entrepreneurs.

We are in the middle of dramatic economic and technological shifts in which entrepreneurs are uniquely positioned to solve large, complex societal challenges, specifically within education. Recent advances in technology present the opportunity to reach every student with the customized education necessary to succeed in school, career, and life.

The real breakthroughs are with new models of education designed around next generation tools and services that deliver a better education experience aligned to student success. New Classrooms' founder Joel Rose suggests, "Our collective change in K–12 innovation today should go beyond merely designing and producing new tools. Rather, our focus should primarily be to design new classroom models that take advantage of what these tools can do."[1] The challenge is not to romanticize any one particular technology, tool, or service, but instead to ask how these new technologies might be used together in new models to solve problems in smarter ways.

Although the models are still emerging and the tools still evolving, one thing is clear: education is no longer limited to a building. It is becoming accessible anywhere, anytime. Current and future generations will experience education as an on-demand service, available anywhere they can tap on an app or click on an online course. It is available to them from school, from home, from the car—anywhere they are connected.

Behind this on-demand revolution is a group of entrepreneurs empowered with low-cost technology platforms, broadband distribution systems, and expanding flows of financial capital. This emerging generation of entrepreneurs is blurring the lines between social and business interests, and though they measure much success based on traditional business metrics, they are driven by something deeper: the desire to have a real social impact. Matt Greenfield of Rethink Education observed that "Successful entrepreneurs have a fascination for a particular kind of intellectual problem and a relentless, unstoppable, endlessly inventive, and improvisational effort to solve that problem."[2]

Problems are like catnip to an entrepreneur. They see every problem as what William Eggers, global public sector research director at Deloitte, describes as a "wicked opportunity."[3] Thus it is no surprise that the long-standing challenges in education are attracting entrepreneurs. Brian Singerman of Founders Fund noted that "today's strongest entrepreneurs are creating technology-enabled models to transform some of the oldest and most established industries in the world. We believe the time has come to reimagine education."[4]

Driven by their passion to challenge the status quo, question long-held assumptions, solve problems, and help students succeed, entrepreneurs are launching new products and services. More than seventy-one tech start-ups were catapulted out of education incubator ImagineK12. Teach For America has grown from 400 corps members in 1989 to 11,031 today, with alumni who have gone on to become leaders of states, schools, and start-ups. The number of public charter schools has grown from 1,542 in 1999 to 6,400 in 2014. Thousands more entrepreneurs are waiting to bring innovations to education. The question is whether our nation will give them the opportunity to do so.

THE TAILWINDS PROPELLING EDUCATION ENTREPRENEURS

Philanthropic and Private Capital

An unprecedented level of capital is flowing into education start-ups, from major foundations to private capital markets. Education technology

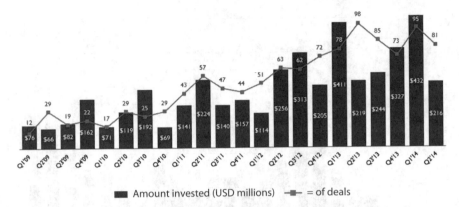

FIGURE 3.1   Ed Tech Financing: Investment Deals and Dollars, Q1 2009–Q2 2014

Source: www.cbinsights.com, "Ed Tech Investment & Exit Report—2014," September 2014.

companies raised $1.36 billion in 201 rounds from more than 386 unique investors in 2014.[5] This represents a nearly 212 percent growth in the sector since 2009.[6] The broader US venture capital market is also on track to have the highest amount of funding since 2000.[7]

The United States is also witnessing the investment of unprecedented levels of philanthropic capital—86,192 foundations holding $715 billion in assets disbursed $52 billion in grants, 22 percent ($5 billion) of which is invested in education.[8] These funds are fueling new social entrepreneurial efforts as well as the advocacy work needed to remove roadblocks and help scale high performers. (See figure 3.1 and figure 3.2 for how funds are distributed.)

Internet Disruption of Traditional Supply Chains

The Internet, app stores, and mobile platforms are disrupting traditional distribution and supply chains. Before the Internet, entrepreneurs had to individually sell products to fifteen thousand separate school systems, all of which had their own byzantine and lengthy procurement processes. "In the past, innovation came to schools in a car," quipped Jennifer Carolan of NewSchools Venture Fund, referring to the salespeople who drove from school to school, providing a demo,and trying to secure a deal.[9]

Today, the Internet reduces this friction and allows entrepreneurs to directly reach teachers, parents, and students. Freemium models offer a free,

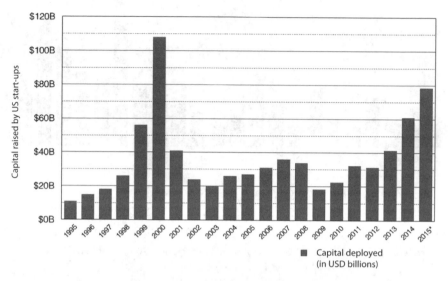

FIGURE 3.2   Annual Capital Disbursed to US Start-ups (All Stages)
Source: Mattermark, "2015 Startup Funding Pace to Reach Highest Levels Since 2000," June 2015.

limited version of the service, while a paid premium version unlocks additional features, allowing teachers to try a service before sinking funds or time into something that may not meet their needs. The result is an incredibly efficient distribution and adoption system. Alan Louie, a Silicon Valley entrepreneur and one of the cofounders of the education incubator ImagineK12, believes that the model "of only going to schools and selling there is the hardest way for a startup to go. Consummating a sale generated by a teacher and then executed by the district is just fine by me. That wasn't possible five years ago."[10]

Lower Costs to Launch New Start-ups

A number of broader technology trends are making it easier, cheaper, and faster to take a concept to market. Cloud computing has made nearly an infinite amount of computing power and storage available and has introduced sophisticated development tools and applications on an inexpensive, pay-as-you-go basis. Even small start-up teams can reach a national audience, often in a targeted way, through paid and organic search optimization, advertising platforms on Google and Facebook, and other digital marketing channels that didn't exist five years ago.

Experts estimate that today's start-up can launch for less than $100,000, nearly one-tenth of the cost a decade ago.[11] Mark Andreesen, one of the early pioneers of the Internet, reflected that in 2000, it cost $150,000 a month to run an Internet-based application. Running that same application today on Amazon's cloud services costs about $1,500 a month.[12] Google executive chairman and ex-CEO Eric Schmidt and former senior vice president of products Jonathan Rosenberg put it this way:

> Many incumbents—aka pre-Internet companies—built their businesses based on assumptions of scarcity: scarce information, scarce distribution resources and market reach, or scarce choice and shelf space. Now, though, these factors are abundant, lowering or eliminating barriers to entry and making entire industries ripe for change.[13]

All of these changes reduce the barriers to entry for entrepreneurs. They allow parents, teachers, and other "non-techies" to be able to take an idea and bring it to market.

Incubators and Accelerators

Incubators and accelerators play a critical role in the start-up ecosystem by providing skills-building opportunities, business planning support, and financial capital startup founders need to bring their idea to reality. The National Business Incubation Association (NBIA) estimates that the number of incubators grew from twelve in 1980 to more than fourteen hundred by the mid-2000s.[14] The number of education technology–specific incubators has surged to over seventeen, including the Jefferson Fund, LearnLaunch, and the Kaplan EdTech Accelerator.

There are also a number of informal incubators that have served to cultivate leaders who go on to start new ventures. TFA not only addressed a teacher pipeline challenge, but has also become a leadership incubator. Alumni have gone on to found KIPP, become state chiefs in Tennessee and Louisiana, launch TNTP, and build School of One and New Classrooms' pioneering personalized learning model. Members of Joel Klein's staff while he was chancellor in the New York City School District have gone on to launch technology start-ups, assume leadership positions in nonprofits, become state chiefs, and lead philanthropies. The experiences gained in these roles have helped shape their work in various social ventures.

Expanded Student Options

Conventional wisdom says the school choice movement, with the exception of public charter schools, has been struggling. In reality, choice has exploded in the form of charters, vouchers, online learning, tax credits, and education savings accounts (ESAs). Over twenty states have school choice programs, forty-two have charter school laws, and twenty-six have statewide virtual schools. Florida alone offers a broad array of options through tax credits, charter schools, virtual schools, McKay Scholarships, Opportunity Scholarships, Course Access policies, and Personal Learning Scholarship Accounts. Far from struggling, the choice movement is gaining momentum. In 2015, at least thirty-four states (up from twenty-nine last year) considered proposals to create or amend programs that offer private education options.

A fresh wave of reform is sweeping the country in three new ways that transcend traditional school choice politics. The first is Course Access policies that allow K–12 students to access a variety of quality courses outside the four walls of the school where they remain enrolled. This policy strengthens the traditional school but also gives students more flexible options, expanded curricular programs, and alternatives to meet their unique needs. Louisiana students and families use this reform to access a simple statewide online catalog, where they select from hundreds of learning opportunities offered by over thirty-seven active providers (online, blended, or face-to-face) that may be unavailable or underserved at their current school. Through the program, students are able to take everything from Advanced Placement to ACT prep to vocational courses.

The second new reform is education savings accounts (ESAs). These flexible, debit card–like accounts allow parents to pay for a variety of education services and supports, including tuition, tutoring, therapy for students with disabilities, instructional materials, online courses, à-la-carte public school courses, and savings for future college costs.[15] The mechanism of a flexible spending account builds on several decades of promising success in the use of similar accounts to allocate government subsidies and empower beneficiaries.

It is only natural that these mechanisms would find their way into elementary and secondary education. Over twenty-two state legislatures debated ESAs in 2015, and Tennessee and Mississippi joined Florida and Arizona in giving parents an education debit card to spend on state-approved purchases. In early June, Nevada governor Brian Sandoval signed into law a universal

ESA that would provide low-income families with, on average, $5,700 of student funds in a restricted bank account to cover tuition fees, textbooks, online courses, or other education services. Unused funds roll over year to year, in some cases rolling over into a college savings account. Doug Tuthill, the president of Step Up for Students, which manages the Florida ESA, calls it "a funding mechanism aligned to customization."[16]

A third reform trend of expanded student options is coming from a somewhat unexpected source—Silicon Valley entrepreneurs. General Assembly is reimagining higher education and job training and has trained more than ten thousand people, with 99 percent of graduates securing a job within a year. The app Duolingo has twenty million active users learning foreign languages, and an early evaluation suggests that using the app for 34 hours could generate the reading and writing skills of a first-year college semester (as much as 130 hours).[17] Students have access to thousands of courses through edX, Coursera, and other massive open online course (MOOC) platforms. Former Google head of personalization Max Ventilla launched AltSchool, which offers a new private school model where students receive weekly "playlists" of individual and group activities customized to their specific strengths and weaknesses.

THE HEADWINDS CHALLENGING TODAY'S ENTREPRENEURS

Entrepreneurs also confront formidable headwinds that slow their progress and keep some from embarking on the journey at all.

Incumbent Protections

Policy can remove barriers to innovative approaches or it can stifle them with restrictions, red tape, and insistence on traditional approaches. It can accelerate reform or it can further entrench the status quo. It can allow innovators to serve students in novel ways or it can protect incumbents. It can make funding more flexible for new solutions or it can reinforce traditional approaches.

Education investor Michael Moe says, "Increasingly, we're worried that a generation of entrepreneurs is facing a 'new innovators dilemma'—where innovation is stymied by regulatory and political environments focused on outdated needs and the wrong set of customers. This isn't about the classic political divide of right versus left. This is about policies and regulations written in a different era that are not easily translated to modern technology. It's no secret that the challenge stems, in part, from the motivations of regulators and the politics of protecting the status quo."[18]

The fragmented system of education monopolies throughout the country creates a scenario where the traditional system is able to use that dominant position to stack the rules and maintain their favored status.[19] For example, online schools can hypothetically serve students anywhere in the country but instead confront student eligibility restrictions, enrollment caps, or policies that require a certified teacher to be in the "line of sight" of a student in order for that instructional time to count.[20]

Government and regulators can disrupt the disruptors. American Enterprise Institute higher education scholar Andrew Kelly notes that "even the most revolutionary innovations are hard-pressed to break up entrenched monopolies that are protected by government policy. Making higher education affordable doesn't require more technology. It requires that policymakers be brave enough to break up the higher-education cartel."[21] Michael Horn, author of *Disrupting Class*, argues these regulatory burdens actually create an incentive to for innovators to "plant themselves outside of the reach of the regulations . . . The reason is that although regulations tend to be put in place to protect consumers initially, over time they become ways for existing institutions to protect themselves, often at the expense of consumers."[22]

Elementary and secondary education is an even more challenging environment. The system is almost perfectly designed to repel innovation, since the road to adoption goes through gates guarded by those with vested interest in not being disrupted. Frederick M. Hess and Chester E. Finn, Jr. observe, "This closed ecosystem alienates creative problem solvers while erecting bureaucratic barriers against those who would devise new solutions." Entrepreneurs eager to help fix the system eventually accept the fact that "the public-school establishment is itself their principal client, customer and sometime regulator. Innovation normally occurs only when that establishment allows it—and only up to the limits that it allows."[23]

Mark Andreessen, whose investment experience includes consumer and enterprise services, believes much of this market is hostile to change: "For a start-up to sell to a school district or in a union or bureaucratic environment, your odds of failure go way up."[24] No wonder that, when asked to identify the perceived obstacles for investment in education, investors ranked "too bureaucratic an industry" (81 percent) and the "role of government" (79 percent) as the highest barriers.[25]

Institutional-Based Systems

The issue confronting education is becoming less about a lack of access to instructional opportunities and more about a system struggling with formally recognizing student learning that occurs outside of school. The system was never designed to formally award credit for a student who learned French through Duolingo or computer science through a Harvard MOOC. This can frustrate the entrepreneur who may design a cutting-edge learning experience and get it into the hands of thousands of students but, in order for the learning to "count," must still secure approval from fifteen thousand school systems.

As the Aspen Taskforce on Learning and the Internet puts it:

> Learning networks not only provide access to a virtually endless array of learning opportunities, but they can offer learners multiple points of entry—both inside the classroom and beyond it—that provide highly individualized pathways toward career, civic and academic success . . . The current reality is that many learner networks are fragmented, organized within silos and not interconnected. Our education system is organized primarily around the learning that occurs within a school and does not capture or recognize the learning that takes place outside of school. New learning networks connect it all.[26]

In other words, there are numerous opportunities and options for students inside and outside of school. The policy and regulatory environment simply lags in formally recognizing this and supporting it through credentialing and funding.

Regulations

Everyone recognizes the need for regulations to ensure student safety, support civil rights, and protect students. But growth in the number and complexity of regulations (see figure 3.3), along with their compliance costs, can make it difficult for entrepreneurs to launch or scale new start-ups. Layers of regulation tend to harden existing ways of doing things and fossilize the underlying models.

According to the Mercatus Center, overall federal regulations alone on elementary and secondary education schools have increased 158 percent since 1997.[27] Another analysis of thirty-four regulations issued by the US Department of Education estimates the total compliance cost to be $4.8 billion, with more than twenty-two million hours of paperwork.[28]

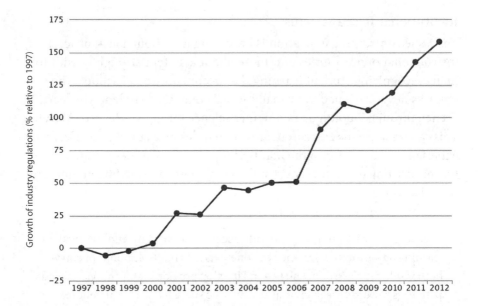

FIGURE 3.3   Historical Regulation of Elementary and Secondary Schools
Source: Provided by regdata.mercatus.org.

Technology-based models of learning confront additional regulatory barriers. Legacy laws, on the books for decades, never imagined a modern-day competency-based model facilitated through sophisticated technologies that blend online and face-to-face instruction. The Family Educational Rights and Privacy Act (FERPA), which guides the protection of student data in education, was passed in 1974—five years before the invention of the cell phone. The legislative drafters could not have possibly imagined today's world of students carrying a device more powerful than a Cray supercomputer in their pockets, connected to a data network and from which they could access thousands of online courses and resources.

An oft-unrecognized regulatory barrier is the byzantine procurement system that rarely works well for schools or entrepreneurs. Freemium adoptions eventually reach a point where, to secure a school- or districtwide adoption, the provider needs a contract with the central office. However, school systems are increasingly more conservative and excessively cautious as they seek to avoid the embarrassment of failed initiatives and perceived misuse of funds. Some regulations are needed to protect schools and taxpayers from fraud, patronage, and other forms of waste or abuse, but there must be easier and simpler ways to achieve the same goals without today's cumbersome processes. State and federal government rules can further complicate matters with contracting preferences for certain groups, requirements that favor entities with an established track record (disqualifying many start-ups), or requirements for physical storage (making it difficult to embrace cloud-based systems). As a result, procurement decisions are shifting away from users into a central office function that is often focused on compliance rather than securing the best solution.

This risk-averse culture leads to long decision cycles, which scare off investors, favor large providers who can afford to wait, and disadvantage smaller start-ups that lack the sales force army needed to compete.[29] It's no surprise that only 4 percent of providers say today's procurement processes meet contemporary needs and fewer than 50 percent of teachers say they were involved in purchasing decisions.[30]

The cumulative effect of these regulations and requirements becomes the problem. Michael McShane and colleagues note, "No raindrop thinks it is responsible for the flood. Individually, each regulation could be sensible and meaningful, but when combined with hundreds of other requirements, the sum becomes incoherent and onerous."[31]

Misaligned Incentives

Incentives matter. To understand how, consider a lesson from the 1800s when the British Empire transported prisoners to penal colonies in Australia. Captains were compensated based on the number of prisoners each ship carried, creating financial incentive to stuff as many prisoners on a ship as possible. As a result, prisoner survival rate was dismally low.

The government responded by pulling the typical levers. They added regulations requiring captains to carry lemons and limes to combat scurvy. Doctors were required to accompany the ships. Salaries were raised for some captains. Inspections were increased. Even the clergy tried appealing to the captains' better nature. None of it worked. Survival rates clung disturbingly to 50 percent.

Then in 1862, economist Edwin Chadwick suggested a change to the incentive structure. Ship captains were no longer compensated for each prisoner who boarded in England, but instead received payment for every prisoner who got off the ship alive in Australia. The survival rate leapt from 50 to 98 percent.

Similarly, we stuff students onto Title I ships and hope they survive their education journey and arrive ready for college or a job. But many do not. Some urban schools face 50 percent dropout rates.[32] Even students who beat the odds arrive at colleges needing remedial courses. And our government's response has mirrored the British government's failure in the 1800s as it pulls policy levers that do not address the underlying failure in the incentive structure.

Not unlike the fee-for-service structure in Medicare, elementary and secondary schools receive government funding based on the number of students served regardless of outcomes, quality of services, or efficiency of service provision. And just as in health care, there is little incentive for the consumers—in this case, students and parents—to seek lower cost services or compare costs. Charles Hugh Smith provides an apt analogy capturing this dilemma: "In effect, fee-for-service is open-ended: It's like going to an auto mechanic and agreeing to pay for whatever services he deems necessary, at whatever price he chooses, with no penalties to the provider if the service is poor."[33]

This broken funding mechanism perpetuates current and antiquated practices, models, and institutions. There are no incentives for school systems to embrace disruptive innovations or use technology to provide more cost-effective ways to accomplish a goal. If funding rewarded student success, schools would have greater incentive to seek out new technologies and innovations to capture the additional dollars.

Suspicion of For-Profits in Education

Launching a for-profit enterprise in education tangles would-be entrepreneurs up in cultural values that are hesitant to fully embrace private enterprises in public education. Public policy reflects and reinforces this.

Traditionally, policy supports efforts that engage the private sector in solving large, complex social challenges, using grants, loans, loan guarantees, and tax credits to incentivize private-sector supply of solutions and stimulate demand for them. In federal policy alone, more than $4 billion in loan guarantees are available to support the development of "technologies that are catalytic, replicable, and market-ready"[34]; a generous tax credit is offered to stimulate demand among consumers to adopt solar[35]; NASA makes billions available to cultivate commercial space programs and replace the vehicles serving the International Space Station[36]; and $22 billion of incentive payments are supporting the adoption of secure, portable, electronic health records—provided by hundreds of for-profit companies—for every American.[37]

Yet those policy levers are virtually nowhere to be found in the education sector. But before exploring why, it is important to emphasize that there is—and should be—a vigorous debate about the appropriateness and merit of these government investments and funding mechanisms. Many federal programs are too vulnerable to political influences over rigorous due diligence, others distort the market by picking winners and losers, and some subsidies can quickly become corporate welfare, propping up companies or sectors that would otherwise have been disrupted long ago. The point in referencing these policies in the context of this discussion is to illustrate how government policy invites, encourages, and celebrates some sets of entrepreneurs in a way unimaginable within the world of education.

Instead of engaging the private sector in education, policymakers actually create regulatory and funding barriers that skew support to nonprofits and prevent for-profit entities from participating in programs aimed at improving student achievement. The Investing in Innovation (i3) competitive grant program was described by secretary of education Arne Duncan as searching for the best innovations to tackle a host of educational challenges from dropouts to helping students achieve higher standards.[38] But rather than being open to the best solutions from the best entrepreneurs regardless of their tax status, the program embedded eligibility limitations in the authorization language that channeled funding only into nonprofits and traditional school-based institutions.[39]

This mind-set stymies more than just eligibility for government programs. Attaching the term "corporate" to a reform has become a way to attack certain reforms and school models. The American Federation of Teachers' president Randi Weingarten characterized her efforts as fighting back on the "unholy alliance of austerity-pushing politicians and the corporate reformers, hedge fund managers, and others who want to destroy public education and profit off kids."[40] These lines of attack used to be directed only at Republicans, but even education entrepreneurs, who often are center-left politically, are surprised to find their motives questioned as a "scheme" to simply profit without regard for students.[41]

This sends the collective signal that for-profit innovators are welcomed (even celebrated) for breakthroughs in other sectors, but are demonized and kept at arm's length if they try to tackle education issues. Consider the example of entrepreneur Elon Musk. Few entrepreneurs can claim to have disrupted one industry, but Musk has disrupted three. He founded PayPal, which paved the way for electronic payments and e-commerce. He launched SpaceX in 2002, leading to a new, lower-cost space vehicle. And he introduced Tesla Motors to offer an innovative electric automobile, rated the safest car ever tested by the National Highway Traffic Safety Administration.[42]

Musk's pioneering ideas were supported by the government through direct subsidies, loan financing, and deregulation. The government even courted Musk as he tackled big challenges. But if Musk wanted to apply his entrepreneurial brain toward an education challenge, he would find only government-imposed disincentives—a system of regulations and structures that would make it difficult for him to bring about a disruptive solution. It isn't surprising, then, that Musk decided to create his own private school rather than change the school his own children would have attended.[43]

CULTIVATING AN INNOVATION ECOSYSTEM

Tomorrow's education innovations require a supportive climate for education entrepreneurs. This climate will require multiple actions by multiple actors, including government and school leaders. It will also require some restraint, particularly from policymakers. Just as government doesn't create jobs, government also can't create entrepreneurs. Michael Trucano, the World Bank's global lead for innovation in education, observed, "When it comes to making accurate prognostications about the future of technology use, education officials do not generally have a track record of great success, and there is always a danger that ill-conceived or overly ambitious policies can stifle, rather than support, the emergence of technology-enabled innovations within various parts of an education system."[44] Policymakers must instead focus on creating conditions that lead to a healthy ecosystem that addresses policy and funding, encourages risk-taking, and creates smarter supply and demand in education.

Creating Room for Innovation

Many have observed that our public education system is simply not set up to demand, reward, and stimulate greater and faster innovation in the ways many other sectors are.[45] The goal for policymakers and regulators should be to create the conditions allowing for a vibrant and self-sustaining entrepreneurial ecosystem that supports student success. Former FCC chairman Julius Genachowski suggests that "policy should begin with admiration for new ways that citizens can build their lives, not with hostility to profits or the impulse to protect entrenched industries."[46] There are two general actions that policymakers can take to create these conditions.

Clear out the regulatory underbrush. Policymakers play an important role in what AEI scholar Frederick M. Hess has dubbed "cage-busting," which enables "promising new providers to challenge education monopolies, [work] to correct the legacy of federal micromanagement, and [help] to free state and local reformers from the burden of their predecessors' bad decisions."[47] It is a simple grand bargain of providing regulatory relief in exchange for a commitment to results-based accountability based on rigorous academic standards and student outcomes. To do so:

- Policymakers should create a more open education system that invites new entrants to serve students, supports new approaches to learning, and empowers new models. *The 10 Elements of High Quality Digital Learning*, unveiled in 2010 and based on input from more than one hundred diverse leaders, offers a roadmap for policymakers.[48]
- Policymakers should incorporate stronger sunset clauses into regulations to shift the burden of proof from those advocating termination to those advocating continuation.[49]
- Policymakers should streamline and modernize procurement regulations to be more accommodating of start-ups. Part of this involves recognition within procurement processes that the rapid development cycles used by many start-ups today may demand a constantly evolving service rather than the purchase of "finished" products in the traditional software sense.
- Policymakers should allow for new authorizers, particularly with charter schools and online learning providers, who can deliver oversight functions but also be open to innovative models. These authorizers should themselves be held accountable by state policymakers, such as in the example set by the Ohio Department of Education in evaluating and rating the state's charter authorizers.[50]
- Policymakers should use reciprocity agreements to formally recognize other state authorizations and approvals. For example, states are using state-level reciprocity process to make state authorization in higher education more efficient, effective, and uniform.[51] This approach could be used to automatically recognize approvals

granted in other states or provide a "fast track" process, saving time and resources for both the state and entrepreneurs. This could be applied to a variety of K–12 segments that require state approvals, including charter schools, supplemental instructional resources, textbook adoption, and online courses.[52]

- Policymakers should have a deep commitment to accountability based on student outcomes and quality. Regulatory flexibility does not mean a reduced commitment to quality. Nobody wants zero regulation. But the regulatory system needs to be flexible enough to accommodate new approaches that can be evaluated against student performance. This would require approval, authorization, and adoption processes to focus more on student outcomes and less on inputs. Entrepreneurial efforts that fail to improve outcomes should be closed or have their approvals revoked. This approach would also allow states to be more agnostic toward nonprofits and for-profits. With a "no labels" approach, policymakers can focus solely on outcomes, not corporate structures.

- Policymakers should release outcome data using open-data formats, not only bringing transparency but also fueling other entrepreneurs. Consider what the GreatSchools rating service could do if every state reported outcome data for all online learning and Course Access programs.

- Philanthropies should invest in advocacy to create the supportive regulatory environment entrepreneurs need to try out their ideas and scale promising models.

- Investors should develop a deeper understanding of the education regulatory landscape, particularly in assessing the risk involved with different business models that could be disrupted by a law or regulation. Better-informed investors will lead to better-informed investments and a better supply of solutions.

Build trusted learning environments. The world of on-demand learning will require deep connections of trust. As the Aspen Task Force on Learning and the Internet noted, "Realizing the benefits of learning networks will necessitate a commitment to establishing trust with teachers, parents and students that children will have safe experiences online and that sensitive personal information is securely protected . . . Without trust, the ultimate success of networked learning could be in jeopardy."[53] To create trust:

- Policymakers, school leaders, and technology providers should use a "trust framework" to guide the use of technology in instruction such as that offered by the Aspen Task Force oriented around transparency, data stewardship, accountability, and oversight.[54]
- Schools should support teacher and leader practices that build trust with parents, not merely training teachers in how to comply with privacy regulations, but also transparently sharing with parents what data is collected, how it is used, and who it is shared with, perhaps through a web-based portal or dashboard. Parents should be able to access their child's education records as easily as they can access their child's electronic health records.
- Technology providers should design their innovations with trust in mind. Privacy and security features must be included up front and not as an afterthought. This will not only entail stronger security measures, but also give users more control over their data and understanding on how the provider is using the data.
- State departments of education, school systems, and technology providers will need chief privacy officers who can not only coordinate regulatory compliance, but also review vendor agreements, assess security risks, provide training and support to teachers, and investigate potential violations.[55]

Catalyzing Innovation

The innovation ecosystem relies on high-risk, high-reward R&D that often only government can support. Any innovation pump must be primed with R&D. This is most needed in education, where only $300 million is invested annually by the US Department of Education, less than 1 percent of the National Institutes of Health's $30 billion research budget. Targeted, long-term investments in basic but expensive research can provide the breakthrough findings that drive new educational advancements.

Such R&D spending must extend to the expensive, but important, rigorous methodologies to evaluate programs and models to measure effectiveness and the conditions under which success is achieved. The complexity and cost to do these evaluations well often makes it difficult for bootstrap start-ups to afford them.

There is also the overlooked policy lever of prizes, which have a long history of attracting innovators to solve complicated problems. Policymakers, philanthropies, and even schools themselves should use prizes to catalyze innovative solutions to pressing challenges. The mechanism is attractive in that it casts a wide net for solutions, often extending outside the traditional players. Prizes are an extremely efficient strategy for mobilizing diverse talent that may be impossible to locate using conventional approaches. It also offers a fiscally conservative solution for policymakers since funds are only paid out once the goal has been achieved.[56]

Philanthropies can greater use of program-related investments (PRIs), which allow for investments as loans, loan guarantees, or even equity stakes with the expectation of recovering the investment plus a reasonable rate of return. Greater use of PRIs will help provide additional capital to scale entrepreneurial entities, particularly in later investment rounds.

Funding Anytime, Anywhere Learning Based on Performance

Transforming education requires rethinking our antiquated funding system to make it not merely fairer, but also more supportive of emerging innovations. Policymakers should adopt policies that are student-centered and acknowledge the evolving system of public education that allows learning to occur not just any time, but anywhere. Greater options inside and outside of traditional education institutions require flexible funding that can follow the child to those options. There are a number of ways to facilitate on-demand learning:

Modernize funding streams to accommodate mobile learners. Policymakers should reform funding streams to reflect the following principles:

- *Weighted funding:* Each child's school receives a certain amount of funding based on the student's characteristics and the cost factors that accompany those characteristics.
- *Flexibility:* Dollars aren't restricted or designated for particular uses. Teachers and leaders are given more autonomy in determining how funds are spent.
- *Portability:* Dollars can follow students to the school or course that best suits their individual needs—including fractional funding for full-time or part-time options. This portability should also extend to opportunities outside schools.
- *Performance-based:* Incentives are tied to student outcomes, and schools are rewarded on the basis of student outcomes.[57] Rewarding performance will in turn create incentives for schools to think more creatively about selecting and using innovations to capture

the additional dollars by reaching the performance goals (see figure 3.4).

For example, Stanford University School of Public Policy and the Foundation for Excellence in Education suggest that this approach be used for online learning. Course providers would decide how much of their payment they are willing to have tied to quality metrics identified by the state, and would receive this

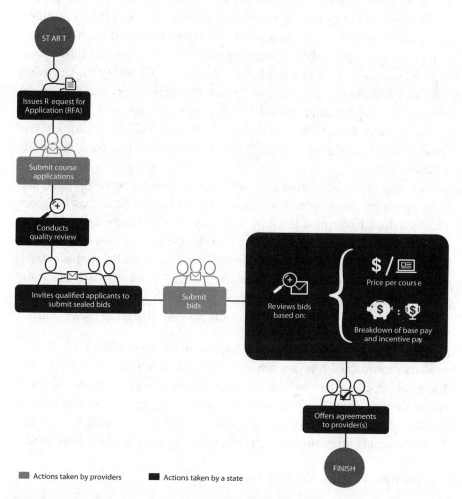

FIGURE 3.4   Visual Framework for Selecting Quality Course Providers at Competitive Prices

Source: "A Framework for Selecting Quality Course Providers at Competitive Prices," Scott Ferron, Paige Gonge, Adeeb Sahar, Kyle Vanderberg, in coordination with the Stanford University Public Policy Program and Digital Learning Now.

incentive portion of their payment only if their students' academic performance meets the bar the state has set. While states may decide to focus on different criteria for evaluation (e.g., proficiency, growth, completion), this payment system will allow them to hold providers accountable for quality.[58]

Allow for dynamic pricing. Setting fixed prices in statutes distorts the market by overpaying some providers and pricing others out. Inflexible pricing structures also fail to take into account different cost structures of different models. An online course may cost less than a blended learning model that combines some online instruction with some face-to-face interaction.

Policymakers will also need to ensure there is flexibility for providers to charge different prices reflecting different levels of services. Louisiana's Course Access program is a model in this regard (figure 3.5). The program allows for dynamic pricing, so courses cost from $275 for online elective courses such as sociology to $1,325 for more resource-intensive, in-person welding courses.[59]

Auctions might be used to assist with price discovery while also incentivizing performance. A diverse coalition of the Center for American Progress, the American Enterprise Institute, and New Profit entrepreneurs suggests that entrepreneurs bid on the level of funding they would need to provide a given service and the proportion of the fee they are willing to have determined by the outcomes they achieve. From this list, states or schools could select the providers offering the lowest price with the highest confidence in outcomes. This shifts the risk from the state or district to the provider.[60]

Leverage ESAs to provide on-demand funding for on-demand learning. Policymakers should use ESAs as a vehicle to provide flexible funding to support the growing ecosystem of education services inside and outside the traditional system. Parents could use the accounts to purchase online courses for their child, pay for the testing fee of an online AP course, fund online tutors, or secure other student supports, including special education services.

Supporting Models, Not Just Technology

Create pathways for competency-based learning. As schooling becomes more dynamic, it makes sense for policymakers to revisit rules that measure learning in terms of time spent sitting in a classroom and instead favor laws and regulation that measure whether students have mastered content and

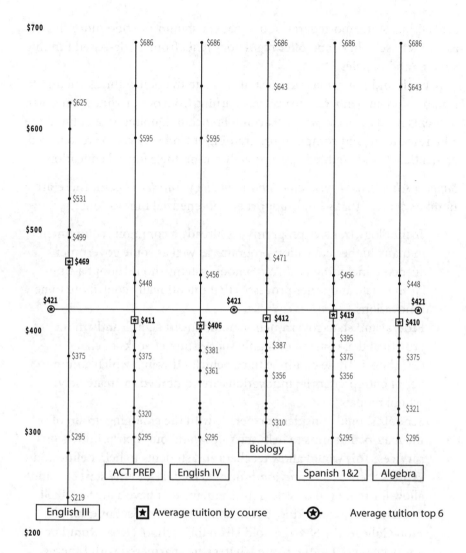

FIGURE 3.5 Louisiana Top Six Course Offerings, Cost By Semester

Louisiana's Course Choice program allows for a vigorous quality review, as well as a unique market framework for course offerings. This chart displays both the range of pricing for these high quailty courses—from $219 to $686 per semester course—along with the average prices for each course. Without this market framework, Louisiana students could be limited in both the number of providers within each course and the variety of courses available.

Source: Digital Learning, *Digital Learning Report Card 2014.*

skills. Thus state and federal policymakers should provide more flexible assessment schedules and offer regulatory relief from grade-based funding streams and policies.

Schools and policymakers must also create the policy infrastructure to support students who want to transfer learning from one provider to another. Students need a system where learning French in Duolingo, calculus at the Khan Academy, and computer programing at Code.org can be recognized, credentialed, and credited appropriately within their formal education.

Support school-based incubators and technology transfer. Again, there are a number of areas that would support entrepreneurial innovation:

- Technology transfer programs are already a common requirement in many higher education programs as well as some government agencies, including NASA.[61] School systems should adopt a similar mandate and other processes that intentionally contribute to new innovations.
- Federal and state governments should invest significantly in the growth and expansion of highly successful networks of charter schools. These continue to be vehicles through which a number of entrepreneurial innovations are combined to create new school models.
- Schools should consider partnering with the emerging group of incubators that aims to help start-ups build out their products or services. This would allow teachers and students to help define and express their needs, provide continual feedback to the start-up, and allow for more rapid cycle improvements that have a greater likelihood of not just working, but meeting users' needs. For example, Eton College, the 574-year-old UK public school (what would be a private school in the United States), has partnered with Emerge Venture Lab, a London-based accelerator, to support tech start-ups.[62]
- Finally, policymakers need to free schools of legacy regulations that make it difficult for schools and companies to collaborate or transfer technology. Joel Rose found himself in such a place when attempting to take one of Time's Innovations of Year, the School of One, and spin it off. Regulations made it nearly impossible to spin off the new model and handcuffed the role Joel could play in negotiating the terms.[63]

CONCLUSION

America is unique in the world for cultivating the conditions that lead to breakthrough, disruptive innovations. Those innovations bring about not merely economic growth, but improvements in the way we work and live. Now more than ever, we need to lower the barriers of entry for entrepreneurs to apply their creative problem solving abilities to help teachers and students succeed.

The cornerstone of this movement is less about available tools and services and more about openness to rethinking traditional approaches and models. This is an opportunity to accomplish the purpose of public education with a system of dynamic solutions, institutions, and services oriented around student success. There is also an opportunity to tackle these issues from a bipartisan center, demonstrated clearly in a paper on education entrepreneurs written by the Center for American Progress, the American Enterprise Institute, and and New Profit:

> Opening the marketplace to a diverse set of new—including private, for-profit and non-profit—providers is not a veiled call for privatization of our education system. Instead, it reflects our recognition that within a public system we must still remain open to various methods of delivery—and a spirit of innovation, whatever its source. Given the crisis in our nation's schools, we must put aside ideological predispositions to support a rational conversation about which providers and approaches have the greatest potential to solve the problems that public education faces.[64]

The United States faces major challenges with global economic trends and addressing economic mobility. The country needs to support the next generation of entrepreneurs who are bringing new ideas to solve old problems. Engaging and supporting these entrepreneurs will help unleash the innovation needed to ensure every child is able to meet his or her full potential through a rich, exciting, and rigorous education.

Barbarians at the Gate?

How Venture Finance Could Support
Radical K–12 Innovation

Dmitri Mehlhorn

> *"Since the early twentieth century, educational entrepreneurs have made major changes to US public school goals, governance, organization, and curriculum, [yet] have seldom altered substantially or permanently classroom regularities and low-income students' academic achievement."*
>
> —Larry Cuban, 2006[1]

> *"Whether it's steamships disrupted by the railroads, or railroads disrupted by the airlines, it's typically the large entrenched incumbents that are displaced by innovators. It happens over and over and over again . . . Why? . . . Companies that depend only on their internal experts cannot possibly evolve fast enough during these times of explosive innovation . . . The day before something is truly a breakthrough, it's a crazy idea. And experimenting with crazy ideas requires a high degree of tolerance for risk-taking. Large companies and government agencies have a lot to protect and therefore are not willing to take big risks."*
>
> —Peter Diamandis, 2013[2]

W hy doesn't every student in America have a tablet computer and smart watch? Why don't those devices engage diverse students with adaptive learning games, every day, all year, including at home and on field trips? Why don't those devices automatically handle routine tasks like grading, testing, and attendance, allowing teachers to act as leaders, coaches, and mentors? More broadly, why haven't diverse ideas from the public, nonprofit, and for-profit sectors found ways to meet the needs of every student? Why, as a century of innovations transformed other sectors, have the changes in American public schools been so incremental?

The answer is not lack of money. Over the past century of incremental K–12 educational change as described by Larry Cuban in the quote above, we have increased public education budgets from 1 percent to 6 percent of GDP, representing a roughly fortyfold increase in constant dollars spent on each pupil.[3] This per-pupil spending is more than enough to cover the rapidly falling costs of hardware and software for all kids. Indeed, aggregate K–12 investments in the United States are greater than those ever made.

Nor is the problem political effort. The past century has seen waves of reform involving teacher wars, testing wars, and many other core principles.

The problem is that America's schools cannot disrupt themselves because radical changes are risky, costly, and uncomfortable. As in all sectors, major innovation must be incubated and sponsored from outside.

This is where venture finance comes in. As explained by Stanford University Graduate School of Business professor Ilya Strebulaev, "Venture capital is the business of failing . . . or the business of failing constructively."[4] Venture finance works by identifying and nurturing those few radical ideas that change things for the better. To do this, it incubates numerous ideas through years of financial losses.

This chapter argues that venture finance has not played this role in K–12 education, as it has only recently begun to emerge from risk-aversion and inadequate scale that have characterized this area. The discussion proceeds in four sections.

- American K–12 education is uniquely change-averse, making venture-backed disruption especially difficult.
- Venture capital in the private sector works because it has the scale and specialization to invest massively over long periods of time, and in the face of widespread failure, to harvest a few truly transformative ideas.
- By comparison, K–12 venture finance is too small and risk-averse; promising recent developments could still be swept away.
- A viable K–12 venture finance ecosystem is possible, but the necessary scale and specialization will happen only if private funders

adapt to the political nature of public schooling—especially by empowering, enabling, and partnering with teachers and teacher organizations.

AMERICAN K–12 EDUCATION IS UNIQUELY CHANGE-AVERSE

For those who lack personal experience, entrepreneurship sounds exciting. In popular imagination, the classic entrepreneur is Virgin's Richard Branson, who started his first business at sixteen, bought his first private island when he was twenty-four, and seems to have spent life since then kite-surfing and exploring outer space.[5] But the reality is that new ventures run the risk of failure and involve levels of uncertainty that few are willing to face.

Successful institutions, by design, discourage such risk-taking. Five factors make these anti-change pressures, common to all organizations, especially powerful in American public schools:

Public bureaucracies lack consensus metrics for success. As James Q. Wilson explored in *Bureaucracy* (1989) constituencies place diverse demands on government, ranging from jobs and regional largesse, to avoidance of scandal, to vaguely defined goals.[6] These conflicting pressures lead civil servants to focus on processes and inputs, rather than outputs. As described by left-of-center billionaire Nick Hanauer and coauthor Eric Liu, this means government focuses more on "how" than on "what," stifling innovation.[7] Furthermore, the lack of consensus on success metrics means that public managers capture few benefits when risky ventures succeed, but face career-destroying criticism when they go wrong. In this environment, rational actors choose low-risk options.

In practice, K–12 stakeholders value conservatism. As Henry Levin wrote in *Educational Entrepreneurship*, schools

> . . . are conservative institutions charged with the primary goal of preparing the young to acclimate to and participate in the cultural, social, economic, and political life of an existing social entity . . . fulfillment of this role means suspicion of and resistance to change by parents, teachers, students, and school administrators, exactly what we find in school culture and in the tendency of schools to modify external attempts to reform them."[8]

Unlike successful school systems abroad that have pushed excellence for decades, the United States has asked its schools to create cohesion and continuity in the face of ethnic and racial tumult.[9]

Parochial cultures reject new ideas.   Diverse social science studies have shown how established experts resist new ideas. Harvard historian of science Thomas Kuhn demonstrated that today's dominant scientific theories were rejected until scholars of previous theories passed away.[10] Geographer Jared Diamond has shown how isolated societies are at a catastrophic disadvantage compared with societies that evolved through the exchange of ideas and immunities.[11] American schools seem prone to this problem of parochialism, especially with regard to ideas from the private sector.[12]

Public discourse casts innovation as morally suspect.   A foundation of modern ethics is that it is morally wrong to use human lives as a means to an end. Thus, those opposed to innovation argue, "We cannot experiment on children."[13] As an empirical matter, this reeks of hypocrisy, as our current education system is full of experiments. Every investment in teacher pensions, classroom supplements, and school buildings that tried and failed to close the achievement gap has been a failed experiment, with lifelong costs for the children whose life outcomes were compromised as a result. The biggest experiment is whether public education can succeed as a government-run monopoly with little parent choice. At the other end of the continuum, new teachers enter the profession every year, individually trying new approaches, often with new curricula and pedagogies. Since we are experimenting no matter what we do, there should be no moral bias against the type of radical innovation that has improved performance in so many other sectors of society. But within individual schools and districts, the "no experiments" argument creates a political barrier to teachers and others who want to pursue new ideas.

Actors throughout the system use idiosyncratic criteria to veto change.   Most state governments give de facto veto power over many types of reform efforts to every district, school, and classroom. As Larry Cuban wrote in 2010, research on classroom practice has shown that "policymakers can legislate changes in teacher practices all they want but teachers, once they close their classroom door, will modify only what they believe will benefit children."[14] Unsurprisingly, individual teachers have diverse ideas about what will benefit children—and since teachers are human, those ideas rarely involve changes to the teachers' own practices. This creates the phenomenon whereby practitioners discard "invented-elsewhere" ideas.[15]

VENTURE CAPITAL: USING SCALE AND TAKING RISKS TO FIND UNICORNS

Popular culture often casts financiers as villains, for good reason. The 1989 book *Barbarians at the Gate*, for instance, told the messy story of a private equity firm fighting to disrupt the workings of the corporate behemoth RJR Nabisco. Financiers operate as outsiders, sharing ideas across companies, aggregating risks to make returns more predictable, and making demands (as partial owners) on the managers of mature companies. As public economist John Kenneth Galbraith wrote, "A banker need not be popular; indeed, a good banker in a healthy capitalist society should probably be much disliked. People do not wish to trust their money to a hail-fellow-well-met but to a misanthrope who can say no."[16]

The very characteristics that earn enmity, however, are useful for innovation. Economist Joseph Schumpeter described this a century ago, arguing that the financial sector spurs innovation by finding and supporting promising entrepreneurs.[17] Since then, theoretical work and empirical evidence across industries, countries, and firms have confirmed Schumpeter's theory by demonstrating that a strong financial sector predicts future development.[18]

Within the financial sector, venture capitalists especially identify and support disruptive new companies. This requires analytic work and rigorous triage. As described by LinkedIn founder Reid Hoffman, "the classic general partner in a venture firm is exposed to around 5,000 pitches; decides to look more closely at 600 to 800 of them; and ends up doing between 0 and 2 deals."[19] Once they have identified potential disruptors, venture financiers provide substantial capital, as disruptive companies' expenses grow much faster than their profits in their early years.[20]

The United States has the world's most successful venture capital sector.[21] Venture-backed firms account for 21 percent of the US economy by output, and 11 percent of its private-sector employment.[22] From 1970 to 2000, venture-backed firms "had almost twice the sales, paid almost three times the federal taxes, generated almost twice the exports, and invested almost three times as much in R&D per $1,000 in assets as did the average non-venture-capital-backed companies," with successes in virtually every sector of the economy.[23]

Like entrepreneurialism itself, venture capital is shaped by failure. Ninety percent of all start-ups fail; despite the careful screening of prospects and the extensive support provided before a project is adopted the failure rate only drops to 75 percent for venture-backed firms.[24] The majority of the industry's profits come from barely 3 percent of investments.[25] Disruptive successes are so rare the industry refers to them as mythical beasts—"unicorns"—if they reach a valuation of more than $1 billion. Unicorns represent 0.07 percent of venture investments, and typically take over eight years from launch to go public.[26] Venture capital as a whole can see decade-long droughts in which aggregate profits are lower than in other investment categories.[27] This harsh environment drives several adaptations:

Scale: Every year, actors throughout the US economy invest roughly $85 billion in young companies, including $9 billion in "bootstrap" financing from founders; $28 billion in "angel" financing by individual investors; and $48 billion in "institutional" venture capital. In that last category, in 2014, institutional venture investors put $48.3 billion into 4,356 deals, for an average deal size of roughly $11 million.[28]

Specialized success definitions by start-up stage: As these numbers suggest, venture finance specializes by the stage of start-up, enabling stage-specific success metrics:

- *Bootstrap investors* put money into their own businesses, often so that they don't have to work for a boss. For many, success simply means survival.
- *Angel investors* tend to be semiretired executives who invest not just money but mentorship. Angel investors vary by sector, size of deal, and nature of support.[29] Metrics for success include product performance and usage levels that justify institutional venture capital investments.
- *Series A funding rounds* represent the transition from individual to institutional investors. Series A investors look for vision and leaders, and expect that their money will capitalize a company for six to eighteen months as it builds its team and tests the vision. Success at this round entails proof of product-market fit, including usage

metrics and revenue. These "first financing" rounds have an average deal size of $2.5 to $4 million.[30]

- *Series B funding* is the first "expansion round" to drive growth at companies that have proven their product-market fit. Entrepreneurs can expect capital in the eight or nine figures in a Series B, along with a highly motivated and well-connected new owner.[31] Series B investors define success in terms of profit potential; their diligence is much more intense than in previous rounds, and includes a hard-nosed look at costs and scaling (proof that the business will be able to see rapid gains in reach and impact).

- *Later stages of investment,* from later private investment rounds, to strategic acquisitions, to initial public offerings (IPOs), also have characteristic sizes, challenges, and benefits. In general, later rounds look more and more for metrics that suggest economy-wide disruptive innovation.[32]

Specialization by sector: A third adaptation is sector specialization, which enables best-practice support in fast-moving niche areas. This allows venture capitalists to collaborate closely when they possess complementary areas of expertise.

ED FINANCE: JUST BEGINNING TO ESCAPE SUBSCALE RISK-AVERSION

Iconic education entrepreneurs of the late 1980s help illustrate the limitations of venture finance to date. In 1988, the late American Federation of Teachers President Al Shanker endorsed charter schools in terms very similar to those later used in Harvard Business School Professor Clayton Christensen's classic *Innovator's Dilemma*: to incubate innovation outside of a central bureaucracy. In 1989, Wendy Kopp submitted her college paper proposing to build Teach For America. Both ideas eventually helped tens of thousands of individual students.[33] Both models, however, faced steadfast political opposition, and twenty-five years later both have achieved only single-digit percentage penetration of their respective markets (number of students educated, and numbers of teachers recruited). Careful research evidence indicates that, on average, both perform only modestly better than traditional approaches.

A robust venture capital ecosystem would accelerate impact in several ways. First, a well-functioning venture sector would invest massively to scale up successes and shut down failures. This alone, even with no further innovation, would create a sea change: today's top charter schools outperform traditional public schools, but sector performance is weighed down by numerous average and subpar charters.[34] Second, early stage venture capital would back many risky but radical ideas for entirely new models incorporating the latest brain science, interactive technologies, and business ideas. Successive investors would discard failures and invest heavily in the successes.

So why hasn't venture finance done this work in education? After all, venture capital has not been entirely absent from the K–12 sector. In the nonprofit sector, for example, venture philanthropists have helped define success, develop entrepreneurial talent, and mobilize new constituencies. In the private sector, initiatives have ranged from for-profit school management to technology.

The historical problem has been one of scale and sophistication. The social sectors have lacked sufficient urgency to innovate, while the private sector has been underfunded by something like $4.5 billion. As Kim Smith and Julie Petersen, then of the NewSchools Venture Fund, described in 2007, education finance across all three funding sectors has lacked the metrics for a competitive, differentiated proliferation of capital providers.[35]

The "Non-Trepreneurial" Public Sector Does Not Innovate

America's K–12 funding has been allocated to worthy causes: buildings, books, salaries, transportation, more equitable services, etc. The fact that these funds have been preallocated to these inputs, however, means that no money has been made available for disruptive experimentation. This result is unsurprising; as noted earlier, the public sector faces constraints that preclude venture-style risk-taking.

The Incremental Philanthropic Sector

As Karl Zinsmeister and colleagues have observed, "More philanthropic donations are channeled into education than to any other sector of American society except religion."[36] Unfortunately, several factors have prevented this money from going to disruptive innovation.

First and most importantly, the philanthropic sector lacks the consensus metrics for success that drive risk-tolerance and accountability in private-sector venture capital. As discussed earlier, venture capitalists deny funding to more than 99 percent of applicants, yet invest millions in organizations that lose money over long periods of time. This selectivity and staying power comes from conviction around metrics that have been developed and honed over many years. Foundations, by contrast, have managed their money by relationships (working closely with a few trusted operators rather than funding new operators) and by sponsoring individual projects with relatively clear, near-term objectives. As a consequence, many radical disruptors cannot even get an audience, and promising start-ups find it difficult to scale (requesting project-level financing to scale an idea would be analogous to a private-sector company seeking board-level approval for regular operating expenses).

The lack of common metrics exacerbates a second problem: the principal-agent problem of donors versus program officers. Whereas clear metrics allow venture funds to delegate decision-making to entrepreneurs, in the absence of such metrics, the philanthropic sector has been necessarily bureaucratic. For example, Facebook founder Mark Zuckerberg invested $100 million to improve schools in Newark, New Jersey, but a substantial amount of money and time were spent building a team that, as its first order of business, had to define success and build a plan. This principal-agent problem gets worse over time, especially after founding donors die; longer-established foundations tend to have larger staffs, better office space, and less urgency.

A third problem is that venture philanthropy doesn't have a virtuous feedback cycle. Rather than successful investors making returns that they then plow back into investments, endowments remain roughly stable regardless of the foundation's "success."

Finally, the psychology of philanthropy often pushes donors to invest less in disruption and more in conservation in the form of libraries and museums. Many donors either want to preserve the society in which they succeeded, or gain reputational benefits vis-à-vis society's current elites. The Annenberg Foundation, for instance, may have an interest in the public image of deceased philanthropist Walter Annenberg. This in turn may have led to relationships with current status quo influencers. As a result, Annenberg contributed substantial sums toward retread ideas. The leaders of Annenberg's massive grant efforts later self-critically assessed their own work as "the classic definition of a professional reform," arguing, "The school districts and the schools gobbled up those grants like lunch, and they were ready for the next one."[37]

While these limitations have begun to change over the past decade, their historical weight has been to make philanthropy conservative rather than disruptive.

Private-Sector Venture Capital: The $4.5 Billion Funding Gap

Virtually every investor who looks at the K–12 sector's failure to adopt new models sees a big opportunity for radical improvement. But the money hasn't come. A 2009 paper by Tom Vander Ark, now a partner at education venture capital firm Learn Capital, estimated that roughly 0 percent of institutional venture capital went to K–12 education, which constituted 6 percent of the national economy.[38] My interviews suggest that this also applies to bootstrap and angel investors. Even the recent peaks, and the peak years of the dot-com boom, have seen annual venture investments of only $500–$600 million.[39] To see the size of this gap, imagine that K–12 education had the same share of the national venture capital investments as it has of the national economy; the result would be $5 billion per year (6 percent of $85 billion). This rough calculation suggests that private-sector education venture finance is an order of magnitude too small for the opportunities presented. As a result of this gap of roughly $4.5 billion per year, we do not see the kind of large-scale specialization or long-term investment that we see in the private sector.

Green Shoots of Progress in Venture Finance . . .

Pessimists look at this landscape and conclude that entrepreneurial innovation will never take root in K–12 education. Optimists push back by noting five recent positive developments:

Measures of performance. Student achievement data, especially measures of growth in student learning such as value-added measures (VAM), provide directionally correct evidence about which schools best help children learn. Recent empirical results confirm the utility of such measures.[40] Parent choice creates another measure; for instance, lottery-based charter schools with longer wait lists have done something to enthuse parents. These two categories of metrics—student achievement and parent choice—allow the government to pay for performance. Both data and choice have started to increase in America over the past decade, thanks to political leadership from both parties; investments by the Gates Foundation in research and pilots; and constituency-building investments by the Walton Family Foundation.

Venture philanthropy. A driver of the trend mentioned above is the increasing entrepreneurialism of the philanthropic sector. Over the past decade, venture philanthropy has made up an ever-larger share of education giving, which has increased donors' impact.[41] Today's philanthropists "are less likely than were donors in the past to think that the solution to that problem lies solely or even primarily in spending more money or even in making the allocation of resources more equitable, which has been a common thread in work that many better-established foundations have pursued."[42] Some of this new philanthropy has taken the form of gap-filling or blended funds, such as the NewSchools Venture Fund, which subsidizes the early finances of entrepreneurs.

Talent. For most venture investors, talent is the single biggest factor in their investment decisions. Hence, one of the achievements of educational entrepreneurs in the 1980s and 1990s was to build a community of experienced entrepreneurs. Pioneers such as Teach For America and KIPP helped develop future leaders in whom venture capitalists can now invest. Entrepreneurs who made it through the lean period after the dot-com bubble may have learned lessons necessary to build great new organizations, which in turn might trigger the virtuous cycle wherein successful founders become venture investors—just as Hewlett-Packard and Apple generated many future leaders in Silicon Valley.

Increased private-sector activity. The trends noted above have renewed interest from private-sector venture capital. Venture capitalists and corporate executives I interviewed reported that they have been seeing a steadily better pipeline of leaders, ideas, and opportunities over the past three to four years.

New political constituencies. Since the barriers to entrepreneurialism have been political, a vital long-term trend has been the mobilization of pro-reform teachers and underserved parent communities. As one hopeful indicator, the 2014 elections saw slim electoral results from massive anti-reform spending efforts.

. . . but a Backlash Could Make This a False Spring
Predictions of imminent revolution in education have been made for decades. Instead of progress, however, the historical pattern has been oscillation, with each generation wiping out the previous generation's initiatives.[43] Each false spring casts a pall on future venture activity; investors lose their

money, retroactively refer to the period as a "bubble," and become less likely to invest in the future. Periods of reform have not lasted long enough for an entrepreneurial ecosystem to deliver big gains.

There could easily be another backlash. To take one possible scenario, a high-profile scandal could spook politicians, donors, and investors.[44] Political moves to reduce data gathering and usage and to further limit choice and charters would take away success stories and momentum, damaging the perceived risk-reward calculus for investors and reversing the recent growth in reform constituencies.

The critical issue, therefore, is whether the recent decade of reform will lead to course corrections (bold behavior moderated with good sense), or to backlash (reckless behavior taking excessive risks).

A PATH FORWARD FOR VENTURE FINANCE IN K–12 EDUCATION

Fortunately, the pessimists do not have a monopoly on the lessons of history. In a best-case scenario, the education venture market will develop in stages. Silicon Valley did not spring into existence overnight; rather, capital, talent, and ideas came together in a series of mutually reinforcing trends. More broadly, scalable innovation has come from symbiotic evolution between platforms and applications.[45] We are starting to see the beginnings of this with platforms such as Common Core, and platform companies such as Clever (which provides a universal interface for schools to share data).

Although the public sector remains the main funder of primary and secondary education, that does not preclude a robust venture capital sector. Venture capitalists have achieved returns and delivered disruptive gains in other sectors with heavy government regulations and spending, including energy, health care, and military defense. Success can create a virtuous cycle, provided that public and philanthropic funders continue to create the conditions for reform, and that private-sector investors engage with the teaching profession.

Public Funders: Defend Results-Based Metrics

If the pendulum swings backward on results-based metrics, it will cripple the prospects for venture finance in education. Despite recent improvement, most US schools still emphasize rigid process controls (for example, all schools must follow a specific operating model) and input controls (for example, teacher quality will be evaluated by how much time those teachers have spent in classrooms). A backlash that reaffirms process and input metrics means no markets for new ideas; no ways to identify the best 1 percent of ideas; and no ways to direct multimillion-dollar "expansion rounds" for money-losing but disruptive start-ups. More than 75 percent of K–12 funding comes from taxes, so the public sector remains the gatekeeper for education ideas. Unless performance measures continue to displace such controls, we will not be able to redirect America's $600 billion budget toward new models of delivery.[46]

Data about *student achievement* and *parent choice* are the two major forms of results-based metrics. Student achievement data allow comparisons of to what extent different kinds of investment help children learn. Choice data show the relative attractiveness of different schooling models to parents. Both forms of results-based metrics are at risk. Although civil rights groups and education reformers have pushed back, reform opponents have stoked public anxiety about overtesting, data privacy, and federal control over education. As of this writing, these concerns have been used to argue for test boycotts, retreats from the Common Core standards, and data restrictions that would cripple research. Attacks on parent choice include lawsuits against Florida's tax credits voucher program, as well as ongoing campaigns against charter schools in many states.

Pessimists reviewing this backlash may claim that a pendulum is inevitable; that publicly funded K–12 education simply cannot maintain momentum toward results-based metrics, or perhaps that results-based metrics are inappropriate for public schools. This claim is belied by the experience of other heavily subsidized sectors of our economy, which encourage choice among providers[47] and link pay to performance.[48] An extreme example is the military, funded entirely with tightly regulated public dollars. In the military sector, venture capitalists select and nurture new ideas, extending the US defense industry's technological lead over adversaries.[49] A more directly analogous sector may be health care, which gets 65 percent of its funding from the public sector (compared with 75 percent of American K–12 education), but allows patients to choose from among government-run, nonprofit, and for-profit hospitals. Health care has focused on empirical measures of performance since the Flexner Report in 1910 led to the closure of half of the then-existing medical schools. Choice and metrics attract investment:

a larger share of the nation's venture capital goes to health care than health care represents as a share of the economy.

Philanthropic Donors: Peripheral Retreats but Defend the Core

Scholars Jay Greene and Sarah Reckhow have separately concluded that total foundation contributions to K–12 education may exceed $1 billion. They both further observe that this sum of money is so small in comparison to the $600 billion spent nationally in K–12 education budgets that donors must invest their money in building constituencies and capacity in order to achieve results.[50] The story of reform success over the past decade has been high-leverage philanthropy, from Gates developing data, to Broad developing leaders, to Walton cultivating political constituencies. Those battles continue today. These investments should be extended in every state to maintain national momentum toward results-based metrics. Each state battleground matters in whether we have a national consensus in favor of results-based metrics.

From the perspective of venture finance, however, high-quality data is central, and everything else must be allowed compromise and tactical retreats. For example, tests do not need to be onerous to generate useful data; reformers should be first in line to criticize overly burdensome implementations. For another instance, value-added measures do not need to be 50 percent of every teacher's evaluation every year in order to generate useful data; they will still play a valuable role if they influence the evaluations of math and reading teachers who have two successive years of top-quintile or bottom-quintile VAM performance. Perhaps most importantly, reformers should respect data themselves. The *Los Angeles Times'* publication of the names of individual teachers and their VAM results was a tactical mistake; such a list implied false precision given the noise around individual VAM scores. The *Times* could have achieved the same result, with much greater reliability, by simply publishing the lists of names of teachers who had been top quintile or bottom quintile two years in a row.

The core challenge for philanthropists and public funders is to ensure that common metrics provide a baseline to enable innovation, rather than a straitjacket. The metrics used by venture capitalists have not kept healthcare and military innovations from saving lives, or energy and consumer innovations from improving quality of life. Indeed, it is the lack of metrics that forces public accountability into a crushing bureaucracy that alienates many teachers, students, and parents. Defenders of common metrics have a great story to tell and need to continue to articulate that vision.

Hybrid Venture Finance: Keep Going in Building Capacity

As noted earlier, entrepreneurial philanthropists have created hybrid investment vehicles that use social impact as part of their definition of success. Many education foundations are putting their assets to work in mission-aligned (related to positive social impact) or mission-driven (directly related to the social mission of the foundation) investments. Others are putting their resources to work through funds like Owl Ventures, New Markets Venture Fund, Rethink Education, and soon Reach Capital (the new for-profit early-stage fund spinning out of NewSchools Venture Fund).

Hybrid finance will never have the incentives or resources to achieve the scale, specialization, and support ecosystem that private-sector venture capital brings to bear. Additionally, as noted above, the top priority for philanthropists is to sustain the political constituencies in favor of "more what, less how" success metrics, as such metrics are critical for venture capital to find and sustain innovations.

That said, hybrid finance is uniquely positioned to coordinate other actors and catalyze new markets. Hybrid finance, for instance, was crucial for Teach For America and many successful charter networks. The best-established institutions in this sector, the NewSchools Venture Fund and the Charter School Growth Fund, invest over $50 million per year, plus added leverage from co-investors such as New Profit, the Robertson Foundation, and the Robin Hood Foundation. Additionally, hybrid grants often catalyze for-profit investments by reducing the risk on a for-profit enterprise. Perhaps most importantly, the hybrid sector mirrors venture capital in finding disruptive ideas and helping them scale when they start to work.

Private-Sector Venture Capitalists: Invest in Teachers

To keep accelerating the flow of capital, energy, and talent into K–12 education, venture capitalists need to make both money and friends. In education, they have thus far been mediocre at both.

Start with making money. Since venture capital on average barely yields a return, venture capitalists avoid sectors of the economy where it is difficult to make money. While the energy, health care, and military sectors have exploited private-sector energy, thus far K–12 education has been harsh terrain due to fragmented jurisdictions, polarized politics, torturous sales cycles, and change-averse budgets. If the current wave of venture-backed companies fails to succeed, the next round of venture funding will be that much harder.

In terms of making friends, venture capitalists would do well to fine-tune their culture, which even they have called arrogant and male-dominated.[51] Venture capitalists can incubate radical ideas without necessarily providing fodder for a political backlash against for-profit interests in public schools. For example, financiers should recognize at least three opportunities to engage productively with teachers:

Empower teachers. Investors can use their disruptive culture to better deploy the assets already in place in K–12 education. Legendary venture capitalist Vinod Khosla has argued that the great power of new technologies is that they will "upskill" professionals by (1) automating the least engaging parts of their jobs and (2) giving them access to the collective insights and capabilities of all of their peers around the world.[52]

Although Khosla was referring to nurses and doctors, Alex Hernandez of the Charter School Growth Fund notes that this idea holds promise for teachers as well. Funders who wish to encourage demand for innovation among teachers have many tools at their disposal, including identifying early adopters and promulgating information about their successes.[53] The teacher-founded Teachers Pay Teachers (TpT), for instance, raised $64 million in venture financing in 2014 to expand their marketplace that allows teachers to buy and sell course materials from other teachers. TpT now has over three million registered users.[54] Since inception it has paid out over $86 million to contributing teachers.[55] Other teacher-empowering companies include BloomBoard, which engages teachers and administrators in a common platform for professional development and evaluations; School-Zilla, which is trying to help teachers visualize student data in a way that helps them figure out how to address next steps; and Remind, which helps teachers send reminders to students.

Find and nurture "teacherpreneurs." Another high-leverage strategy is to support teachers as entrepreneurs. Teachers throughout the country innovate daily in leadership settings. Many look beyond their own walls for ways to leverage the talent of others, extend their own impact, and collaborate. The most entrepreneurial professionals are already building new models and attracting funding. The nonprofit 4.0 Schools funds competitions and incubation tools to create "teacherpreneur communities" to help individual teachers succeed as entrepreneurs, while Teach For America has encouraged its alumni to become entrepreneurs.[56] Former teacher Barnett Berry, who popularized the term *teacherpreneur*, has predicted that this work will empower and upgrade the entire profession in ways that move far beyond current reforms.[57] A virtuous cycle is entirely plausible, where teacher entrepreneurs build and sell tools that enable other teachers to also become more entrepreneurial.

Encourage unions as venture funders. Although America's teachers' unions have a reputation for resisting change, politics within the unions are fluid, giving unions (like other funders) a combination of altruistic and self-interested reasons to sponsor innovation. As charters and choice expand, evidence suggests that traditional public schools feel more urgency to improve. As I have discussed elsewhere, pro-reform teachers are underrepresented in low-turnout internal union elections, but charters and choice can enhance the internal political power of the unions' reform wing.[58] Reform skeptics have an interest in showing that union-controlled school systems can innovate on behalf of students. To that end, unions have begun allocating some of their considerable discretionary resources toward venture funds such as the American Federation of Teachers' Innovation Fund. Although most of the innovations have been incremental, pro-innovation constituencies within the unions can push for investments to scale promising initiatives such as peer assistance and review[59] or labor-led pay-for-performance programs.[60] Venture capitalists who want to make money in education should embrace unions as funders; union sponsorship can ease the path for teacher-friendly innovations, while reducing the risk of a destructive political backlash. Some specific steps venture funders can take would include: give the unions credit for taking risks when they do; share ideas; and even co-invest. As a case study, for-profit education start-up BetterLesson received a $13.5 million grant from the Gates Foundation and then partnered with the National Education Association to identify and codify the work of master teachers.

This paean to investing in teachers declines to endorse near-term investments in whole schools. Recently, some have pushed for greater urgency in building whole schools that dramatically improve student outcomes. Investors generated excitement by putting $100 million into the tech-powered customized schooling model of AltSchool. While this enthusiasm has both analytic merit and moral weight, the politics are not favorable. The K^{12} virtual schooling company represents only the most recent cautionary tale. Education experts and market analysts are both pessimistic about the company's performance to date. In a functional marketplace, competitors would raid K^{12}'s customers and talent, and get funding for alternative approaches. Instead, rivals and funders have looked at K^{12} as a proof point that the market is not ready (ironically, giving K^{12} more runway than it would have in a functional market). This example shows the weakness of the current for-profit schooling market, and may dampen investor enthusiasm if performance degrades further.

All this suggests an unappealing risk-reward profile. For the next several years, funders and regulators should view for-profit schools with caution. Those seeking to innovate at the school level should focus on nonprofit charters, which face somewhat better politics than for-profits, yet remain able to purchase services from disruptive for-profit companies. Indeed, AltSchool itself may be taking the smart course by licensing its model to other schools, rather than building charter schools that would take public funds.[61] This puts AltSchool in the position of serving other schools, which creates a political and market buffer between AltSchool and taxpayer funds.

The clash of cultures between the homeostasis of public schools and the barbarians of finance can be harnessed for the benefit of students. In the immediate term, the best path forward is to protect political gains already made, while engaging entrepreneurial teachers. The virtuous cycle of building teacher-oriented businesses and supporting teacher entrepreneurs can generate accelerating returns in performance, political capital, and profits, which in turn will attract the next wave of venture capital. Before long, America's innovation and educational investments will drive radical customization and improvement in our K–12 schools.

5

The View from Abroad

Does American Education Suffer from
a Deficit of Innovation?

Marc S. Tucker

N o one who has even the slightest acquaintance with the international comparative statistics on national education performance needs to be persuaded that the United States has been falling further and further behind a growing group of countries whose students outperform our own on average, countries in which the gap between the best- and worst-performing students is much smaller than in the United States.[1] Many people believe this growing deficit in performance can best be reversed by creating powerful incentives for innovation, entrepreneurship and competition in the schools sector. I, however, am of dissenting view.

THE ARGUMENT FOR INNOVATION, ENTREPRENEURSHIP, AND COMPETITION

The argument for innovation, entrepreneurship, and competition is not hard to make. In one arena after another, US capitalism has conquered the global competition. Competition drives prices down and functionality, quality, and customer satisfaction up by rewarding the efficient and punishing the inefficient. Constant creative destruction in the economy is unforgiving; there's a graveyard full of formerly dominant players who failed to adapt and a warm welcome to entrepreneurs with innovative and powerful ideas. More recently, the idea that has gripped proponents is the notion of disruptive firms that do not merely improve on what went before, but render existing firms obsolete with entirely new approaches to performing the functions performed by those previously dominant players. In this conception, governments that nurture such providers will be rewarded with whole new industries that leapfrog the competition, capturing our imagination and our money with products and services from left field, the very frontier of innovation.

What I have just described is the American way, the engine that made this country the dominant economic power in the world for much of the twentieth century. So why not apply this magic fairy dust to public school education—where critics maintain that the growth of the bureaucracy and absence of competition has led to the capture of the institution by the monopolists who run it, with the predictable result that costs have skyrocketed and the needle of performance for high school graduates has hardly moved for decades?

The argument seems so reasonable.

Testing the Proposition . . . to Find It Wanting

What should follow from this argument? You would expect that countries with higher achievement and equity would have more powerful incentives for innovation, much wider scope for innovation, much more innovation than one can find in the United States. You would expect to find government playing a smaller role in education than is the case in the United States. You would expect individual and corporate entrepreneurs to play a much more prominent role in designing and delivering educational services than they do in the United States. In short, you would expect to find that there would be more of everything in the competition, innovation, and entrepreneurship prescription than exists in the United States. After all, if America is lagging in performance and that is due to an insufficiency of competition, innovation, and entrepreneurship, you would expect top-performing countries to have more of all these things than we do.

But that is not what you would find. You would find less competition, innovation, and entrepreneurship than you find in the United States. To put it simply, countries that are outperforming the United States by considerable margins have not relied on the competition, innovation, and entrepreneurship agenda. The United States, which has implemented the competition, innovation, and entrepreneurships agenda on a much more ambitious scale than any other industrialized country, has seen those other countries outperform us by wider and wider margins. If competition, innovation and entrepreneurship are the key to building successful education systems, this could not be true—but it is. Why?

Let's take the underlying propositions apart. We'll start with competition. I made the case for competition as a driver of improved outcomes at lower prices to the consumer above. But markets are not especially equitable. Not everyone gets to have a Lamborghini, only those who have a lot of discretionary income and choose to spend it that way. Those who have a great deal less may not be able to afford a car at all. The same thing is true of vacations in Bali, designer clothing, and washing machines that steam your clothing.

But in the language of the economist, these goodies are all *private goods*. If someone else has a Lamborghini, it neither helps nor hurts me. Public schooling is different. If a lot of other people don't have a good elementary and secondary education, employers might well choose to pull up stakes and put their factories and research labs in some other city, region, state, or country, and my own standard of living falls. I have a big stake in the quality and access to education of others. Schooling is a *public good*, not a private good.

You won't find Brooks Brothers stores, Lincoln dealerships, and Whole Foods Markets in our inner cities for the simple reason that no one there has the discretionary income to buy what they sell. In fact, it is hard to find any supermarket at all in many inner cities. But the situation is much more challenging than that. Low-income minority children often come to school facing a host of problems that more advantaged children don't. That is why more experienced teachers typically don't want to teach in schools that serve them. Getting children from these areas up to high standards requires not fewer resources than it takes to get wealthy suburban children to such standards, but a whole lot more. Why would a schooling organization want to go into business delivering a very costly service to a poor population when it could do much better delivering a less costly and more easily delivered service to a customer base prepared to spend much more money on it? These questions don't arise when we are talking about markets in which private goods are traded. But they are very important when we are talking about public goods like education delivered to low-income populations.

What I am describing is an arena in which the situation is beautifully positioned for massive market failure. It simply won't work under these circumstances if the aim is to provide a superior education to all students.

Economists have known this for a long time. What this analysis leads to is the understanding that, for vigorous markets providing private goods to work well, government must provide services outside the market system in the public sector that complement the market economy for private goods. More simply, this means that for private markets to deliver the goods in a modern capitalistic system, government needs to make sure that airports, seaports, high-speed rail, higher education institutions, certain arenas of research and development, and, yes, elementary and secondary education, are all supplied at a high level of quality for the rest of the economy to work well, even if government has to provide the service and it has to run at a loss. A well-functioning economy is the result of the public and private sectors playing complementary and vitally necessary roles. Government must step into the public goods arena because the true measure of the worth of each of those sectors is not whether it is directly recovering its costs and making a profit, as is the case in the private sector, but whether the overall economy is improved by the way these key elements of infrastructure function.

EVEN IF COMPETITION DID WORK, THERE ARE OUTCOMES MUCH MORE IMPORTANT TO PARENTS THAN STUDENT ACHIEVEMENT

Early advocates of market solutions to the education challenge worked hard to prove that if parents were given choices of providers of education and the money to exercise those choices, they would select schools that offered the best education they could get for the dollars they had to spend. Inefficient providers of high-quality education would fold and efficient ones would grow in number.

But that is not what actually happens when parents are given those choices and dollars. It turns out they put the safety of their children way above their performance on standardized tests when they are selecting schools. For most parents, this means selecting a school that is close to home over one that is further away. For some parents, there isn't a choice at all. Many don't have the money to pay for their children to attend a school that is not the closest school. Some, including the poorest, don't have the time, because they have two or more jobs, or don't have a car, or, more likely, both. School choice, in such circumstances, exacerbates income differences among parents and their children, rather than ameliorating them. The poorest get worse schools than the ones they used to attend. The richest get to go to school with more advantaged students than they used to go to school with. The gap widens. Another case of market failure.

But the safety of their children is not the only factor that is more important to parents than student performance on standardized tests. Nor is access to transportation the only factor limiting the free exercise of choice. Students want to go to schools their friends are going to, and parents try to accommodate them. At the high school level, both students and parents will often choose schools with winning sports teams. Some parents will pick the schools they themselves attended, out of loyalty. Some will pick the schools with the newest facilities. Many will pick schools with teachers they have heard are nice to the students. Many, confused by the choices they are asked to make, will not pick a school at all, usually defaulting to the nearest school, whatever its reputation.

Many advocates of choice are perfectly comfortable with these decisions, because for them, it is better to have choices in a democracy than not to have them. But that is a very different thing from advocating choice on the grounds that it will improve the academic performance of the students. At the level of a state or nation, there is no evidence for that proposition.

WHY INNOVATION IS NOT THE ISSUE

Many believe that, more than anything else, our schools need innovation. It seems obvious to them: "If we are not getting good value for our money," they say, "then clearly, we need to do things differently. That means we need innovation."

But the truth is that the United States is already the education innovation center of the world in elementary and secondary education, and we are getting very little benefit from it. Lack of innovation is not the problem.

The American education system has been a magnet for educators and education researchers all over the world for decades. They come to see US schools, bone up on our latest ideas, talk with our researchers and policymakers, examine the latest interventions and more. Then they go home and think hard about how to take the best of what they have seen, adapt it to their situation, and implement it at scale, carefully integrating it with the rest of their system so that they innovations they are bringing into their country work in close harmony with the rest of their system.

When we at the NCEE talk to educators and policymakers in the top-performing countries and ask them where they got their ideas and innovations, more often than not, the answer is the United States. America is the world's cauldron for innovations in education, and all the world uses them.

Educators from the rest of the world also tell us that one thing they do not come to the United States to see is education systems that work. In their own countries, the Ministry of Education is responsible for the smooth functioning of the whole system. These educators pay a lot of attention to how all the parts and pieces of the system fit together. When they look at the United States, they see no one and no agency of government anywhere at any level that plays that role. The result is a non-system—something resembling Brownian motion—that consists of conflicting policies and practices, often canceling one another out.

When we talk to Asian educators, they describe their activity in the United States as a search for "peaks of excellence." They find a lot—the US education system is a treasure trove of innovations. When we ask what education research they pay attention to, invariably they tell us that most of the research on which they rely was done in the United States. America is the world's leading source of innovations in education. But few of these innovations go beyond their original creators and very little of the research is actually put into wide practice in in this country. The innovations that *are* enacted are rarely integrated with other features of the education system in a way that would make them truly effective. The problem is not lack of innovation. It is the lack of effective systems, especially effective systems for the governance of education.

ENTREPRENEURS WHO THINK OF THEMSELVES AS IN THE VANGUARD OF "DISRUPTIVE CHANGE" ARE THE LAST THING WE NEED

In Asia, companies get bigger with processes based on slow incremental change. In the United States, companies don't improve with the industry; new players blow industries up, destroying them with innovations that completely redefine the industry. So there's a lot of talk about how education is the only industry that uses methods of production that have not changed in at least a century. "Surely," advocates of reform say, "the time is ripe for some entrepreneur to put the schools out of business with a completely new, digitally based alternative to the now-ancient model we have been using for so long. What we really need is an internal combustion engine to replace the horse and buggy, or an Amazon to create a whole new model of retail sales."

I have been hearing this refrain since I first went to work, producing (black-and-white) TV instructional shows for the Boston schools more than half a century ago. And I have yet to see it happen.

Digital solutions, of course, have much more potential for explosive change in education than TV or film ever did. But the real issue here is that that none of these tools is yet anywhere near smart enough or capable enough to get inside students' heads to understand why they are making the mistakes they make; none has what it takes to earn enough of any student's confidence and trust to get him or her to open up about personal troubles in ways that would enable the teacher to provide the right kind of help; none yet has what it takes to evaluate a truly creative performance and help students get better and better. Maybe someday, but not yet. And even when then those things do happen, we need to remember that learning is really hard and even disagreeable work for most students. Very few people are autodidacts. For most of us, most of what needs to be learned will not be learned outside the social setting provided by school.

But this is not the main issue. The most determined advocates of entrepreneurship as the savior of our schools are or have been entrepreneurs, or have made their fortunes investing in them. Many are from the Silicon Valley, some from Wall Street. A large fraction of them have no use for government. They see government as an unimaginative, bureaucratic restraining force.

Around twenty years ago, I had a chance to make my case for change in education to John Doerr, a founding partner in the legendary venture capital firm Kleiner, Perkins, in the heart of Silicon Valley, and Reed Hastings, the founding CEO and chairman of Netflix. I saw myself as an entrepreneur, too. Over the years, I had built a nonprofit organization employing, at one time, 250 people. We had taken one of our programs, turned it into a for-profit subsidiary, overseen its growth, and then sold it for enough money to provide the nonprofit with a reserve fund that functions like an endowment. I had to make payroll every month. Our books had to balance. We had no debt. We were widely recognized for the quality of our work and our prospects were rosy. It all sounded pretty entrepreneurial to me.

But no—when I started talking about how the problem was the way the system works and how the only solution was a redesigned system with a much-improved system of governing education, their eyes glazed over. Then they became angry, making it clear I was wasting their time. For them, government and the bureaucracy were the enemy. What was needed, in their view, was people like them and the people they funded—people, preferably young people, who were prepared to work around the clock to turn the system upside down, to reduce government's role to a bare minimum, and to simply get rid of the bureaucracy. Bright, highly motivated, and very well-educated young people with the right entrepreneurial spirit, they thought, would make short work of the old, outmoded education system. People like me, interested in making the system work rather than burying it, were the problem, not the solution.

I don't think so. Once again, my touchstone is the growing number of countries that are outperforming the United States in elementary and secondary education. Not a single one accomplished this feat by unleashing a small number of inexperienced young people on their system with the express mission of tearing it down and building another in its place, using a design for a new system that no one had discussed (not discussed because the system was essentially uninteresting to the Silicon Valley entrepreneurs). This model of reform by entrepreneurship stands on feet of clay. Its advocates can point to no country, state, or province that has embraced this model and, as a result, entered the ranks of the high performers. We are supposed to take the efficacy of the entrepreneurial model entirely on faith.

But why should we do that? Public education is not Silicon Valley. There is no promise of riches at the end for the successful entrepreneurs. Unlike the Silicon Valley firms, education is fundamentally government employees performing a government function in the hot spotlight of the public eye. Politics is not incidental to the work. At many levels, it *is* the work, because we are in a public arena in which, at the operating level, there is disagreement about almost everything, everyone is entitled to an opinion, enormous sums of public money are at stake, and how that money is spent spells the difference between stable employment and perhaps no job at all for everyone from the teachers to the school bus drivers. In a firm, these choices are made by the executives, and the verdict on their performance is made by the market, which means on the basis of whether or not they were able to turn a good profit. But, in the very public arena of public schooling, the verdict on performance of the executive or the entity employing the executive is made by a public with many and often conflicting interests. This is not the world in which the Silicon Valley executives made their money and it is not an environment they know very much about. It is certainly not an environment in which young, bright, inexperienced people just a few years out of graduate schools are likely to succeed at scale. If we take our cue not from people who have been successful in a very different industry, but from those countries that have had great success in the educational arena, what we need are highly capable, well-trained, and very experienced educators who can design and inhabit schools and districts, who can build effective institutions to educate our children, who are themselves professionals and who know how to manage teachers—also as professionals. We don't need people who are expected to blow up the system but have no plan for a new system and no interest in coming up with such a plan.

WHAT IT ALL COMES DOWN TO

We don't need more innovation. We have plenty of it. The problem is that we don't make use of the innovation we have because we have a highly dys-functional system of education. That is what we have to fix.

Entrepreneurs, as that term has been defined by the Silicon Valley and Wall Street communities, does not mean creative people with a lot of energy who are prepared to devote their lives to education. It means people who want to blow the system up or work outside the system. But if the *design* of the system is the problem and the *redesign* of the system is the solution, as it has been in the top-performing countries, then the last thing we need is a bunch of people who want to do away with the current system but have no clear idea of what a better system would look like or any interest in building one.

Competition is fine if you want choice because you think that choice is an important value in a democratic society. But don't go down the entre-preneurship route if you see entrepreneurship as the principal driver of improvement in school and student performance, because there is no record of that happening anywhere.

6

But Does It Work?

Evaluating the Fruits of Entrepreneurship

Jon Fullerton

A new wave of entrepreneurship is changing the educational landscape. In many urban areas, the district monopoly on public schools is a thing of the past. Parents can now choose whether to send their children to district schools or to new charter schools founded by educational entrepreneurs. Likewise, other entrepreneurs have begun to transform the content that is delivered. Teachers, parents, and schools can now use easily available online offerings to supplement curriculum (e.g., Khan Academy), to replace existing textbooks (e.g., LearnZillion), or even to replace entire classes led by local teachers (e.g., the Florida Virtual School). Entrepreneurs have also provided teachers with a new class of resources allowing them to access curated lessons from across the country (Better Lesson), better track student performance (Kickboard), and better access targeted professional development (BloomBoard).

Both the providers of new schools and the providers of new software claim that their products will improve outcomes for students (and sometimes teachers). Learning strategies will be "differentiated" or "reimagined" to be better adapted to student needs than the traditional one-size-fits-all approaches of the past, and motivated kids and their families will see student achievement dramatically improve.

Given these straightforward promises, we might expect that we would be feasting from a cornucopia of evidence about school and product efficacy. All products trying to command the attention of potential consumers (district leaders, principals, teachers, or parents) would begin their pitch with strong evidence of effectiveness. However, anyone with even a cursory familiarity with US education knows that while one can find plenty of testimonials and vendor-selected examples of test score outcomes, few providers of schools, software, or anything else have rigorous evidence to back up their claims. In fact, a 2010 report from the US Department of Education found that of the 1,132 research studies on online learning published from 1996 to 2008, only four rigorous studies compared outcomes for students who used online learning programs to outcomes for those who did not.[1]

This chapter examines the role evaluation of efficacy should play, why so little evidence of efficacy exists, and potential infrastructures to provide more evidence on an ongoing basis.

WHY DO WE NEED EVIDENCE AT ALL?

Some might hold that the reason for the relatively rare use of strong efficacy evidence is that we don't really need it. The point of the markets in which entrepreneurs flourish or flounder is to allow more consumer choice. Families will match to schools, and schools will match to programs and providers. If a school, program, or provider is not effective, families, schools, and teachers will abandon it for better alternatives. A functioning market will, in fact, maximize educational outcomes.

The above argument would be most plausible if we were worried only about maximizing consumer preference—*and there were no objective measures of higher priority outcomes than preference.* When we are talking about what mobile phone to buy or what movies to download it is hard to say that there is a right outcome beyond what the market supports. However, education is different in important ways.

First, the efficacy of schools and products matters for children's long-term well-being. If a school or product fails to teach math, students exposed will suffer long-term and lasting impacts to their opportunities in life. Poor choices mean poor outcomes. In this way, educational offerings are analogous to pharmaceutical or medical offerings. Just as with pharmaceuticals, we should demand some evidence of efficacy—or at least harmlessness. Simply leaving it to the market to determine which treatments result in mortality is unacceptable.

Second, the purchaser of educational products (e.g., a district or a school) is often distinct from the consumer. The penalty for poor choices and instructional failure falls on children who generally do not have the ability *not* to use the product. Thus, while the market may respond to the preferences of district and school administrators, it does not necessarily respond to the needs of students.

Finally, at least for now, accountability goals are imposed from other levels of the system. Therefore, purchasers are buying products for goals they did not set for themselves—and are desperate for help. Providing neutral and valid evidence of what purchasers can expect would be a positive step toward making accountability work.

For all of the above reasons, simply letting market preferences drive which schools and products succeed may not drive student success. Markets need reliable information and appropriate incentives to function properly.

WHO CARES? (AND WHAT DO THEY CARE ABOUT?)

Even once we agree that we need a stronger evidence base to support educational progress in an entrepreneurial setting, we should recognize that evidence has many different users and uses. There are at least four different stakeholders in this market, all of whom have somewhat different needs and interests. Some of these interests can even line up against better evidence.

I will discuss four groups of stakeholders—entrepreneurs, teachers and school leaders, parents, and policymakers.

Entrepreneurs

Entrepreneurs need evidence for three primary purposes: product design, product improvement, and marketing.

Product design. Many new products are the result of a felt or discovered need on the part of an entrepreneur. For instance, the founder of Kickboard was a teacher struggling to collate and coordinate data on student progress across a multitude of sources. She designed a product to help teachers easily manage data on student progress. No research or evidence base was needed (beyond the clear pain in the marketplace).

However, other products and ventures are a direct response to research findings. For instance, recent work on the importance of noncognitive skills for long-term outcomes has jump-started a new mini-industry focused on products and resources to measure and improve student grit, perseverance, and growth mind-sets. While the research provides the motivation for product design, it does not allow us to know whether the products and services based on "research" actually *do* make a difference.

Product improvement. Any entrepreneur worth his or her salt will be constantly testing, updating, and improving the product—whether that be a school (could any school open with a perfect program in place?) or a new learning technology (what tweaks to the interface can cause students to spend more time involved with the product and answer more or harder questions?).

The challenge is that entrepreneurs often do not have access to the data they need. While software providers can easily run A/B tests (discussed below) against their own internal metrics, they generally do not have access to student performance on assessments and outcomes that teachers and parents care about. Without access to student outcomes outside of the platform, providers run the risk of testing their product against shadows on the wall.

School and service providers face a different challenge. While they may have more insight into their own students' outcomes, they often don't know how these outcomes compare with those of students they did not serve. In addition, the outcomes are often extraordinarily delayed. Consider a middle school aiming to get kids on the path to college. One could see whether the school is achieving its goal only *seven years* after founding. That's a long time to wait to get feedback on a program.

Marketing. While credible proofs of efficacy are rare, those that do exist can be used to convince more people to purchase a product or go to a particular school. But what matters in this case is the signal that there is evidence of effectiveness, not the actual quality or external validity of the research. And, of course, negative findings are unlikely to find their way into marketing brochures. Organizational theorists call this the *symbolic utilization of research*, or "using research results to legitimate and sustain predetermined positions."[2] Obviously, this approach to evidence is aimed at improving outcomes for entrepreneurs, not children. (Some strategies for ensuring that evidence is not simply selectively presented to advance business interests are discussed below.)

School Leaders and Teachers

Districts, schools, and teachers have different needs than entrepreneurs. In order to make wise decisions, they need to know how products compare to one another in terms of student outcomes as well as how products compare to "business as usual." What's more, school personnel need to be able to find information quickly about multiple products applicable to their specific circumstances, and many do not have the time or capacity to do this tremendous amount of data gathering on their own.

Once products are selected, the information needs of school personnel are not over. Schools, or at least school systems, must monitor usage and outcomes for themselves.

All of the above assume that school personnel want to use research and evidence to guide their decision making. This is not a given. A 2009 article by Cynthia Coburn and her colleagues provides a somewhat dispiriting account of how often the symbolic use of evidence is used to justify decisions already reached.[3] While this is clearly a challenge to using efficacy evidence to improve outcomes, we should recognize that without much easier access to a broad range of relevant findings, it is hard to imagine how school systems could regularly use data otherwise. Both the lack of timely information and the cost of gathering new information make the non-symbolic use of research exceedingly difficult.

Even so, when thinking about evidence in terms of informing teachers and leaders, there are three important things to keep in mind. First, the evidence base will never provide simple, universal rankings of products. Instead, we would expect individual products to work better with certain students and worse with others. Second, schools and teachers may use a bundle of products with their students—making it hard or even impossible to isolate an individual product's effect. Finally, products are unlikely to be effective unless they are used. If teachers are not invested in a product, we would expect low usage. If students learn how to goof off while apparently using the product, we might see high "usage" but no impacts. Thus, in choosing products, teachers and school leaders also need information about how much teachers and students like the product and how it gets used in practice (and the implications of this for the rest of the school day).

Parents

To be wise consumers of education services, parents need information on both school effectiveness (assuming that there is school choice) and product effectiveness (as parts of the educational experience decouple from the school).

In many ways, parents have the simplest information needs among the four stakeholders discussed here: they have to keep track of only a few students, decision-making processes are organizationally simple, and their incentives are generally aligned with the long-term interests of their children.

The primary question they are looking to answer is straightforward: Will a given school or product improve outcomes for their children?

Unfortunately, parents have the least direct access to data on effectiveness and generally the least capacity to sift through conflicting evidence of any of the stakeholders.

Policymakers

Policymakers monitoring and encouraging educational entrepreneurship have a somewhat distinct set of needs.

At the most basic level, they need to assure the public that at least basic protections are provided in the education market. Schools and programs must meet a minimum standard. Given the importance of education to the future of children, if schools or programs are shown to be actively harmful to educational outcomes, policymakers will likely want to exclude them from the market. On the other hand, if a product or approach is successful, policymakers may want to encourage its rapid spread. In short, they want to demonstrate that success is scaling while failure is excluded.

Timing, however, is important. Once a policymaker has introduced or supported the spread of a program, efficacy evaluations may have a much larger downside than upside, since having one's favored program shown ineffective or harmful can have high political and organizational costs.

BARRIERS TO THE SPREAD OF EVALUATION PRACTICES

Given the apparent usefulness of better evaluation to all stakeholders, it seems reasonable that there would be a strong evidence base on most new providers of schools, services, and software. But this is manifestly not the case. Few emerging products can show evaluations of their causal impact, and schools are still judged primarily according to crude proficiency rates and word-of-mouth. Too few high-scoring schools have strong evidence that they, rather than the preexisting characteristics of their student body, are the cause of student scores.[4]

There are four barriers to the spread of evaluation practices in the entrepreneurial education space: data, time, money, and interest.

Data

No single entity (entrepreneur, education agency, or parent) has access to all of the sources of data needed to evaluate outcomes credibly. Software providers can, of course, track users' progress against internal metrics within the software—but these may not be aligned with the external assessments (teacher and state tests) that are most valued. Charter schools (and other organizations offering classes) have access to state assessment outcomes—but they generally do not have access to a well-controlled comparison group. School systems, on the other hand, often do not have easy access to usage data from software providers, nor the capacity to analyze and use it in determining a product's efficacy.

Most evaluations will require carefully connecting data from across multiple sources. Linking and cleaning data is not a trivial process—though many firms can help with this. More challenging, however, may be confidentiality and privacy issues. States and districts are rightly concerned about simply sharing back to vendors student data the vendors themselves did not create—but without this information, it is hard for vendors to determine much about the efficacy of their products. We need a way to allow for analysis and learning for the field while simultaneously preserving privacy and protecting student data from being used for marketing or other purposes.

Time

For evaluation data to be useful to entrepreneurs or to customers, it must be timely. Unfortunately, in the traditional program evaluation model, the amount of time required to produce results may well be too long for the results to be useful.

For instance, in 2003, the federal government, contracting with Mathematica Policy Research and SRI International, undertook a massive study on the effectiveness of mathematics and reading software products.[5] The study ultimately examined sixteen products, with the first wave of results released in 2007 and the second in 2009. While the results were disappointing (generally finding no effects by any of the software on student assessment outcomes), they were also largely irrelevant. It is as if a study were released today on the economic impact of PalmPilots on companies that use them. The world has moved on. As importantly, software providers are able to say, "Yes, our software was less effective when this evaluation was conducted. We have made many changes since then and are confident that they have paid off in terms of additional student learning."

In a world changing at Internet speed and in which superintendents' average tenure is 3.2 years,[6] five-year impact studies won't work.

Money

The two barriers above lead to a third challenge—money. Rigorous evaluations often run into the hundreds of thousands, if not millions, of dollars. In fact, the evaluation contracts issued by IES's National Center for Educational Evaluation (NCEE) have typically cost over $10 million in recent years.[7]

The high cost of evaluation is not (only) the result of universities and contract research firms having inflated rates while dealing with naive procurement officers. High costs are inevitable, given the way education research is currently structured. For each new project, researchers must (1) recruit students, teachers, schools, and districts, (2) develop data collection tools, (3) execute data transfer and confidentiality agreements and consents with each public agency involved and with research subjects, (4) clean the data received from each agency (with different issues across different agencies), (5) complete the actual analysis, and (6) write the report. Essentially, a brand new research infrastructure is created for every evaluation project undertaken. It is no wonder that costs run high.

Entrepreneurs managing limited cash are unlikely to have funds to support such work (or prioritize evaluation over further product development). School districts and states, likewise, may feel that they have limited funds to take on this type of work, particularly given that whichever district runs an evaluation takes on 100 percent of the costs, while other districts and states receive the same benefits in terms of knowledge of what works and what does not. Current cost structures make the routine use of evaluation unlikely.

(Self) Interest

Finally, not every entrepreneur has an interest in being evaluated. Experienced researchers know that many to most studies of new interventions find zero effects.[8] This is not specific to education—a large majority of pharmaceutical trials also fail—but it is hard to understand why entrepreneurs should risk having their product perceived this way *when they are not required to.*

There is plenty of collusion in this. Investors may have little interest in seeing their millions of dollars proved ineffectual. Whoever recommended and adopted the software for schools will not be pleased and may very well be embarrassed by unflattering results. And parents who have already chosen and sent their child to a school may not want to know it was ineffective!

As a result, as long as marketing of individual stories remains a plausible alternative to research and rigorous evidence, we should expect little movement.

So how can we create an efficient evaluation infrastructure that provides results in a timely manner, protects privacy while leveraging the data needed to prove efficacy, and ensures participation? The next two sections cover some existing efforts and possible solutions that are emerging.

EXISTING SOLUTIONS

User and Expert Reviews

Perhaps the most intuitive way to inform consumers about the usefulness of new products and schools is simply to connect them with one another and give them the opportunity to rate schools, software, and other products. Just as Yelp!, Amazon, and thousands of other sites already allow users to take advantage of the "wisdom of crowds" that emerges from consumer ratings, so too a number of sites allow consumers to weigh in about their experience in the education sector. For instance, Common Sense Media has collected ratings on a few thousand educational apps, and GreatSchools has collected parent and student ratings on schools.

As in the private sector, a number of "expert" sites have arisen to provide guides to perplexed teachers and families navigating a barrage of new offerings. Much as CNET provides overviews of trends and expert reviews in consumer technology products, EdSurge seeks to provide information on the burgeoning ed tech sector. Another organization, EdReports, aims to be a "*Consumer Reports* for school materials" and has assembled a team of experts to rate various curricular offerings' alignment with the Common Core.[9]

Such sites can be of great value to teachers, parents, and educators in selecting products, services and schools. They can provide information about what teachers and students like and, by implication, how engaged they will be with the school or service. They can also be of value to entrepreneurs in providing feedback and direction on how to improve their offerings. Finally, reviews are relatively easy to produce and disseminate. Unfortunately, the review solution has major limitations.

First, at least as of now, user reviews of education products have not created the active review community that is typical in other sectors. As I have noted elsewhere, there are often very few user reviews of schools, and those that do exist are largely information free.[10] Common Sense Media also has a thin set of user reviews—with none of the useful detail typical of vacuum cleaner reviews on Amazon. Without a large number of active users dedicating time to reviews, it is hard for any "wisdom" to emerge.

But even if the user community were to increase dramatically, it is unclear what the relation of user ratings would be to efficacy. Ease or pleasure of use may trump efficacy, and in the ratings, even if parents and teachers explicitly attempt to rate on efficacy, it is very unlikely that they have sufficient data to determine impact.

Expert reviews might seem to provide a way out of this dilemma, but this is an illusion. How experts are chosen, what rubrics they use, and how either of these are related to student outcomes are critical and generally unanswered questions. The EdReports reviews of curricula provide a good example. Out of sixteen curricula rated, all but one were deemed "unaligned" by an expert panel. Unsurprisingly, publishers immediately attacked the methodology used by the ratings panel as well as the efforts of the raters.[11] But all of this debate is somewhat futile—as of Spring 2015, nobody knows the outcomes for any of these curricula as no student results on Common Core assessments are available yet. Once student performance is known—controlling for prior performance, of course—it should be possible to know whether students using the favored curriculum do indeed outperform others.

This suggests that one potentially important line of research is carefully correlating both user and expert ratings with growth on student achievement (or other measures). If the correlations are high, ratings might serve as a proxy for effectiveness. Until we know this, however, ratings should be considered as evidence of user preference, not evidence of efficacy.

IES and the What Works Clearinghouse

In 2002, the Institute of Education Sciences created the What Works Clearinghouse (WWC). As described on its website, "The goal of the WWC is to be a resource for informed education decision making. To reach this goal, the WWC identifies studies that provide credible and reliable evidence of the effectiveness of a given practice, program, or policy (referred to as 'interventions'), and disseminates summary information and reports on the WWC website."[12] The WWC even has interactive forms that allow searches for interventions and programs that work on user-identified topics and grades. From this description, it sounds as if the WWC could be an answer to the evaluation needs of the sector—providing easily accessible, yet rigorous, evidence about what works.

Unfortunately, the reality falls somewhat short of the vision. First, while WWC has an admirable emphasis on rigor of study design, the result is that

relatively few studies pass its screening criteria. The methodological requirements are quite high and favor randomized controlled trials.[13] Findings from
studies that do not meet the requirements are simply not reported—even if
they might provide suggestive evidence. Furthermore, studies that almost
meet the requirements (say, studies that have slightly more attrition than
WWC has determined is appropriate) are lumped together with very low-
quality studies—unreviewed and their findings ignored.

But shouldn't entrepreneurs and product providers be held to the highest
standards of proof? Perhaps. But the research acceptable to WWC faces the
time and money challenges discussed in the previous section. Assuming a
start-up can find the substantial funds needed to run a WWC-acceptable
evaluation, the results are out of date by the time they come out.

Even if this were not the case, the results reported by WWC are of limited use to practitioners trying to figure out what works in their own situations. Typically, WWC methods require researchers to treat products and
interventions as "black boxes"—providing impact estimates on whether the
product works overall, with little information about why it works, how it is
used, and how usage is related to outcomes. (Almost no study on the relation
between usage rates and outcomes could meet the WWC criteria, as either
compliance with a specific usage level would need to be randomly distrib-
uted or the researcher would need to demonstrate that high and low users
have no other observable differences at baseline—a tall order.) While some
studies will show impact estimates for different subgroups (e.g., economi-
cally disadvantaged students)—selecting even a few criteria on the WWC's
Find What Works website can reduce the number of endorsed studies to
zero in many areas.

But there is still worse news. Even studies that get over the methodological
hurdles are still likely to have substantially different measures of outcomes
and substantially different comparison groups—meaning that results will
not be comparable across studies examining similar products. For instance,
the recent *Blended Learning Report* released by the Michael & Susan Dell
Foundation examines blended learning outcomes across five charter management organizations (CMOs), and the report adheres as much as possible
to WWC standards.[14] Impacts of blended learning are examined across the
Alliance College-Ready Public Schools, FirstLine Schools, KIPP Los Angeles,
Rocketship Education, and Summit Public Schools. Unfortunately, both the
assessments used to gauge impact and the comparison groups varied across
each of these sites—student growth in some CMOs was compared with a

"virtual control group" of students identified as similar nationwide, whereas in others, student growth in the schools adopting blended programs was compared with growth in other schools within the same CMO. As a result, the growth estimates reported mean wildly different things depending on the specific CMO, and it is impossible to compare programs across them. Note that this is not the fault of the authors of the report (or the CMOs), but the result of different data being available for different schools: some schools took internally developed benchmark tests, others used NWEA Measures of Academic Progress, others had only end-of-year state assessments. The result is that different studies give us incomparable estimates—*even when conducted by the same research team.*

So, while WWC scores high on rigor, it fails in terms of timeliness, affordability, and comparability. The WWC design is thus unlikely to be a fount of evidence for entrepreneurial ventures and school leaders seeking to find what will work for them.[15]

A/B Testing

A third approach to evaluating efficacy is "A/B testing." This approach evolved in the private sector as a means of improving business decisions. In its canonical form, a company would be considering one or more pricing strategies or promotions and eager to select the one that would reap the most profit. A subset of customers or locations is randomly assigned to one of two treatment groups (A and B), and each group then receives a different offer (e.g., 30 percent off widgets versus a two-for-one widget offer). The results of each group are compared, and the action that generates the higher profit (or more page views) is adopted. Because customers are randomly assigned to the treatment group, the differences between the two groups reflect actual differences in treatment effects.

The astute reader will note that an A/B test is, in fact, simply a randomized controlled trial (RCT) with a new name. Any differences from traditional RCTs are in terms of scope, time, and cost. First, businesses using A/B testing typically run tests on marginal improvements, not their core business. In other words, whether or not to add an item to a menu at an existing restaurant chain is more amenable to A/B testing than whether or not the same chain should focus on Thai cuisine or American comfort food.

Second, given the speed at which the business environment can change, the long wait time for results typical of traditional RCTs would make many answers moot by the time they are received. Businesses are less interested in learning about the best strategy to reach BlackBerry users now than they were five years ago. In the corporate world, tests are designed to run for days, weeks, or months—not years. Finally, insofar as these A/B tests are focused on conducting short-cycle experiments on marginal improvements, businesses will likely want to conduct frequent tests. All of this puts a fairly tight constraint on cost—if the marginal cost of a test is too high, the tests will not pay for themselves.

While A/B testing has been used for several decades (though sometimes under a different name), it has taken off with Internet-based businesses that can easily tweak what users see and what offers they get as well as track the results on their own platform—for almost no cost.[16] Not surprisingly, many Internet-based entrepreneurial ventures in education have turned to A/B testing; even the US Department of Education recommends the technique in its guide for ed tech developers.[17] In addition, A/B testing is moving beyond developers' own databases. A few organizations have begun working with schools and vendors to run A/B tests using learning assessments external to those generated by the lesson provider. For instance, PowerMyLearning (formerly CFY) has a network and technology platform that allows teachers to create individualized playlists for students drawing on content from multiple sources. As part of its work, PowerMyLearning has set up the platform to allow providers to test "granular pieces of digital content—such as games, interactives, video, short simulations—to help software developers improve their products and know 'what works.'"[18]

Thus far, it sounds like the A/B testing approach might be the answer to our needs. It is fast, cheap, and rigorous. Again, though, some serious limitations will limit progress.

Entrepreneurs testing their own products face a fundamental limitation. Most providers will not have external student assessments available to them. *Internal* measures of student progress might not line up to the *external* measures that schools and parents care about. Without access to outcomes external to the system, it is hard to know if a change actually did anything in the broader world.[19]

The second and more concerning issue with internal A/B testing is that even if individual entrepreneurs are able to continually improve their products, there is no reason for them to share those findings. Doing so would give an unearned leg up to competitors. Part of a company's competitive advantage comes from keeping knowledge private—but this slows down learning for the field as a whole.

The emergence of third-party A/B testing platforms such as that provided by PowerMyLearning might be a solution to this, given their ability to test across products and use outcomes external to product providers, but there are still some difficulties.

First, at least so far, these platforms are designed to work with schools taking an à la carte approach to blended learning (creating individual playlists from multiple sources), rather than with schools implementing an integrated curriculum from one or two sources per subject. Second, the granularity of what is tested (e.g., individual lessons) is often quite small. While this information is valuable at the tactical level, it provides little guidance as to what overall approaches might work best with a specific set of students. Third, existing platforms were almost exclusively designed around testing learning software. While learning software is becoming more and more important, and testing its efficacy is critical, schools and systems are choosing much more than student facing learning platforms. Systems must decide how and who should provide professional trainings and supports for their teachers, and parents must decide what schools to send their children to. As currently implemented, A/B testing has little to offer these parts of the entrepreneurial landscape.

Table 6.1 provides an overview of the strengths and weaknesses of each approach discussed above.

While each has some attractive features, each also has limitations that hamper its usefulness in guiding stakeholders. Moreover, the table as a whole illustrates what Martin West has called the *relevance/rigor trade-off*.[20] The evidence that we can collect most quickly is either unreliable and biased (user reviews) or so specific to a context that it provides little guidance to others (A/B testing).

CORE REQUIREMENTS FOR A LEARNING NETWORK

If we really want evaluation to inform the sector, thinking in terms of one-offs is not going to work. We need to think about creating an infrastructure for evaluation that can provide timely evidence to stakeholders for relatively low cost in terms of both money and time. This means creating a network of schools and districts, ideally united by common measures and willing to participate in experimentation. What would requirements be for

TABLE 6.1   Overview of existing evaluation approaches

	User and expert reviews	"Traditional" evaluation; WWC	A/B testing
Timeliness	Medium/high: Users can rate instantly, experts take more time	Low: Generally years to results and results rarely updated	High: Months to results (in education)
Affordability	High	Low	High: Once infrastructure in place, incremental tests are very cheap
Comparability	Medium: Users implicitly test across products or services; however, they may not have enough experience with other products (e.g., schools) to provide comparability	Low	Low: Best at testing incremental changes within a product or service
Rigor/quality of evidence	Low	High	High
Usability for stakeholders	High: Easily used if sufficient reviews exist	Medium: Easily used, though lacking in granularity	Low: Testing completed within a product or approach. Little applicability to larger decisions (e.g., which school to choose)
Likelihood of vendor/ entrepreneur participation	High: Even if vendors not interested, there is little they can do	Low/medium: Large cost barriers. Also, methodology typically results in "all or nothing" conclusions, creating high risk for the vendor. On the other hand, slow timelines allow vendor disavowal of negative results ("we have already fixed that")	Medium/high: Vendors are most likely to participate if results are primarily for their own learning and not public evaluation; method also reduces risk by providing information on only small portions of offering, not offering as a whole

the network infrastructure that combined speed, comparability, rigor, and relevance to stakeholders? In this section, I will discuss the requirements for a potential new evaluation infrastructure conceptualized by Tom Kane, myself, and other researchers at the Center for Education Policy Research that could combine the strengths of the above approaches while overcoming at least some of their limitations.[21]

Speed

Current evaluation timelines are generally too long to be of use to entrepreneurs and their customers. In order to transform timelines from three to five years to three to five months (or, at the least, under a year), a number of requirements must be met.

Most importantly, a *frequently updated, longitudinal data warehouse* for network schools must be in place. As noted above, one of the major barriers to rapid evaluation is the challenge for researchers of obtaining and cleaning data. Evaluators build a new research infrastructure for each project at great cost in time and money. What is needed are analysis files with standard data elements that could be used across projects and that are regularly updated (including the benchmark assessments that act as key external measures of progress, which are covered below). Over the past ten years, most states have created longitudinal data systems that house many (though not all) of the variables needed for evaluation analysis. Properly cleaned and with data masked to protect student privacy, these databases could serve as a basis for the evaluation work. Alternatively, districts, CMOs, and other schools could work together to come up with their own data specification and warehouse system. Importantly, access to the data and analysis would all be granted at the behest of and for the participating districts and schools. Learning platform vendors and others would not have direct access to the student data—though they would have access to reports.

Note that we do not expect all impacts from all products and services to be seen in less than five months (or even a year). However, frequent usage reporting will allow participants to track implementation and course correct as necessary. Frequent outcome collection will allow users to track growing impacts over time (should they exist).

Comparability

To ensure comparability, it is useful for network members to use *common annual assessments and benchmark assessments*. While it is possible to standardize assessment results, this can reduce the precision of impact estimates. In addition, if assessments are, in fact, testing very different content areas, differences in outcomes may be the result of differences in measures, not actual impact. This can be important for benchmark tests in particular, as they can have very different strategies for measuring progress (e.g., adaptive versus not) or may have different assumptions about sequence and pacing of topics.

Potential new resources in this area include the new Common Core assessments (PARCC and Smarter Balanced). *If* the two Common Core tests end up widely adopted by states, for the first time it will be easy to compare outcomes for specific products and services across states, speeding the ability of districts and states to learn across state lines.

The network will also require a sufficiently *large number of schools and students* in order to have the statistical power needed to test interventions and understand differential impacts by subgroup. In addition, if the network has multiple types of schools (e.g., charter and traditional), policymakers and school leaders will be able to see if certain products work better in some environments than others. Essentially, analysts would be able to run multiple tests in multiple contexts.

Finally, *standardized teacher and student surveys* collected several times over the course of the year could provide additional insights into school culture, "noncognitive" outcomes, and student and teacher usage of technology products.

Rigor

An *analytic infrastructure* must be created that is able to process multiple high-quality evaluations quickly. At first, this might be done by a small team of dedicated analysts that combine technical expertise in evaluation with knowledge of the analytic files in the data warehouse. Over time, however, many evaluation approaches should be routinized through software. Indeed, in the private sector there are already companies to easily design and analyze short-cycle experiments (e.g., Applied Predictive Technologies) and numerous firms that provide software to analyze the results of web-based A/B testing automatically. The network should *publish the methods used*, inviting feedback and improvement from other experts.

Relevance

Four elements are key to creating relevance in an evaluation infrastructure. First, the evaluations conducted should be focused on *products that a portion of schools in the network are already using or are considering using*. The network members themselves (as opposed to researchers) should guide the order in which products are studied to ensure that network participants care about the results.

To provide more than a crude thumbs-up or -down on a product, it will also be essential that *usage data* be collected from providers. For schools, this is simple (enrollment, attendance, etc.), but standard data needs to be collected for other providers as well. Learning software providers should be able to provide usage time, activity, and progress by student. Teacher-focused providers should be able to provide information on which teachers used the service, for how long, and what they did with it.

As noted above, *standard impact reports* should be created so that network participants and others can quickly identify results across many programs and interventions. The language of the reports should be clear and accessible to the layperson. As evaluation processes become more automated, products and services should be retested on a regular basis.

Finally, *all results should be published and easily searched*. One of the significant challenges facing practitioners attempting to rely on evidence is publication bias. High-quality studies that find an impact for an intervention are more likely to be published than those that do not. In addition, an unknown number of evaluations may not be released due to negative or null results. To prevent this, all results from the network evaluations should automatically be published and easily searched. Across large networks and over time, this may mean that there are multiple and conflicting findings of efficacy for individual products. This is okay and even expected[22]—efficacy is likely to be highly context dependent, and having more information about variability of results will help parents and leaders make more realistic decisions.

Likelihood of Entrepreneur Participation

The above requirements are challenging, but they leave aside the question of why school or product entrepreneurs would want to expose themselves to a network that will publish efficacy data that they do not control. While many entrepreneurs no doubt would welcome the opportunity to test their offerings for mission-driven reasons, it is not clearly in their narrow self-interest. Why would entrepreneurs provide data under these circumstances?

First, some of this evaluation can be done without cooperation. Districts and schools presumably know (or could know) which products are being purchased and assigned to which classrooms. Without detailed usage data, all that can really be done will be a black box evaluation without regard to intensity or fidelity of use. Vendors would likely prefer to have a more nuanced story told about their product—and so have some incentive to provide usage data from the start.

Second, members of the learning network should contractually require vendors to participate as a condition of adoption of their product. If a network is sufficiently large or contains high profile schools, few vendors will walk away.

Third, over time vendors that are not part of these learning networks will find it harder to market without evidence. As purchasers come to expect non-symbolic evidence of outcomes, vendors will appreciate the opportunity to generate this evidence (if their product works with at least some populations).

Note that the above arguments apply primarily to providers of services and software. School operators are unlikely to find the publication of results particularly threatening. They already have accountability data posted about their results every year.

Benefits of a Learning Network

While setting up such an infrastructure will not be easy, the benefits would be great. School leaders and teachers within the network will gain easy access to evaluation data on their own students. They will be able to see variation in impacts across user types and sites, and the reduced evaluation cycle time will allow leaders and teachers to course correct quickly. With better and more timely information, administrators, principals, and teachers will be less likely merely to use research symbolically and instead see research as a practical tool that can provide useful guidance and feedback. Finally, a searchable database for those outside the network will allow others to benefit from the network learning, and, one hopes, spread the approach to more school systems.

If appropriately constructed, the findings database could help parents identify potential programs and products that that match their individual child's needs. For policymakers, supporting and/or funding learning networks could provide major benefits. It allows them (1) to demonstrate that there is, in fact, quality control over programs and interventions entering the schools and (2) protects them from needing to "pick winners" themselves (and, perhaps more importantly, from the consequences of picking ineffective programs).

Ultimately, despite the challenges noted above, entrepreneurs also stand to benefit from such networks. They will be able to receive timely, regular, direct evidence on what is and is not working in their products. Importantly, though, this evidence will generally not be "all or nothing." The variation in impacts will allow them to better focus their products and suggest specific areas for improvement. By taking part in learning networks that they do not control, they can demonstrate to customers a commitment to following where the evidence leads and provide reassurance that positive findings are not just the result of selective marketing hype.

THE LIMITS OF EVALUATION

A just machine to make big decisions
Programmed by fellows with compassion and vision
We'll be clean when their work is done
We'll be eternally free, yes, and eternally young

—Donald Fagen, "I.G.Y."[23]

Before ending, I want to be clear about one possible misinterpretation of the argument and the proposed infrastructure. Raising the standard of evidence and creating a strong demand for the evaluation of products, interventions, courses, and schools is critical to separating dangerous educational tonics from efficacious products and improving educational outcomes. However, this does not imply that with enough good evaluation data, parents, teachers, and policymakers can simply "know what works" and mechanically implement it. Two products may be individually effective but contradictory when combined. Interventions that work in general may not be effective with a particular child. Education is a complex, context-dependent endeavor that will always require thoughtful organizational strategies and an ability to be responsive to feedback from the field.

This should not be surprising. In medicine, if one drug or dosage does not work for a patient, doctors will look for alternatives. Likewise, if a prescribed lifestyle change proves difficult to implement ("eat less, exercise more"), doctors may move on to other treatments. However, (we hope), the treatments recommended all have some evidence behind them and possible negative consequences of the treatment. Few doctors today recommend taking up smoking or ingesting tapeworms to lose weight!

With better efficacy data comes the opportunity to make better decisions—but not the opportunity to avoid decision making. Donald Fagen's retro-futurist irony highlights that only the foolish believe that access to better science, data, and evaluation will eliminate the need for thought and judgment.

A Matter of Practice

Entrepreneurship in Teaching and Learning

Elizabeth City

D oes entrepreneurship matter in education practice? The answer, in most classrooms on most days, is *not much*.

Could entrepreneurship matter in education practice? *Maybe.*

Should it? *Yes*—depending on what we mean by "entrepreneurship."

Many people think of entrepreneurship as starting something new, but entrepreneurship has many important roles. As described in the introduction to this volume, entrepreneurship includes finding a need, filling it, and taking risks. We don't necessarily need to start something new as much as we need initiative and willingness to take risks to fill needs and pursue opportunities while being creative with resources.

I want entrepreneurship because I am getting impatient. It has now been over twenty years since I first was entrusted with the responsibility of helping children in my classroom, seventeen years since I helped to start my first school, and five years since I helped to start a doctoral program in education leadership. And still, when I visit most classrooms, I see compliant, bored (if mostly happy) children and teachers who are either giving out more worksheets or are (understandably) bewildered by the array of skills, motivations, and learning differences in their students.

We must move farther faster.

For all the attention and resources that entrepreneurship, entrepreneurs, "disruption," and technologies garner, it's worth pausing to look at the core of the learning enterprise—the interactions between students, teachers, and content—in other words, what is actually happening in classrooms. How much is really disrupted there, and how much should and could be?

This chapter will look at entrepreneurship as a potentially promising strategy of school (and in particular, learning) reform, including how amenable our education system is to innovation, the inevitable trade-offs, the important equity concerns, and the fundamental question of who the entrepreneurs could and should be.

HOW AMENABLE IS OUR EDUCATION SYSTEM TO ENTREPRENEURSHIP?

American education has been quite resilient and resistant to most entrepreneurial attempts—that is, schools today by and large look like schools of one hundred years ago.[1] Of course, there have been lots of changes within the careers of our most experienced educators. I heard one thirty-year veteran ask a group of seventy colleagues, "How many of you remember having to crank the mimeograph machine to make copies?" She got nods from the most experienced educators in the room and puzzled looks from the rest of us. "How many of you remember the smell of the fresh ink on the papers from the mimeograph machine?" More nods, now with the twenty-year veterans included. "How many of you remember beating the chalk off erasers?" " . . . when there was only one phone in the entire school building?" " . . . punching holes in cards to program computers?" Finally, a ten-year veteran teacher leader held up his smartphone and said, "And now look at what you can do with this!" The group went on to talk about what it would take to help over one hundred schools innovate and move to more personalized learning.

While the format of producing and consuming assignments has changed, at the core, much of the work we ask children to do in school is still, in essence, worksheets. If we're asking students to fill in right answers in response to questions someone else has generated, even if the student fills them in on an iPad, it's a worksheet. Here's an example: A student said, "I'm so tired of [a tech-based math program]!" The coach working with the teacher said, "You're not engaging your students. Put away the iPads and the laptops. Write a problem on the board and invite students to solve it." The coach wanted the teacher to engage the students in mathematical thinking, not a technology-based worksheet.

The problem is not just that one particular teacher did not fully understand the potential of technology, it's far more widespread. Take, for example, a real school I'll call Typical High School. It has about fifteen hundred students, a dizzying array of extracurricular activities, and academic performance heavily correlated with race, language, and disability. It was founded over one hundred years ago, and for the most part, the classroom tasks look essentially the same as they have since the school opened. You might see more students sitting in groups these days (although they are often working on individual tasks). You might see more technology in the room (computers, projectors, interactive whiteboards, smartphones, etc.). Yet the fundamental tasks and the teacher-student interactions are not dissimilar from those of a century ago or from what the TIMSS study showed twenty years ago— namely, that American students spend a lot of time doing recall and procedural-level learning without really understanding the underlying concepts.

To give examples of actual practice, here are snapshots of three math classes I visited in spring 2015.

Classroom A

On the board: "Today's Topic: Simplify Radical Expressions. Outcome— Students will work with properties of radicals to simplify radical expressions. Do Now: Make corrections from the following radical expressions: (1) $\sqrt{80} = 2\sqrt{20}$" [and three more like this]

Teacher: "Hey, there's a Do Now up there. Remember that worksheet I gave you the other day? These are some of the mistakes I found."

The teacher calls roll, sitting at her desk at the back of the room. Students write problems down from the board and try to do them on small dry-erase boards at their desks. Out of five students whose work-in-progress I observe, one is doing the first problem correctly.

Teacher: "Are you guys struggling? That's what I found out. That's why I decided to do a review."

Several students: "Thank you!"

The teacher hands out graphic organizer: "Guess what we're going to title this." She writes, "How to determine if a radical is simplified" on board at the front of the room. "Who can remember one?"

Three different students respond: "No fractions in the radical." "No perfect squares in the radical." "No radicals in the denominator."

The teacher walks through one example of a problem in each category, asking students questions along the way like, "The square root of 25 is . . . ?" "Does this number come out from under the radical?" "Can it be simplified?" Students write each example down in their graphic organizer.

The teacher returns corrected worksheet to each student. The worksheet asks students to simplify radicals and lists the numbers 15 through 100, each underneath a radical (i.e., $\sqrt{15}$, $\sqrt{16}$, $\sqrt{17}$, $\sqrt{18}$ . . . $\sqrt{98}$, $\sqrt{99}$, $\sqrt{100}$). Of the papers I observe, none has more than half the answers marked as correct, and most have one-quarter to one-half of the answers correct.

The teacher tells students to return to the Do Now and try to do the problems again, using their notes in the graphic organizer.

On the plus side, Teacher A checked to see whether students understood how to simplify radicals, then paused to revisit the topic rather than moving on, and finally provided a graphic organizer to help students organize their notes. On the minus side, she gave them the same rules for simplifying radicals that she had supplied before their misunderstanding (now recorded in different parts of a graphic organizer), she gave them eighty-five tries at the same task when likely a handful would have covered all the varieties of simplifying radicals, and there was no evidence that students had a better understanding the second time they tried to simplify radicals.

Classroom B

On the board: "Outcome—Students will know how to find all the side lengths and angle measure of a triangle that has two known sides and an angle between them or three known sides. *Class work:* p. 734, #1–8. *Homework:* p. 735, 9–41 odd"

Students are sitting in groups of three or four, working on a problem. For the most part, they are working on their own. Several are wearing headphones while working. Some are chatting while working: "I'm so glad it's almost the weekend! I don't know what I'm going to do this weekend." "I don't lift weights." "I'm going to start an a capella group." "Hey, what did you get for #4? Yup, that's what I got, too."

The teacher circulates, looking at students' work and answering one or two questions that arise. When students are done with the problem, some sit and listen to their headphones, others chat, and others look at a packet of worksheets. Most students have the same answer to the problem; three students have different answers.

Teacher: "I think most people got it." He calls on a student.

The student comes to the front of the room, explains her process of applying the law of cosines, and writes the process and answer down, which are projected on the front board.

Teacher: "Did everyone follow? Did everyone get that?"

Nods from students. No questions.

Teacher: "Now we'll do the class work. I'll display [the problem from the textbook] on the board—you can come up and take a picture with your phone so that you don't have to squint."

Students go to the front of the room, take a picture of the problems, head back to their seats, and start working on the problems. Again, they chat with each other, a mixture of life outside of math class and discussion of the problems.

Student to another student: "Is there another way to do that? Isn't it the same problem as the one we did yesterday?"

Some students sitting next to each other have different answers. They don't compare answers and don't know they have different ones. When asked what they are working on, students say they have to figure out which equation to use and apply it.

On the plus side, students seemed both relaxed and focused on mathematics (in contrast to Classroom A, in which students were focused on mathematics, but seemed quite anxious about having lots of wrong answers and not understanding the math), technology was used to make things easier (no lugging heavy textbooks) or more pleasant (listening to music on headphones), and the teacher was circulating and checking in to see whether students had the right answers. On the minus side, some students did not have the right answer and did not say anything when the teacher asked, "Did everyone get that?", the mathematics was entirely based on applying equations (procedural), and the homework was sixteen more practices of the same thing they did in class. Those students who did it right in class could do it right sixteen more times, and those students who did it wrong in class had sixteen more opportunities with no feedback on what they did wrong the first time.

Classroom C

On the board: "I will learn how to solve quadratic functions by graphing. *Homework:* 12 problems. I'll know I have learned this when I can graph: $y=x^2-6x-3$."

Each student is sitting at a computer.

Teacher: "I've uploaded the notes on what we just did on the board. You can reference those while you work. Each of you has three or four problems to get correct, and then you can move on to your homework."

Students are at the Khan Academy website, working on graphing parabolas in standard form. They are trying to graph quadratic equations. They move the points of the graph around with their mouse. The teacher circulates, spending a couple of minutes with each student. He reminds them how to start with 0 as one of the x-values, and together they calculate y. He also reminds them that they can use a table to keep track of other x and y values. He asks questions to make them do the calculations: "What's 4+8?"

Student: "12."

Teacher draws a y-axis and x-axis, marks 4 on the x-axis and says, "What happens when we go back 8?"

Student: "–4."

Another adult, who appears to be a student teacher, circulates on the other side of the room, spending a few minutes with each student. Students sitting next to each other have different problems generated by the Khan Academy site. They try to help each other.

Student 1: "What do you do with these two points?"

Student 2: "I'm checking the hints."

Student 3: "Find the x-value instead of the y-value."

In the twenty minutes I am in the classroom, I observe nine students working. In that time, four do one problem correctly, then start working on another one, while the others still work on the first one.

On the plus side, the students had somewhat individualized lesson plans—the teacher had selected which part of the Khan Academy quadratic functions each student should be working on, and students could access help through the hints on the Khan Academy site; the teacher used technology to capture the notes for students' reference in real time rather than using their time to copy things from the board; and students who understood the mathematics could accelerate without waiting for the teacher. The teacher was recognized by administrators and teacher colleagues for trying new things with technology in his classroom. On the minus side, most students didn't understand quadratic functions and the hints weren't enough, so they moved their mouse around to guess and waited for the teacher to be available to help; because they were working on different problems, it was harder for them to support each other, though they were willing to try. In twenty minutes, fewer than half the students had done one problem correctly, and they had twelve more for homework.

Why do we need entrepreneurial behavior in American education? Because what I just described is modal math instruction in the United States: apply a procedure over and over again to a lot of problems, and if students don't get it right, the teacher explains again and they practice it again, sometimes still making the same mistakes. If they do get it right, they probably won't be able to apply it in a situation different than the one in which they practiced. That's not good enough. We now have computers to solve procedural problems and apply algorithms. But most jobs that support a decent living require problem solving and figuring out things that computers don't do as well. Students are compliant, and generally will try to do what the teacher asks. But they're not learning much about mathematical concepts or reasoning.

Of course, these examples do not describe every math classroom in America, nor every classroom in America. Some look more like Classroom D, which I also visited in Typical High School.

Classroom D (an Engineering Class)

Students are in groups, some sitting, some standing, and at first it's not clear what they're doing. Two students are starting to grow mushrooms. A student wanders over from another group and asks: "What is that?"

Student 2: "Mushrooms."

Student 1: "Why do you all want to grow mushrooms? How long will it take?"

Student 2: "It's for our greenhouse project. Plus, Mr. [Teacher] had a mushroom kit, and this seemed like a good day to grow them, since some of our group members are missing because of testing. I don't know how long they'll take to grow."

Students request a big pot from the teacher. The teacher leaves the classroom and comes back a few minutes later holding one: "Will this work?"

Another group of students has a map of the high school campus spread out on a table and is figuring out where to propose a bike path and where the bike racks would best go. When they see the principal enter the room, they tell her they want to meet with her to share their bike path proposal.

Another group of students is designing a solar-powered charging station for the carts that are used by campus security. The teacher is looking at their design and asking questions: "Is the L-bracket going to go into the metal or the wood?" Students explain their design choices.

Teacher: "I want a list of supplies that you need by Monday."

Students: "Okay."

Students in this class also periodically go to the local community college, where they get dual credit (high school and community college) for learning about energy sources.

Students look least busy in Classroom D, but that's where the most learning is happening. When I ask students what they're doing, they don't say "−4" or "the law of cosines"; they tell me about the projects they're designing to solve a problem or build something they think will make their school better. When I ask them how this class compares to their other classes, they say they like this one more because they get to do "hands-on stuff," they get to go to the community college, they learn about energy and the future, and it's fun. They also show some understanding of the content they're engaged in. When I ask a student what energy source seems most promising for the future, he describes a few currently used energy sources, then says: "I consider the present the past. The energy of the future hasn't been discovered yet." Then he tells me he's going to be an engineer so he can help discover it.

Who was being entrepreneurial in these classrooms? In classrooms A and B, nobody. In classroom C, the teacher was trying to be. In classroom D, the students, with the teacher's support.

Lots of things get in the way of changing the kinds of tasks and interactions teachers and students engage in. Fear of failure is one. A student doesn't want to admit he didn't get the right answer because he doesn't want to show he didn't know something. A teacher doesn't want to try to explain something differently because if she does and students still don't understand, maybe the problem is the teacher's practice, not the students' effort. Neither one of them wants to try a task that doesn't have a clear right answer or that requires deeper understanding because that would make it easier to be wrong, or at least less sure of being right, and that doesn't feel good, especially in school, which seems to be mostly about right answers.

Policies that reinforce incrementalism and hold teachers or schools accountable for test scores also inhibit change or risk-taking: Why try something if it won't show up on the test results fast? What if test scores get worse before they get better? There's a strong culture of "do what we've always done." The prevailing attitude seems to be "We all know what schools look like because we've spent a lot of time in them as learners, and the schools most of us grew up in were not hotbeds of innovation. Those of us making decisions about what happens in schools managed to figure out school well enough to succeed, which means that at some level it was good enough for us."

Also on the list of why classrooms continue to look like those of 1915 (with electronic slates): myriad activities going on in schools and school systems with no systematic ways of learning from them. In fact, most schools and school systems I work with will list somewhere between twenty and seventy initiatives when asked to map what they're doing. One could see those as lots of mini-experiments, but they're not. They're a mixture of mandates, things we've done forever, things we really hope will help solve a real problem we have, things we have special funding for, and ideas somebody had (maybe even cool, promising ideas). Mostly, they're tried without enough support to really do them well and without careful learning loops to see what's working and how to adjust for the next attempt.

Add to that a parochialism that uses context as an excuse not to learn from other places and research. I confess to having fully ascribed to the philosophy of "our students and school are unique, so we have to figure everything out ourselves" until I got into schools outside my own and realized that there are enough similarities across schools that I would serve children better to learn quickly from others. There's also a tendency to think of solutions as either-or rather than both-and—algorithms *or* concepts; phonics *or* whole language; lectures *or* projects; accountability *or* support. All of that adds up to inertial learning environments unless there are powerful forces to shake things up beyond window dressing.

Disruption on the Horizon?

The good news is that there *are* some of those powerful forces at work, and they are slowly permeating the boundaries of school. Current conditions work both for and against more entrepreneurial behavior in American education, which is why we have pockets of promise in a sea of status quo. On the plus side, technology, long looked to as a possible harbinger of changes in schooling, is now inexpensive and ubiquitous enough that it is accessible in many forms. In Typical High School, although over half the students qualify for free and reduced-price lunch, nearly all had phones that they could use to listen to music and take pictures of the assignment. This availability of technology also means that the role of school as source of knowledge for students has fundamentally shifted—students no longer need to rely solely on a school or teacher to give them access to learning or to decide what learning matters. They can now easily ask their own questions and find their own answers through the Internet. That doesn't mean the school and teachers have no role in exposing students to things they don't know or in helping them learn things that might be easier to learn with support, but it does mean that educators no longer have nearly as much power to decide what matters for learning, and that a lot more learning can happen outside of school.[2]

While there is a too-small set of schools in which learning looks and sounds truly different (often most notable in the roles students and teachers play in driving learning), there are increasing shifts at the edges of learning. An urban school in Massachusetts asks visiting educators to observe in classrooms based on a problem of practice that emerged in survey data of students' experiences generated with tools from Panorama Education. A high school student in rural Kentucky talks about feeling "college- and career-ready" because he has tracked his progress on the WINLearning system and applied his skills in his first job interview. A teacher listens to a first-grade reader and tracks her progress on a handheld device. A team of teachers uses Google Docs to track their agendas and next steps from their collaborative planning time. And so on.

That said, in the average classroom on the average day, there is not much evidence of entrepreneurship, especially if it's defined in terms of shifting the core tasks and interactions—i.e., moving beyond worksheets and right answers to the land of rich questions, problem-solving, communication, creativity, and challenge. Most teachers and principals and system leaders feel so burdened to keep up with a pacing guide or hit learning targets that they don't have (or make) room for innovation and entrepreneurial behavior. For example, the Common Core State Standards should be a great opportunity to be entrepreneurial, but instead they feel limiting or overwhelming. Instead of educators asking questions like, "How might we do things differently to help students learn to use their minds as described in the Common Core?" they are more frequently asking questions like, "How do we get enough technology for all students to take PARCC?"

Years of improvement plans do not mean educators are very good at improvement. We seem stuck, whether doing status quo, or trying new initiatives or programs but not learning systematically from them. There are more and more entrepreneurs in education, some of whom are making a real difference in the lives of children, but they are still not serving very many of them.

WHAT ARE THE TRADE-OFFS FOR IMPROVEMENT AND INNOVATION?

When it comes to helping all children learn, we need to be able to hold the possibility of multiple strategies simultaneously while still recognizing and making trade-offs. Learning is complicated, learners are different, and rarely will one approach work for all children (or the adults who serve them).

Here are a few examples of the trade-offs to consider:

Improvement and Innovation

Why spend energy on inventing approaches when we in fact know some things about what works? Why can't we simply continue to improve them? This argument, while persuasive in the sense that we would surely be better off if we did more of what we know works, ignores the importance of context and learner differences and also assumes more of a knowledge base than we have in education. But innovation is not the only answer, either.

An innovation-oriented approach ignores the knowledge base we do have and can be irresponsible toward the children in front of us right now, who deserve the best of what is known, not just the best efforts of whoever is working with them. Ted Kolderie, who helped start some of the earliest charter schools in the United States, is now advocating a "split-screen strategy," which includes both improvement and innovation.[3] This approach makes a lot of sense, as long as we recognize that both improvement and innovation take discipline to do well. There is an embedded trade-off in trying to do both improvement and innovation—the potential of doing one or both less well than if you just did one, and the potential that neither one will inform the other in a meaningful way. One principal I know describes *improvement* as the obligation of all educators—"getting better every day"—and *innovation* as the great hope.

Initiative

Being opportunistic is an important part of being entrepreneurial, and yet following opportunities that aren't tethered to a need or problem or aren't working toward a clear, ambitious vision can quickly make an organization less strategic and effective. This can cause a frustrating churn of initiatives. On the flip side, being entirely problem-oriented can make an organization reactionary and not a lot of fun to be in, unless problem-solving efforts are wildly successful (and even so, focusing on our weaknesses all the time can be very discouraging).

Technology

Technology is often viewed as the equivalent of innovation, but you can have technology without innovation, and innovation without technology. Take Classroom C in Typical High School. Doing worksheets on the computer is not innovative. The mode of delivery is new, but the task is not. A superintendent in Georgia told me he is selling and giving away his Smart-Boards in favor of iPads throughout his district, and both teachers and students are engaging in learning in whole new ways as a result. He had seen SmartBoards used as modern chalkboards with the teacher directing all the learning, whereas the iPads were helping students have (and teachers release) more control. In stark contrast to that approach, the head of some of the highest-performing schools in Boston talks about technology as a "resource choice" and limits technology in the classrooms in favor of investing in developing teachers.

Equity

A core entrepreneurship equity paradox is that the people who most need breakthrough ideas are also the ones who have the most to lose if the ideas fail. The potential danger of entrepreneurship is clear when one looks at entrepreneurship through an equity lens. What if we take risks and leave the most vulnerable learners even worse off? What if the schools and communities with the most resources get the most promising ideas and technologies—that is, the rich get richer? What if we absolve ourselves of responsibility for excellence for every child in the name of personalization?

It used to be that education entrepreneurs were mostly of a certain color and class—white and middle- to upper-class—and invention was the luxury and privilege of a few. That is beginning to be less true, and is certainly not true in less developed parts of the world, where innovation springs, out of necessity, from all corners.

A few ideas can help the equity-driven entrepreneurial educator out of this potentially harmful conundrum. First, one element of Clay Christensen's disruptive innovation theory is helpful as an ethical guidepost—whatever we're providing to children shouldn't be worse than what they're already getting, particularly for the children who rely most on schooling for opportunity and access. That means that it might very well make sense to channel resources (people and dollars) to fringe issues or populations rather than where the bulk of children are, particularly as a starting strategy.

But that's only defensible from an equity perspective if the purpose is to serve current nonusers really well (like students in the juvenile justice system or those who have dropped out of school or students without access to particular content and experiences, like those in rural areas) or to learn about the new approach in order to help more kids, particularly the ones who need better learning opportunities most.

A related question is: *On/with whom are we experimenting?* I sometimes get a visceral reaction, particularly from my doctoral students, when I describe the need to "place bets" as a part of effective strategy. I am then careful to add that we're not betting on children, but instead that there's a level of uncertainty whether any strategy we choose will work, and we need to be comfortable enough with that uncertainty to focus the efforts of the organization on really trying to make the strategy happen. While all that's true, my students make a strong and persuasive equity argument that we shouldn't be experimenting on children, especially when the "we" are often white and embedded in institutions long dominated by white privilege and the children we're talking about are often brown and have been failed by those institutions. One way to ameliorate this issue is to run the riskiest experiments on children with the most privilege (though this has the double risk of the rich getting richer if the experiment works well and of the experiment working well for this group, but not all children).

Another approach is to do things *with* people rather than *to* them or *on* them. In this regard, the empathy component of design thinking is a helpful starting point. Who are the "users"? What do they identify as a need (instead of the entrepreneurs telling them what they need)? How does one design for them? How might one engage them in the design process?

WHO COULD—AND SHOULD—BE ENTREPRENEURS?

Another way to address equity is to broaden the scope of who the entrepreneurs are. Currently, most entrepreneurs come from outside of education, and they often come with solutions in search of problems. Thus, it is no surprise that many of the (often attractive) ideas and products they come up with don't fundamentally change learning. They weren't really meant to, and/or they weren't designed by people who really understand learning. What if people closest to the learning were entrepreneurs?

Students. The students at Typical High School have lots of ideas about what could be done to improve their learning experience and their school. Students of every age have lots of ideas. That doesn't mean we necessarily need to give more recess or better lunch (two ideas I reliably hear across schools), but even these innovations might be worth considering—maybe learning would improve, at least for some students. Students also have ideas about how to make school less boring, what kinds of questions or comments help them switch from disengaged to engaged, and so on, and they could probably come up with some very different ideas about what their learning environment could look and sound like.

Teachers. Teachers are the group (after students) most likely to have entrepreneurship done to them rather than with or from them. How much are teachers driving innovation agendas? How often do ed tech start-ups have learning and teaching expertise at the core of the enterprise? Schools could have teacher roles like "entrepreneur in residence" (perhaps instead of a department chair). On a smaller scale, being entrepreneurial could be a particular role to play during teacher team meetings. The younger generation of teachers are generally more facile and fluid with technologies. Unlocking the agency of the people most comfortable with technology in our school systems (often not the ones with the most power) and linking that to some outcome we cared about could lead to more engagement and increased learning by today's students, who have yet another degree of fluency as "digital natives."

Leaders. Leaders often contract or delegate entrepreneurial behavior. There's nothing wrong with that, but what if all school and system leaders had an entrepreneurial disposition? The doctoral program in education leadership (Ed.L.D.) that I run at the Harvard Graduate School of Education aims to develop entrepreneurial leaders, no matter what role they're in, because we know they will be facing complex problems with numerous constraints, and that they'll have to get creative about what they do with their resources to address those problems and seize opportunities as they arise. We also know that they're going to have to be comfortable with a lot of uncertainty.

Parents and community members. These groups too can turn their concerns into entrepreneurial ideas. Families should be given the opportunity to name a need or opportunity and generate concrete ideas as a response.

This is not to say that only the people in education should be entrepreneurial. Educators (and parents) can get a little parochial in our hundred-plus-year-old school box. We definitely need some non-educators, people who don't think of twenty reasons why something won't work based on their experience in schools. We need people who ask different questions and see different possibilities. Sometimes, outsiders are better at listening because there isn't a particular answer they're expecting when they're designing something.

How Might We Develop Entrepreneurs and Entrepreneurial Behavior?

Like most things, some people seem to have particular talent or disposition for being entrepreneurial. But that doesn't mean that others can't develop that disposition or unlock that talent. One leader said to me, "I never thought of myself as an entrepreneur. But now I think I might be. Or could be at least entrepreneurial. It's funny—I almost feel like I'm not allowed to call myself that, and I'm talking with a friend who is a proud entrepreneur, and she's telling me it's okay."

Four mechanisms can help develop entrepreneurs and entrepreneurial behavior:

Teach. In preparing educators, include an entrepreneurial mind-set as part of the curriculum. For example, in the first year of the Ed.L.D. program, students read cases about entrepreneurial leaders, write a paper about what it means to be an entrepreneurial leader, and complete a "sector change project," which is their idea for how they might help improve the education sector. Programs for school leaders and teachers could include examples of people in those positions acting entrepreneurially and could ask people to complete relevant assignments related to entrepreneurship.

Within existing schools and school systems, free people up to imagine possibilities. Protocols like "Back to the Future"[4] or asking "what if" questions like "What if children were grouped by interest, not age?" help people step out of the boundaries of their current conditions. Ask people to design things specifically tied to a problem: a redesigned more productive parent-teacher conference; a welcoming school lobby; an opening ten minutes of class that got students excited to learn.

Incentivize. How do you signal the value of entrepreneurial behavior? First, make time for it. That is no small task. Even Google no longer allows employees to spend 20 percent of their time on personal projects. But it's not impossible. Teachers might take one common planning time a month to innovate (as opposed to thinking about how to improve their practice). One districtwide principal meeting could focus on a common need and designing a new approach. Students could have one day a month to develop entrepreneurial ideas.

Time, of course, might not be enough. Dollars would likely help generate more and better ideas. What if a school ran a competition open to students, faculty, and families to generate ideas that would solve some real need, preferably connected to learning, and awarded some money to help enact the winning ideas? What if there were some designated innovation dollars in the school system's budget? This might seem like an impossible luxury within tight budgets, and maybe you would need a community organization to fund the competition or line item.

A less grand, but also effective incentive would be to show you value entrepreneurial behavior by talking about it and by recognizing those who do it. One superintendent I know gives out Apple TVs to the teachers he calls his "speedboats"—the ones he observes leading rich learning, often using technology.

Support. As a sector, we don't systematically support entrepreneurs well. Some organizations like NewSchools Venture Fund and Imagine K12 have infrastructure to support education entrepreneurs. We could have more accelerators and supports for entrepreneurs, and school systems could do more partnering with such organizations.

Convene. Convenings are a great way to share and generate ideas, as well as build energy (which can be important in the face of the inevitable failures that come with entrepreneurship). There are an increasing number of convenings for education entrepreneurs, and some of them are including more educators. School systems could hold a convening for entrepreneurs within the system and the surrounding community. Or how about a weekend hackathon about a pressing need? And if calling special entrepreneurial convenings is not feasible, standard educator conferences could include pre-convenings related to entrepreneurship, like giving feedback to entrepreneurs with emerging ideas or generating new ideas by the people convened, rather than just sharing existing practices.

CONCLUSION

When I ask educators why innovation is worth the effort, they tell me it's because they want the children they serve and the children and grandchildren in their own families to dream big, to fulfill their dreams, and to make their communities thrive. They know that children are capable of big things, and that means the adults who serve them need to try some big things—and also get out of the learners' way.

To do all that, to help children live up to their potential and to see potential in themselves they don't yet know is there, we need both improvement *and* innovation. Leaders and organizations should be able to do both. We need people in education who will be *entrepreneurial.* I don't think of myself as an entrepreneur, but I am attracted to entrepreneurial behavior because being entrepreneurial is about efficacy—I see a problem, I can do something about it; I see an opportunity, I can seize it. I am willing to sit with uncertainty, ambiguity, and risk because the goal we are after is worth the risk and because the process itself is challenging, rewarding, and fun, especially when done with colleagues.

We will not build a thriving democracy in which success is predicted by effort rather than skin color or zip code or home language solely through bold innovation. Nor will we build it and tap into the most underutilized resource we have—our children, all of them—solely by doing what we know how to do well and learning how to do it better. Both are necessary. And both will accelerate progress much faster if the people who do them engage in entrepreneurial behavior *and* focus on going beyond worksheets in myriad forms to fundamentally shift the way learning looks and sounds. We need to help insiders be more entrepreneurial and outsiders be more focused on learning.

An experienced educator I know predicts that learning will look really different across lots of classrooms in five years. I'm a bit less sanguine about the timeline, but no less hopeful about the possibilities.

8

Go Small or Go Home

Innovation in Schooling

Matt Candler

In 2010, I created a nonprofit called 4.0 Schools for curious, gutsy people to test better ways of doing school. 4.0 is an early-stage incubator of innovative schools and education organizations led by entrepreneurs committed to rethinking education in the United States. Some of the people in our community create new tools for education. Others create what we call "tiny schools"—small pilots of bold new school designs. This chapter is about how that works, and what it's taught us about entrepreneurship and learning.

A REFORMER GETS SCHOOLED

For the first fifteen years of my career as a school reformer, I had a stubborn "kids' lives are at stake" mind-set that championed certainty and perfection. I've since realized that what kids need more is what Stanford psychologist Carol Dweck calls a *growth mind-set*—one that champions curiosity over certainty and iteration over perfection.[1]

My call to other reformers was to avoid settling for "sucking less" than our predecessors. I saw the world like this: "Someone has broken school; it is our job to fix it." And further, if we were in the business of fixing schools that the establishment had broken, we'd have to get it right. Lots of pressure, high stakes, no room for mess-ups. That's what Dweck calls a *fixed mind-set*—where anything new might risk your identity as someone who's successful; growth and new ideas are mostly downside.[2]

Beyond the irony of a reformer being stuck in a fixed mind-set, there were two really big things wrong with this approach:

1. My arrogance.
2. My definition of the problem.

Since our first attempt in 1647, the idea of compulsory schooling in the United States has grown increasingly complex. The school model we have is a like a 360-year-old hiker who's given more rocks to carry every year, never once asked if she might need some help. Schools, especially public schools, have been asked to do more and more for more and more. And much of that has been good. Things are more equitable (school should serve all kids, not just white boys (*Brown v. Board of Education*), school should strive to educate all to higher level of achievement (NCLB). But it's a complicated thing. There are many things about the current way we do school that are now obsolete.

A better starting place for the conversation is the actual obsolescence of the system—specifically, the incapacity to test new ideas without risking the entire system itself. The lack of any real sustainable approach to research and development in public schooling is one big reason why something as promising as the charter movement, in relatively short order—a decade or so—has become a place where reform ends up being more about doing the status quo better than your predecessor instead of actually trying new ideas.

As positions have hardened and dialogue between reformers and critics has calcified over the last decade, too few people have invested any real effort into achieving a balanced mix between doing what works and doing what might work better.

We reformers need to admit we've invested too little in trying new ideas, choosing instead to tell people, "We know what works, now please get out of our way." These are phrases I hear often, sometimes from reform leaders who serve many kids, and sometimes from funders who support those reformers.

Sometimes people who've resisted reformers have gone too far, too, defending the status quo at all costs, even when it's pretty obvious—especially when you ask families and kids—that parts of the status quo have outlived their utility and better solutions deserve to be explored.

A Mix of Scaling What Works and Trying New Things

I'm not preaching some Silicon Valley–style disruption for disruption's sake, even though as an entrepreneur, I do use the word *disruption*. And others like *iteration*, and *lean development*, and *design thinking*. But I write to you as a teacher, as a principal, as a district office employee, as a parent. Our system is due some upgrades, specifically ones that solve problems for those at the core of the system—children, teachers, and families.

I don't advocate blowing the whole system up. I'm preaching what we've been working on at 4.0 for the last five years—portfolio, risk, balance: a mix of investments in scaling what we've found to work along with deliberate, disciplined exploration of the things that we don't have yet but can scale later, once they show us a better way.

Here are my three big takeaways thus far—things that make up a robust approach to finding the next wave of breakthrough ideas in schooling:

- *Be user-centric:* Entrepreneurs and leaders of large systems need to focus on the problems facing their users—students and families— instead of the problems facing the people who serve them.
- *Be curious:* Kids don't need to see us modeling "I know what works; just let me show you." They know the world's changing faster than their school is. What they need to hear us modeling is, "Wow, this is hard! I don't know what the future will hold, but I am excited about it. Let's be curious and explore it in a thoughtful way."
- *Start messy, then focus on the frequency of your edits, not the perfection of your first draft:* In the pursuit of a better way, we must make many, many more, smaller, faster bets. This requires a bias to action, not a bias to certainty. Shipping an early version of a new idea to your users is scary. But when you get this right, they appreciate that you've involved them in the process of finding new ways to meet their needs. And if you respond quickly to their feedback, you'll create deeper loyalty and investment than you ever could trying to read their minds.

BUILDING A PLACE WHERE PEOPLE CAN TRY BIG IDEAS BY STARTING SMALL

4.0 Schools exists because there are very few places to innovate in education in the United States. We are, above all else, a community—a diverse group of people who believe schools can be dramatically better, especially for kids whose families don't have the resources to exercise choice by moving to another neighborhood or paying for private schools. We believe that big change in education is more likely to come from disciplined focus on acute, granular problems faced by the people who matter most in education—students, families and teachers—than from complex plans trickling down from the top.

What We Do

4.0 Schools equips entrepreneurial people to create new education start-up companies and schools. We solve problems like how to respond to student behavior you're not familiar with—for example, Branching Minds is an online tool built by a special ed teacher and a neuroscientist to give parents and teachers real-time feedback on how to best respond to unfamiliar student behavior. And problems like a culture that discourages girls from pursuing science, technology, engineering and math: Blink Blink's wearable technology kits and Vidcode's online video effect tools were built by women who code and design themselves. Finally, we train them to launch effective solutions as a start-up or new school, within a cohort of other passionate entrepreneurs. At 4.0, we are dedicated to testing ideas early, at a small scale, and in close partnership with students, families, and teachers. We don't create a start-up or new school until a leader in the community proves that someone we care about needs it and wants it. Our unique training in leading innovation in education happens in three stages:

- *Essentials:* Eight to ten times a year, we host Essentials, a multiday experience where up to twenty leaders from the 4.0 Schools community move their ideas forward. Participants define the person they're serving, the problem they're solving, and ways to test solutions. Essentials alums walk out the door with a plan to test their ideas quickly and cheaply.
- *Individualized coaching:* Leaders who show a willingness to test quickly and adjust to feedback from people they're serving get small-group and one-on-one coaching from highly trained 4.0 staff throughout the year.
- *Launch:* Twice a year, we offer our Launch program to up to ten teams of entrepreneurial founders who've validated new solutions to important problems. They bring new start-ups to life based on these ideas in under ninety days. The Launch program gives leaders an environment to fine-tune solutions, figure out what type of venture makes the most sense, and build the foundation for launching a new start-up or running a miniature version of a new school. The expanded 4.0 community serves as an extensive test-bed where

founders can iterate rapidly during Launch as they secure their first customers. Cohorts spend one month of the program in New Orleans or New York receiving daily coaching and support to beta-test their startups and school designs. They also have access to up to $5,000 of equity-free start-up capital.

We're convinced that leaders who work within a community of people who give them feedback and context for their work create change that lasts longer and digs deeper than those who work in isolated silos. And we've seen the promise of this approach pay off:

- We've trained 750 people in our Essentials course.
- Our Launch program—starting point for fifty-two new ventures including new schools and tools—is now more selective than Harvard.
- 75 percent of the ventures we have launched so far are still operating and serve more than 200,000 students, teachers, and families across the United States.
- Our pipeline is diverse: 81 percent of recent Launch alums are first-time entrepreneurs; 50 percent are women; 36 percent are people of color; 26 percent are parents.
- 4.0 start-ups have raised $7 million in capital, earned $3 million, and entered prestigious downstream programs like Echoing Green, Imagine K12, and LearnLaunch.
- 4.0-trained entrepreneurs have swept the podium three times at Startup Education Weekend.

While there are other organizations focused on early-stage investments in education, we don't have nearly enough people doing this type of work. And although 4.0 generally invests much earlier in the process than others, what really separates us from other ed-tech accelerators or school incubators is the expectations we have of the leaders we train, beyond the start-up or school they create at 4.0. Because for us, the unit of change in education isn't the superhero superintendent, or the charter management operator, or the mayor who takes control. Nor is it the entrepreneur or the disruptive ed tech start up. It is the local start-up community where local leaders make the future of school radically better regardless of how much policy work and traditional structural reform is under way. We expect these leaders to continue to drive systemic reform as the architects and founders of sustainable start-up communities that can thrive in their hometowns. When each community in our nation has its own stunning example of the future of school and enough momentum to sustain its own local innovation, regardless of the policy environment or elected leadership, 4.0's work will be done.

To make that vision a reality, we're creating a national network of local start-up communities led by the entrepreneurs and school founders we're training right now. Over time, this network people will transform how we do school, and how we approach school reform. Last year, 4.0 Schools' events and programming drew more than 1,750 people together to imagine and test ideas for the future of school.

Big Ideas That People Have Brought to Life at 4.0

Entrepreneurial individuals rely on Essentials and our early-stage coaching to turn their ideas into actionable pilots like:

Uncommon Construction, New Orleans. New Orleans youth lack the exposure, experience, resources, and soft skills that are necessary to successfully pursue the career of their choice. Aaron Frumin is piloting unCommon Construction, an initiative in which currently enrolled high school students build houses, and the profits are used to provide these apprentices with expanded academic or career opportunities. They're currently planning for this summer's "Tiny House Institute," where they'll test their program and process by building and selling a tiny (but complete!) house on a trailer with a small cohort of apprentices.

Bridge the Gap, New Orleans. College mentoring programs exist in low-income communities, but very few provide support to high-achieving students attempting to prepare for and apply to the country's most competitive universities. Founder Clara Baron-Hippolyte believes students can match into better universities through more personalized advising, mentoring, and academic enrichment opportunities early in their high school careers. Her project, Bridge the Gap, is now testing information sessions and workshops to educate students and families about steps they can take to prepare for the admissions process.

Li'l Stories, New York. Many schools talk about the need for teaching soft skills, but most of the curriculum created to teach them are unnecessarily boring, ugly, and ineffective. Designer Anke Stohlmann is exploring how to teach elementary students twenty-first-century soft skills—creativity, creative thinking, communication, and collaboration—with a play-based approach. She's testing a visual storytelling framework that teaches abstract thinking and collaboration through visual, oral, and written storytelling, working with first- through third-graders in schools and museums.

Yang Camp, Los Angeles. Vivy Chao is focused on equipping students with the skills they need to succeed beyond high school. She is testing how students respond to hands-on, experiential learning of entrepreneurship and is getting feedback through piloting in schools, the General Assembly computer programming school, the homeschooling community, and a maker studio. (The maker movement, once the realm of late-night garage tinkerers, has now become a vibrant community of people embracing nontraditional approaches to making things. The maker movement takes education far more seriously than it used to. 3-D printing, robotics, drones, and high-tech fashion design now serve as incredibly engaging avenues for kids to learn about technology. Some of our most interesting startups are striving to bring the energy and passion of this movement into schools.)

Not all our pilot tests work, and neither do all of our start-ups. But we don't hear the people involved say they were reckless experiments. By starting small and including parents, teachers, and students in the process, the leaders we work with start off asking for help, admitting they don't have a perfect solution yet, and ask for support and feedback. If they adapt when people give them good feedback, not only do they get better faster than they would have if working alone, but they build trust and buy-in.

This posture of curiosity and openness to feedback is what makes these leaders so effective in the finding new ways to do school.

THE TINY SCHOOLS PROJECT

Over the last twenty years, I've been involved in more than one hundred school start-ups. Until about four years ago, I stuck with a pretty consistent approach to get a new school up and running:

1. Find effective classroom teachers and give them a chance to have more impact as the founders of new schools.
2. Have teachers spend six to twelve months incubating in one or two quality schools in order to understand the culture and shadow a proven school leader.

3. Help teachers write a charter application detailing a school as close to the one they'd worked in as possible. Authorizers are mostly concerned with approving schools based on models that have been proven effective, so convincing them they are making a safe bet was key.

4. Cross fingers on the authorizer approving the two-hundred- to four-hundred-page application on a school that I never actually tested with any of the people who were going to run it.

5. Get ready to launch. This included things like: build a board, rent or renovate a private building or negotiate with the district for one, hire a pretty large staff (plan for growth), start recruiting families, plan marketing, raise funds, talk to local political leaders for support, reach out to local community and convince them of the benefits the school would bring, get insurance, find vendors, buy books, buy furniture, find buses or hire someone, plan routes, train staff, get school uniforms, plan the first few weeks down to the minute, and so on. I dug up an old checklist for a start-up; it contained almost four hundred tasks.

6. Go from zero to running a $1–4 million operation, serving eighty-two hundred kids out of the gate.

I used to think chartering this way was a great approach. It was safer, faster, and lower-risk than the traditional district-led school improvement plan, where a powerful champion would show up at a huge school and promise the moon to families, but be equipped with control over only a few variables— a school-site budget line here, a few staff changes there, and a coat of paint here. So the chance to start anew, with a new culture and a new team, with only a few hundred kids, seemed a huge upgrade.

I'm not saying that there's no merit in finding ways to replicate what's working in good schools and train more leaders to take those models to more families. But my approach had a big flaw. I rarely tested the models before families and kids showed up! I was scrupulous (and proud) to have leaders do test runs with staff and run role-playing and practice scenarios, but I rarely asked anyone to actually test a simple version of the school in action.

Chartering Isn't So Tiny Anymore

The charter movement has shifted away from its original promise of offering a tiny way to test new models and ideas in a way that might inspire and inform bigger systems. These days, charter schooling is less about trying new things than "scaling what works"—at least that's where the money's going. And increasingly, this approach is where the laws are leaning, too, with many favoring "proven operators" over new ones. I'm optimistic that we'll rekindle the original spirit of the movement, especially if charter advocates dial back the "we know what works" bit, but for now, even though the charter movement has fallen short of its potential, I think we can still find ways to validate and explore new schools. We're already finding a few new ways to test new models without getting a charter school approved.

A Tinier Way

At 4.0, we're starting schools in a very different way than I used to. Our first cohort of school founders and start-up entrepreneurs was a group of six innovative people. I got started with them the same way I'd always started; I asked them to commit a year soaking up proven concepts in existing high-quality schools.

Not long into that year, Josh Densen, a member of that first cohort, challenged my approach. He started hosting sessions in living rooms around New Orleans, asking parents what they wanted in a new school. He didn't sell anything; he just listened. And when he crunched the numbers from his surveys, the two things that parents wanted were socioeconomic diversity and a focus on creative thinking. So we sat and sat and Googled and called friends trying to find a school he could replicate that had that stuff. But we couldn't.

Then Josh came up with a crazy idea, informed by the big fight going on at the time between old-school New Orleans restaurants and the food trucks roaming around selling new types of food. What if he tried a food-truck version of his school?

Josh bought a table and some creative thinking manipulatives he wanted to use in his school and started doing pop-up versions of his school at free music festivals at the Mahalia Jackson Center. He'd cleverly set up his table close to the inflatable bounce house that all these festivals had for the audience's bored children. He had no brochures, no propaganda. He'd just have a sign with the school name, a blank sign-up sheet, and himself standing next to a big groundcloth with some really fun toys on it. He'd usually have his kids playing with the stuff once he got set up. Families making their way to the bounce house do a double-take. Was it OK for their kids to play with this stuff? Could they do that *and* do the bounce house? Josh would encourage them to let their kids to try they toys out and when it felt safe, geek out about how he thought the building blocks might boost creative confidence.

A mix of families started showing up repeatedly at the pop-ups. Josh felt it was time to test his creative confidence ideas at a deeper level, so he struck a deal with Jay Altman, the CEO of FirstLine Schools, to show up at Samuel Green Charter School one afternoon a week with some of the kids who had participated in the pop-up and have them join Green students in a test run of his design thinking class. He wasn't driving a food truck, but he might as well have been. It took Josh a year beyond what I hoped to start Bricolage Academy—now one of the most diverse schools in New Orleans—and he spent much of that extra year doing these pop-up and small-scale pilots.

Ever since watching Josh's experiment, we've been trying to de-risk the process of new school creation and make it more iterative, more responsive, and more agile. We've studied everything we can find on agile development and lean start-up. Four years after Josh's first pop-up, we're formalizing this new approach to school creation we call the Tiny Schools Project.

The goal of the project is to reduce the risk of creating new schools by testing promising concepts at a very small scale in intimate environments where willing families and students provide high-frequency feedback to school leaders before they build a full-scale school. We provide design guidance, real-time feedback, leadership coaching, and financial support of between $25,000 and $150,000 for each pilot, depending on the pilot design and duration.

Too many school incubation efforts prioritize writing about what a school might look like. In fact, the average charter school application in many states is hundreds of pages long and yet requires no evidence of actual field testing of the school model itself. Our school incubation program prioritizes real life testing with a small community of willing participants-families and students who want to be a part of testing the new design and exploring its potential. It is best suited for leaders who've completed the 4.0 Launch program or can demonstrate a similar level of preparation, including at least ten hours of field-testing with students.

As a follow up to our three-month Launch program, 4.0 Schools will help small teams of school builders run small-scale (*tiny*—smaller than a typical private school classroom) pilots of ambitious new school models with families and students who want to participate in well-structured, carefully monitored schooling experiments.

Tiny Cohort 1

There are four groups in our first cohort in The Tiny Schools Project:

- *1881 Institute:* The 1881 Research Institute is a hands-on training high school that builds community and hope while using the power of STEM.[3]
- *NOLA Micro Schools:* NOLA Micro Schools prepares students to pursue their passions and creativity through a blending of state-of-the-art software, quest-like projects with real-world applications, Socratic discussions, and apprenticeships in diverse, student-centered, multi-age classrooms.[4]
- *Rooted School:* Rooted School is an open-enrollment high school that prepares students for employment in high-growth, high-wage industries.[5]
- *Noble Minds Institute:* The Noble Minds institute for Whole Child Learning is a New Orleans–based learning lab that focuses on academic and personal development (set to open in 2016).[6]

Each team is led by an alum of our Launch program, where they conduct a series of day- or weeklong pop-up school experiences in New Orleans.[7] Based on the feedback they received in the pop-ups and coaching from 4.0, each team has designed a more extensive real-world pilot of its school model—something we call a *tiny school*.

Each tiny school pilot will last between two and twelve months, serve fewer than fifteen students, include no more than two teachers, focus heavily on self-directed learning, include lots of data about how students are doing, and explore cost-saving approaches that improve sustainability. Public school models should run without philanthropy after three years; private schools must aim for tuition of less than $6,000 per child.

We challenged each founder to ask existing schools and organizations to carry as much of the operational load as possible during the pilot so they could focus on testing academic elements of their models.

What they've come up is far more creative than I expected. Here are their four very different approaches:

- *The tiny two-month summer school:* 1881 partnered with Adinkra NOLA (a home school collective that doesn't have extensive high school student summer programming) and Tuskegee Institute on its tiny pilot—a two-month, full-day summer program.

- *The tiny low-cost private school:* NOLA Micro is subletting unused space in a local private school (that's also leased to public charter schools) to run a tiny version of its low-cost private school.
- *The tiny school within a public charter school:* Rooted is contracting with a local public charter school for a year to run a tiny version of the tiny school with kids who will volunteer to be in the pilot but stay enrolled at the host school.
- *The tiny school within a district public school:* Noble Minds is still finalizing where it will pilot, but one option (and the one that most fascinates me) is contracting with a local district for a year to run its tiny school with kids who will volunteer to be in the pilot but stay enrolled at the host school.

This collaboration—especially between the aspiring charters and existing public schools—is a big deal to me. That leaders of existing schools would so willingly help out here is extraordinary. A fixed mind-set, like the one I used to have, would lead many to avoid this kind of thing.

4.0 is working closely with each founder and their host partners to craft smart agreements that maximize their chances for success. We'll miss some things, and partnering like this will come with some challenges. We'll try and adapt as fast as we can during each pilot. If we get something that starts to work, we're planning to share what we know in the form of a *model tiny school agreement* that anyone can use.

Is building a tiny ten- to fifteen-student version of a new school model a perfect test? No. I can give you a long list of operational and financial mistakes easily made once a school gets bigger—even if the tiny pilot works flawlessly.

But even a few months into this effort, the support from willing partners in existing schools has allowed each tiny school team to pay far more attention to the core work of educating students than the politics, logistics, and operational details that tend to overwhelm founders of schools that have to start bigger than these four do. I think these schools will learn far more in these constrained, simpler pilots than they would starting the way most new charters do. And over the long term, that willingness to go slow at first may in fact let them grow faster later on. And best of all, the students in these pilots will get the full attention of the model founders because other schools are willing to help them out.

That's one of the tiny victories we've had that I'm going to celebrate.

WHAT NEXT?

Fifty-eight start-ups and schools into our work at 4.0, we're starting to see some interesting trends that might suggest where school might go in the future:

- Schools can get smaller, more responsive, and more flexible by relying on technology and customer-centric thinking instead of chasing "economies of scale" in huge buildings and huge bureaucracies.
- Students and families will be able to choose from a network of providers within their community offering a wide variety of more personalized schooling options instead of having to exercise choice by moving to new communities.
- Students will exercise more ownership over their learning than in the past.
- We'll supplement teacher qualitative judgment about student progress with data from a variety of learning channels (independent learning platforms, student-to-student learning, parent-to-teacher, and student-created data).
- Family members will understand what's happening in class and know how to support from home in real time instead of at the end of a grading period or school year.
- Students will spend more time outside the school building, relying on mobile platforms to capture learning and share work with teachers and each other.
- Schools will be more connected to their communities through partnerships with civic institutions like museums as well as employers to more closely align learning to the most promising local careers.

And there's a lot more to see at 4pt0.org/ventures.

Stay Tiny Out There!

I believe in taking many more but much smaller bets on the future of school—that the best way to innovate is to start small and grow only when we've built something parents, teachers, and students want.

This process must take place within a community, not because we believe in some abstract idea of the power of communities, but because in the early exploratory stages, that community of volunteers plays a critical role in the development of the schools; people who willingly volunteer give our entrepreneurs critical feedback when they are still testing things out. Without that community, entrepreneurs and leaders have nowhere to test, so they must choose between doing nothing and experimenting—and risk wreaking havoc—with teachers, kids, and families who haven't volunteered.

And that's why I pause when I hear someone, as I used to, too quickly draw the conclusion that the methods and incentives we see in places like Silicon Valley should just be ported over to education. This is a public good in our democracy, so the concept of testing and exploring new solutions requires a little more care and deliberation.

If we do our testing thoughtfully, we can get bolder ideas to come to life with less risk to the public. We *can* create the conditions for more ideas to surface, for more of those ideas to get tuned before they're thrown at hundreds or thousands of children.

My view of the future of school? I think it starts with an army of humble leaders getting to know the human issues that students, teachers, and families face every day, setting out to solve those problems, even if they start with just a handful of people. Those students, teachers, and families are talking to them, telling them what's working, cheering them on as they make the next version better.

That may sound like a tiny idea, but someday, I think it could be big.

Transparency, Authenticity, Civility

*The Prerequisites to Sustainable
Entrepreneurship in Education*

John Katzman and Jillian Youngblood

A market philosophy in education is both obvious and powerfully aligned to American values. People often think of marketplaces in terms of competition, but they are more about fit. There's no best mobile phone; there are a bunch of great phones with different screens, operating systems, and prices. And there doesn't need to be an objectively best school, teacher, curriculum, or ed tech company—there is the right school for your son or daughter, or the right technology or curriculum for your school. In a top-down world, players don't find novel ways to good outcomes; rather, they seek to be like each other. In a marketplace, players differentiate themselves and optimize for their target audiences.

Further, every complex question has a simple answer that's wrong. Are bananas healthy? If you're diabetic or eat ten in one sitting, probably not. Is that college for you? It depends on who you are and what you need. A marketplace can handle *complexity* in a way that a blunt tool—like a list of college rankings—cannot.

John has spent a three-decade career at the intersection of education, technology, and business. He founded The Princeton Review in 1981. By the time he left some two decades later, the company was helping over half of the students applying to US colleges each year, from researching the options to preparing for the SAT to paying for school. In 2008, he founded 2U, a technology company that helps build and administer online graduate programs in partnership with top-tier universities like the University of Southern California, Georgetown, and the University of North Carolina at Chapel Hill. In 2012, he left to found The Noodle Companies, a studio designed to bring radical transparency and market-driven change to our education system.

At Noodle, Jillian has exhaustively studied how consumers make decisions about education, including parents comparing traditional public schools and charter schools and veterans stumbling into lousy for-profit colleges via predatory lead generation websites.

Our experience shows resoundingly that top-down approaches don't work. So why do so many people disagree with a marketplace approach, and how do we convince them to adopt it? Let's looks at some of the issues.

FOR-PROFITS HAVE BEEN TERRIBLE

A big hurdle for adoption of a marketplace approach is that educators and policymakers often conflate markets with for-profits, and equate for-profits with bad motives and bad outcomes. They're skeptical for good reasons.

For-profit organizations have a weak track record when compared with nonprofit organizations. For-profit universities have a six-year graduation rate of 22 percent, far below the 60 percent at nonprofit institutions. At the same time, for-profit marketing budgets dwarf those of their nonprofit peers; they spend 23 percent of revenue on recruiting new students, compared with 1 percent by nonprofits. At the K–12 level, charters run by for-profit companies meet proficiency standards about 20 percent less often than those run by nonprofits.

Some of these statistics speak more to the student population and selection process than to the quality of the education at these schools. But all speak to a need to realign the incentives of our education system. The promise of the private sector—that it can raise quality while lowering costs—makes it that much more important that we create marketplaces that are both trusted and worthy of that trust.

And there are many reasons to be distrustful. Consider the lead generation business in education. Lead generators are marketers who create attractive websites that appear to offer reliable data and advice on higher education (they're also adept at telemarketing, display ads, search engine optimization, and search engine marketing). In reality, they are little more than advertisements for colleges and graduate schools, largely low-quality ones. Once prospective students register—often providing information about themselves, their college interests, and their financial aid needs—they become sales "leads." The lead generators then sell those names and contact information to paying schools. Almost no education lead generation sites clearly state that they are advertisements; disclosures are usually difficult to find, opaquely worded, or simply nonexistent.

A reputable search site will at least produce a list of schools that nominally meet some set of student criteria (e.g., located in the Northeast, urban campus, focus on finance), and will flag results that are actually advertisements. But search for, say, an MBA on a lead generation site, and you won't get actual search results; you'll get a list of advertisers. The results have nothing to do with student needs and everything to do with how much the schools paid to be listed.

The companies running these sites mislead prospective students, as Noodle confirmed in a January 2015 white paper.[1] Working with an independent research firm, we surveyed people who were planning to begin a college or graduate program in the next two years, and found that a majority of respondents believed that their search results on these sites were based on a neutral evaluation of their search criteria. As a result, a significant portion of respondents said they were influenced by lead generator site recommendations—had they known their search results were paid for by schools, it would have influenced their decisions on where they ultimately enrolled.

Such sites are now omnipresent online, and focus intensely on ranking well in online search results. And they often target students who are searching without much guidance or information.

Some argue that trying to perfect the education marketplace is a waste of time. Some educators dismiss for-profit education simply by pointing to the numbers mentioned above. They are concerned that educators, parents, and students will make unwise decisions regardless of the data given them, and thus we need stronger regulation. Others—free-market fundamentalists, to use the economist Joseph Stiglitz's term—argue that the education system will work better if we simply let organizations compete with no rules.

But the for-profit sector isn't going away, and the marketplace isn't functioning well. Moreover, most people actually agree on what we want from our educational system: adults who are happy, healthy members of the community, are financially stable, and have careers they enjoy. We can also see that both the current and proposed accountability structures have very little proven correlation to those goals. Since we will inevitably get what we measure and incentivize, we will need to erect structures that reflect these values, and are limber enough to adapt to change. For-profits will continue to deploy capital to maximize return. Traditional educators will struggle with budget pressure and a flood of new opportunities and challenges springing from new technologies. As a result, our goals will evolve.

THE WRONG KIND OF TRANSPARENCY

We also talk about the critical need for market transparency, but we focus on the wrong kind of transparency. Consider a few examples of the unintended consequences.

Economist Charles Goodhart found in the financial system what many people in education also know: when a measure becomes a target, it ceases to be a good measure.[2] In her excellent book on testing, Anya Kamenetz writes, "The more you turn up the pressure to hit that number, the worse the distortion and corruption gets."[3] The 2015 conviction of Atlanta teachers and administrators for changing students' test answers and scores highlights just one particularly troubling pattern of institutional cheating. But we see irrational measures at every level of our education system.

In *Lies My Teacher Told Me*, James Loewen describes the dynamics of distorted incentives through the evolution of American history textbooks.[4] K–12 publishers have traditionally catered to states with textbook adoption boards for simple economic reasons: getting adopted by a few large states—often California, Texas, and Florida—could make or break a publisher's multimillion-dollar investment. Paradoxically, many states have volunteer boards to determine whether the text is adopted. They often have little time (and sometimes, even less expertise) to judge the numerous and voluminous offerings in a meaningful way. They simply look for the number of facts, topics, colorful pictures and graphics, and special subsections. Publishers then further strip their books of anything that might provoke parochial objections (best of luck to the textbook that frames Texans' defense of the Alamo as a defense of slavery). What's left is a compilation of easily scannable headers and flashy signifiers.

Whether the material is accurate, relevant, and compelling to students is a secondary consideration. Says Loewen: "While textbook authors tend to include most of the trees and all too many twigs, they neglect to give readers even a glimpse of what they might find memorable: the forests. Textbooks stifle meaning by suppressing causation. Students exit history textbooks without having developed the ability to think coherently about social life."[5] If we rewrote our history textbooks with outcomes in mind, the new volumes would bear no resemblance to the old ones we scrapped.

SAT prep is another ghost of unintended consequences. The College Board continues to make grand claims that it measures a broad range of reasoning skills, but good tutors know what is actually getting measured, and they teach those things to the exclusion of others. Early at The Princeton Review, we called our favorite technique "the Force" because it called on students to solve a type of math question with their eyes closed.[6] This question tested little more than students' ability to pay money to learn how to answer it. It certainly did not test their chances of success as a college student or employee.

One of the best (or worst) examples of lack of transparency in higher ed are the *U.S. News & World Report* rankings. They are enormously influential, and for college administrators, much of the past thirty years has been about gaming those rankings. Rather than rate a college on real outcomes connected to its mission (which varies by type of school), *U.S. News* uses input metrics like selectivity for elite schools and for the 350-odd colleges that want to be perceived as elite (for the 2,700 other colleges and universities in the United States, it uses almost nothing). We care about our kids' happiness, health, financial stability, and career satisfaction, yet efforts to tie those outcomes back to college choice are few.

So what kinds of misguided transparency got us here?

Inauthentic Measures

The accountability systems we have in place now revolve around inauthentic, hamfisted measures. While policymakers remain devoted to them, they have been largely unpersuasive to parents, who sense how far removed they are from meaningful outcomes. When parents lie down in front of bulldozers to save terrible schools, it's not because they're victims of Stockholm Syndrome; they are simply unconvinced that we should institute a burdensome testing requirement to narrowly define degrees of achievement, then fire teachers and shut down schools based on weak scores. When Mrs. Jones doesn't see the connection between accountability metrics and who her child is, she won't take them seriously. Imagine, instead, offering information about school quality in the form of figure 9.1: When a child like yours

Springfield Independent School District

For a student like yours:	John Adams Middle School	John Q. Adams Middle School
Chance of graduating high school	50%	75%
Chance of graduating college	74%	86%
Chance of incarceration	35%	4%
Best fit	5 (mediocre)	19 (very good)

FIGURE 9.1   Sample Parent Choice Form

goes to *this* school, he has an 8 percent chance of going to college and a 25 percent chance of going to prison. But when he goes to this other school, it's 30 percent and 5 percent. Now she's engaged.

Parents will take accountability seriously only when we talk about their children as individuals, and when we speak honestly about real outcomes rather than gameable metrics like test scores. A pioneer in this way of thinking is KIPP schools. KIPP is known for its long school year and strict code of conduct. Its students' test scores are considerably higher than those of nearby district schools. But it recently released some much more compelling and authentic numbers: 45 percent of students who had graduated from a KIPP middle school went on to earn a four-year college degree. That's more than *five times* the rate of the average low-income student they work with.[7] This is the kind of metric that matters to a parent. Test scores are both abstraction and distraction. A four-year college degree, however, is real. Any parents, given the information in a usable way, would make the decision to push their children toward that outcome.

That parents care about outcomes over arbitrary, short-term metrics is not a hypothesis that needs to be proven at any economic level. An upper-income Manhattan independent school parent assumes that every child who enrolls at her child's school will go to college; she's interested in *where*. She doesn't look at test scores (other than as they relate to college acceptance). Instead, she speaks the language of Gallup's research, of general well-being over time. Gallup, in partnership with Purdue University and the Lumina Foundation, surveyed more than thirty thousand US college graduates to identify formative experiences in college that prepared graduates not just for "great jobs" but for "great lives." They mounted the survey on Gallup's "tentpoles" of well-being—social, financial, purpose, community and physical—and looked at how well colleges positively impacted their graduates in the long-term.[8] A teacher might be able to make the case that value-added test scores are meaningless, but she'll never convince a parent that graduating some college is meaningless—and she won't try.

The Evaluative Mind-Set

A misguided evaluative mind-set further hinders attempts at transparency. The metrics of school accountability and school choice are different. Accountability metrics are designed to *evaluate* students, faculty, or schools against a common yardstick; the accountability is to an accreditor or supervisor. Choice metrics are built to *persuade* students to make wise choices, given their unique backgrounds, goals, and resources. These prospective uses lead to quite different data sets and reports.

Our current reports are the result of an evaluative mind-set. We test K–12 students to determine if they're ready for promotion and if their teachers and schools are competent. The next logical step—and a popular topic among reformers—is to fire incompetent teachers and close bad schools. Such reports speak to overall performance, like the average gains made by students, or the percent achieving proficiency.

Most of these metrics are less precise than they appear and take more time to provide meaningful information than we give them. According to the American Statistical Association (ASA), a teacher's performance as measured by value-added models has "large standard errors, even when calculated using several years of data. These large standard errors make rankings unstable, even under the best scenarios for modeling." The ASA finds that performance in one year has only a 0.5 correlation to performance in the next—notable but not overwhelming.[9] And that's based on tests that add seven hours of testing and untold hours of prep (sophisticated schools now give two full-length practice tests beforehand, in addition to targeted review).

Even if these evaluative statistics were more precise and less intrusive, they would still get less than optimal use. Because they are geared to teacher and school evaluation, they are (and always will be) disparaged by a significant percentage of the teachers and administrators around them, especially in weaker schools. Groups of educators have worked hard and so far successfully to discredit and marginalize these metrics.

These badly thought-out metrics have a huge cost. As is both intuitively obvious and well proven, they drive schools to narrow their curricula to the material on high-stakes tests.[10] Since these tests promote the unproven notion that every student should learn the same things at the same time, they push schools across the country to become even more homogenous, and choice becomes less important.

What we should be asking is: What data do policymakers need, and what data do decision makers need? A policymaker looks at a school and asks, "Is it great?" A parent looks at that school and asks "Is it great for my kid?" We've asked several state accountability people to use their scores to tell us where to send a kid, and no one can. How do we expect regular parents to make good decisions?

The Criminal Justice Approach

There are two judicial systems in America. The criminal judicial system addresses misdeeds so serious that the government prosecutes the wrong-doer on society's behalf. The civil code, on the other hand, is a framework for citizens to enforce their rights against one another. If someone violates the terms of a contract, you can sue; the government will merely supply the legal and logistic structure. Our current approach to education reform has only one mode—the metaphorical equivalent of the criminal code. Educators and students are not held responsible by each other, but by the state. This top-down approach makes meaningful transparency impossible.

The US education system applies this criminal code approach not only to critical problems (diploma mills or the very worst elementary schools) but for everyday situations (laws governing how teachers are to be trained, standards that every school must teach to, rating systems for colleges that set the same metrics for liberal arts and vocational schools). What constitutes good education is laid out in a sort of criminally stringent statute, as if the keys to a great education have been settled beyond reasonable doubt.

This rigid approach is surprising, given the egregious track record of top-down reform. Beyond a handful of unimpeachable truths—say, that every child should be able to read—education is better left to a more nuanced civil code. In a bottom-up, civil code world, we talk about *fit*. Providers differentiate, and consumers try to figure out which approach works best for them. Over time, we start to see which approaches result in which outcomes for which consumers. When it comes to exactly what your sixth-grader needs to know, where your daughter should attend college, and how to measure their knowledge and skills, we need the transparency and energy of a well-regulated marketplace where ideas and schools are tested against one another, and the search is for best individual fit.

In a criminal-law, top-down system, we create metrics to rate every teacher on a given scale. In a civil-law system, a principal picks her team based on the school's goals, philosophy, and ethos.

In many other cases where the government does step in—like shutting down weaker schools or lowering debt levels—it need not act unilaterally. It can function like the civil code, and allow people and organizations to hold each other accountable.

The Standards Movement

States and school districts are now in the process of trying to create transparency by spending billions of dollars implementing the Common Core, despite research showing that standards simply do not matter. A 2012 report by the Brown Center found that between 2003 and 2009, states with excellent standards and states with terrible standards raised their scores on the National Assessment of Educational Progress (NAEP) by roughly the same margin. The report further notes that the variation in NAEP scores is far more dramatic within states than among them.[11] If rigorous standards have the power to raise achievement, then why have we not seen improvements among school districts within states that have been using the same standards for years?

Standards aren't all bad. They can be neutral, like nuts and bolts. They provide a common language to more easily connect an assessment with the appropriate remediation or enrichment. And indeed the Common Core standards themselves are probably better than most state standards as descriptors of the things that students might learn. It's when they become prescriptive—every third-grader must master *this* standard versus *that* one—that they move from enabling a market to preempting it. When we tell teachers that we've decided they should deemphasize geometry, or spend less time on fiction and more on close reading of nonfiction, we're doing much more than giving them a framework. We simply don't trust educators to differentiate their schools and choose curricula. Now add tests that enforce those prescriptions and we end any conversation about the best approach to a child's education. Some people theorize that a commitment to uniform measures will beget innovation around achieving them, but our experience suggests the reverse. The standards movement isn't another raindrop that eventually drowns innovation; it's a tsunami.

The most disruptive change in K–12 has been charter schools, an area where the market approach is yielding strong results. Now, charters need to show they're better, and the movement embraces more testing. But there are a lot of ways to measure schools without this one-size approach: by *authentic metrics* like the long-term outcomes that Gallup and Purdue measure, and (for shorter-term results) by NAEP. By embracing the accountability and Common Core folks, the charter movement makes itself less popular and less persuasive, and allies itself with those who don't trust parents to choose a school any more than they trust educators to choose a curriculum.

THE EDUCATION MARKETPLACE

A transparent, well-functioning marketplace provides brutal accountability. BlackBerry and Nokia were not terrible companies, but both plummeted in just a few years because they didn't innovate as fast and as well as Apple. This brutality springs from millions of individual decisions based on both emotion and hard data. Consumers and employers know what they want and should have a transparent marketplace where they can assess their options. Choice without information is a rigged game.

Experimentation and Innovation

Imagine an education marketplace where different schools are driving meaningful choice by adopting a broad variety of curricula. As different methods are shown to produce better outcomes for certain kinds of students, networks of schools could adopt these methods and specialize in them. Parents could choose the right school based on simple, useful information.

In higher education, imagine that professors could truly implement flipped-model approaches to learning, having access not only to modular content but to modular technologies. Working within an ecosystem of learning management systems, content management systems, and guidance counseling tools, professors could enable the right course for every student at any moment in time. With no barriers to entering the market, this model is endlessly scalable and would allow for continual improvement.

But as long as we continue to focus on performance against a set of externally generated goals, innovations in teaching die as caterpillars. We're terrified of innovating because it requires something we feel is morally dubious: experimenting on kids. Hypothetically, we want to encourage progress in education in the same way we encourage it for everything from medical devices to photo sharing apps. But when it comes to actually giving teachers or principals any authority to try out new methods—much less new structures—we get stuck.

Most innovation fails, even at companies like Google. We often have trouble recognizing promising innovations and find it even more challenging to implement and scale them. The US Department of Education's What Works Clearinghouse was originally mocked as the "Nothing Works Clearinghouse." Despite knowing this, we seem to want innovation only if every experiment is a success.

I don't mean to make light of this concern; it's just that the status quo is not working for a lot of students. And some parts are not working for anyone. Did you take a foreign language in high school? If you didn't immerse yourself in that language by spending a few months in a country where it's the native tongue, you're probably not fluent. And while it's possible that American schools are worse at teaching language than anything else, it's more likely that we're equally imperfect at teaching everything; it's just not as obvious when we teach math because there are no native calculus speakers.

Plenty of schools are experimenting every day, of course, but we need smarter, larger-scale, more thoughtful experimentation against authentic metrics—even if these experiments might fail. We can't test out educational theories on computer models or lab rats—we have to test them on children. That might make us uncomfortable, but by avoiding it, we'll never make any scientific progress. Only through the long process of building a strong, diverse evidence base did we stop treating illness with leeches (*before we started again*). There's an important lesson here: you have to try something to find out if it works.

Some of the most successful ideas will offer benefits to a wide range of children, but never to all. A one-size-fits-all approach to experimentation will generally overlook not only pedagogies that engage students in non-core topics, but also those that work well only with a subset of students. Similarly, it encourages us to prematurely scale up programs that work well only in a controlled environment, like Head Start or whole language.

In fact, just about every time we've made a grand proclamation and implemented a large-scale plan, we've wasted a decade of time, energy, and money. Usually, we've pushed against teachers to force a prescribed change. What we need is a bottom-up approach, in which good ideas become more nuanced as they scale. Scientists are ecstatic when a new fact disproves current thinking; it means the race is on, that a new theory is beginning to bubble up. As hard as it is to accept the proposition, we are merely in the foothills of pedagogy. Let's let ideas slug it out. That will help us understand what moves the meter for which types of learners. The key is to increase transparency and reduce friction so that evolution occurs much, much faster.

Like the rest of the top-down, criminal-law framework in which it sits, evaluative reporting is of little use for parents making a choice. They don't know what to make of value-added methodologies, which are abstruse at best and which speak to performance in only a few areas. In a world with increasing choice in everything from fast food to anticholesterol drugs, with everyone from *Consumer Reports* to the First Lady helping them choose from among myriad options, parents get very little useful professional advice as to which learning approach and school are right for their children.

Any parent with two children knows that each has different interests, learning styles, and strengths. The desire to shield children from ongoing testing is well meant, but it also shields our education system from the competing ideas that recognize and nurture students' individual needs and abilities.

As we go about setting metrics that measure what is really important, we would be wise to assume our own ignorance about what we're measuring. Only in the past few years have we really begun to understand how children learn. Work by Kurt Fischer of the Harvard Graduate School of Education, for instance, suggests that learning isn't about recalling facts, but about building entirely new neural networks in the brain, then reorganizing those networks as we learn more. Mary Helen Immordino-Yang, an affective neuroscientist at the University of Southern California's Rossier School of Education, has studied the connection between learning and emotion, and found that we "think in the service of emotional goals."[12] And data showing that frequent testing improves student performance should be viewed through the lens of Nathaniel von der Embse and Ramzi Hasson's work, which suggests that students with test anxiety don't perform as well on tests, and that their anxiety creates a cycle of low performance.[13] These findings have barely begun to trickle down to teacher training, let alone to our systems of measuring learning. As in any field ripe for innovation, new discoveries are making us more confident that we don't really know much at all—except that as our understanding of learning evolves, so will our conception of what (and how) we should be teaching.

In higher education, there is a new and growing market for nontraditional programs that focus intensely on outcomes. Programs that teach web development—at places like General Assembly, the Flatiron School, and Dev Bootcamp—make a value proposition up front. They tell you they'll train you for a job as a junior web developer at a tech start-up, and measure themselves against a common yardstick. These programs show great promise, but we will need a few years of evidence before we jettison everything else we know about teaching computer science and drive every STEM-inclined millennial to a three-month web development immersive.

Any conversation about educational quality should assume a quickly changing world where we are still learning about how to teach. It also requires that we open up to changing the structure of learning. Today, that means focusing on adaptive learning and breaking education into smaller units. But what will we know in six months or two years about brain development or technology that we don't know today? And how will we be able to adapt that new knowledge to better help students?

Transparency for Consumers

A marketplace can be a playground where any number of players—schools, tutors, companies, nonprofits—test different learning approaches. But that won't improve education unless both providers and consumers have unbiased, accessible information on the choices it enables. Markets function well only when both parties in a transaction know roughly the same amount about each other—that was a Nobel Prize–winning idea for economists George Akerlof, Michael Spence, and Joseph Stiglitz. Buyers and sellers are often unevenly matched, of course, which compromises outcomes for both parties. Akerlof, Spence, and Stiglitz cite a number of examples: "The seller of a car may know more about his car than the buyer; the buyer of insurance may know more about his prospects of having an accident (such as how he drives) than the seller; a worker may know more about his ability than a prospective employer; a borrower may know more about his prospects for repaying a loan than the lender."[14] When Stiglitz studied information asymmetry in the insurance market, he concluded that "if individuals were willing or able to reveal their information, everybody could be made better off."[15]

Now think about the consumer of a college. You apply to a college and tell it everything about yourself. In turn, you know some things: its reputation, the fields of study it offers, students' favorite local bar. But there is a lot more that you don't know, and when the price is a quarter of a million dollars over four-plus years, those unknowns matter. In fact, you know very little. Your investment has an unknowable return until we do the hard work of defining metrics that are as close as possible to real life. Making a smart decision about college requires actual longitudinal data. Without it, colleges and students engage in an elaborate dance of signaling and screening that often produces bad fits. Any group that says it can tell you how good a college is based on such things as the math and language test scores of incoming freshmen should instantly lose credibility. Yet in this system of severely imbalanced information, publications like *U.S. News & World Report* do not.

Consumers have always had choice in higher education, but without reliable data on outcomes that matter, they have never been able to exercise it effectively. The information available to a college-bound student is broad, deep, and confusing as more and more publications offer their own version of rankings. Lots of websites aggregate student comments about campuses—and if you want to know which bar in town has the best live music, this is terrific information. No matter how noble the intentions or sophisticated the methodology of all these rankers, the results always seem to fall short. In order for education data to be useful to learners, the data points must be specifically relevant to them as individuals and must be presented in an understandable way.

Consumers shopping for toasters have access to multiple sources—from user reviews on Amazon to professional assessments on *Consumer Reports*—that can give a good idea of which toaster is right for them. Importantly, these consumers can get information based on metrics they care about. A consumer whose primary intention is to toast bagels does not need or want a bunch of information on how well a particular toaster oven doubles as a broiler. In fact, that information could be so confusing as to skew his purchase irrationally. A parent looking for a preschool for her three-year-old currently has no way of knowing, say, if the Waldorf method is effective, if a particular school implements it well, and if that method and school are a good fit for her child. The parent can see that a Waldorf school offers play-based learning that emphasizes creativity within a set of routines, but can only guess as to how her child will fare in that environment.

Transparency should exist in both inputs and outcomes. In higher education, the steps we are taking to assess quality focus on narrow criteria, like average first-year salary and loan default rates. These criteria do tell us something about outcomes. But they tell us more about the inputs than anything else, and need to be disaggregated to help a student make a wise choice. Further, all the narrow criteria described above are top-down metrics designed to treat complex problems as criminal matters. A market-based, civil-code mind-set would be to mandate data systems that allow a student to ask "What are the likely outcomes for someone like me?" An upper-middle-class kid may care how good a job his school does of recruiting Pell students (although Noodle surveyed a few hundred parents and found that astoundingly few cared about economic diversity[16]), but that information is relevant to him in a different way than for a student who needs a Pell grant.

A bold example of commitment to outcomes is the aforementioned partnership between Purdue University and Gallup, which measures student outcomes beyond short-term financials. Any parent will tell you that "great jobs" and "great lives" are the factors they care about when helping their child choose a school. Schools would serve themselves well by taking broader life goals seriously.[17]

Creating ways to give people better data and better tools to use that data is truly daunting. The University of Texas at Austin's national ranking is 76, according to *Forbes*, 53 according to *U.S. News & World Report*, and 28 according to *Times Higher Education*. How do we present that, and what do we want a parent or student to do with it? Better information is already available in every other sector, on sites like Zillow (real estate), TripAdvisor (travel), Houzz (home design), and Rotten Tomatoes (movies). Relevant, transparent information is obviously good for students. But it's also good for providers, who struggle constantly with the challenges of finding the right students.

At every level, every person with a stake in the education marketplace—parents, students, educators, administrators, policymakers—must have access to meaningful, useable data about the options available. One of the primary goals of Noodle is aggregating K–12 data, making it useful, and getting it in front of parents. Choice without information is not choice.

E CORPS

As we stated at the outset, the term *marketplace* makes educators cringe—and legitimately so. Skepticism about for-profit education companies is well-earned because so many for-profit companies serve their students poorly, and at times catastrophically. Behind decisions that are short-sighted and counter to the interests of students and institutions are investors and management focused on maximizing return on investment. The legendary investor

Peter Lynch remarked that he only invested in a company that "any idiot can run—because sooner or later, any idiot is probably going to run it."[18] A corollary might be that no matter how interested the management team is in serving both students and investors—a dual bottom line—companies will, sooner or later, bend toward profit.

One approach to creating well-functioning, transparent markets is the *benefit corporation* model. This is a status now recognized in thirty states that requires for-profit companies to consider not only their impact on share-holders, but also on society and the environment.[19] These companies agree to meet high standards of transparency and accountability, each putting its mission side by side with its fiduciary duty to stockholders.

B Corp, the organization that advocates for this approach, says "Government and the nonprofit sector are necessary but insufficient to address society's greatest challenges. Business, the most powerful man-made force on the planet, must create value for society, not just shareholders. Systemic challenges require systemic solutions and the B Corp movement offers a concrete, market-based and scalable solution."[20] Electing B Corp status requires transparency, and some great companies have done it, like Warby Parker, Patagonia, Etsy, and Seventh Generation.

The B Corp certification serves as a badge of distinction. It says to consumers who care about social or environmental values, "We share your concerns and your goals." Does it help improve customer loyalty or the bottom line? The companies that have elected to go the B Corp route—and endure the demanding transparency requirements—believe it does.

How can we drive more for-profit institutions to focus genuinely on outcomes? In education, we might create a variant of B Corps—let's call them *E Corps*—and hope they can help channel the energy of capitalism to the social mission of education. Organizations electing E Corp status would be completely transparent about their values and outcomes, and demonstrate that they provide a worthwhile service to students. Imagine how powerful transparency would be in higher education. Prospective college students interested in E Corp schools could easily see short- and long-term metrics like graduation rates; student debt levels; compensation after one, five, and ten years; and other important factors, not for an average student but for *students like them*.

E Corp–owned schools might go further by showing students how they spend their money, broken down by instruction, marketing, executive

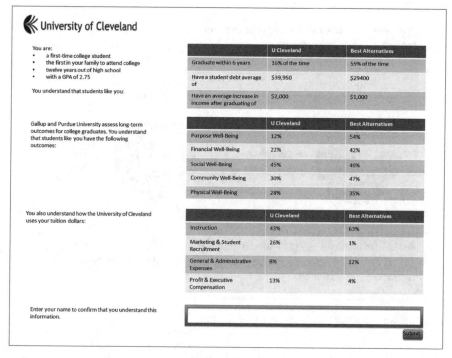

University of Cleveland

You are:
- a first-time college student
- the first in your family to attend college
- twelve years out of high school
- with a GPA of 2.75

You understand that students like you:

	U Cleveland	Best Alternatives
Graduate within 6 years	16% of the time	59% of the time
Have a student debt average of	$39,950	$29400
Have an average increase in income after graduating of	$2,000	$1,000

Gallup and Purdue University assess long-term outcomes for college graduates. You understand that students like you have the following outcomes:

	U Cleveland	Best Alternatives
Purpose Well-Being	12%	54%
Financial Well-Being	22%	42%
Social Well-Being	45%	49%
Community Well-Being	30%	47%
Physical Well-Being	28%	35%

You also understand how the University of Cleveland uses your tuition dollars:

	U Cleveland	Best Alternatives
Instruction	43%	63%
Marketing & Student Recruitment	26%	1%
General & Administrative Expenses	8%	12%
Profit & Executive Compensation	13%	4%

Enter your name to confirm that you understand this information.

`[                              ]`   Submit

FIGURE 9.2   Sample College Choice Form

compensation, profit, and, ideally, the long-term Gallup metrics. Imagine if every college student saw a form like figure 9.2 before enrolling.

The example in figure 9.2 is very much a first draft. But as we learn more about how students and parents use the information to make better choices, the presentation can improve. Working this way, we can make it easier for students to find the right fit and easier for great schools to attract the students they serve best.

E Corp–owned colleges could go even further by improving the success rates of college transfers. A third of students transfer at least once during six years of college, and nearly 40 percent of them lose all their earned credits in the process.[21] That translates to lower graduation rates and wasted dollars, both private and public. Similarly, students who switch majors often find themselves even farther from graduation. It's not surprising that students see tens of thousands of tuition dollars vanish. Tracking credits is complex, and schools often don't tell transfer students which credits they'll accept until after they've enrolled.

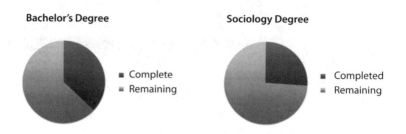

You have now completed **37%** of the courses necessary for your BA and **26%** of the courses necessary for your Sociology degree.

Bachelor's Degree   **Sociology Degree**

■ Complete   ■ Completed
■ Remaining   ■ Remaining

Impact of Transferring Schools:
Transferring to the University of Cleveland would result in the loss of 14% of your course credits, about one semester. The courses necessary to regain these credits would cost $11,000 at our current tuition.

FIGURE 9.3   Sample College Transfer Form

The top-down approach—the criminal-law approach—to fixing this would be to mandate that colleges accept all transfer credits, but that's both bad policy and unlikely to happen. Imagine, however, if we required E Corp–owned colleges to tell students each semester about their progress toward graduation, using clear metrics and language. It might look something like figure 9.3. Note that at the bottom of this figure, students are clearly told the impact of a transfer.

The E Corp concept need not be open only to for-profit companies. Traditional nonprofit schools could either apply for E Corp status or simply adhere to its transparency requirements. And setting up this construct would require no act of Congress or Department of Education regulation; we could build this under existing laws regulating benefit corporations. If some key schools lead, those that opted *not* to become E Corps would have to explain why.

How might E Corps address unethical lead generation practices? Requiring schools to be transparent could and should apply to their proxies (perhaps by expanding the scope of the third-party servicer regulations). Gaining E Corp status would, in turn, require those providers to properly disclose the nature of their listings.

CONCLUSION

We need to replace the accountability movement with a focus on perfecting the marketplace. The impulse to manage education from the top down is powerful because it doesn't require us to trust one another. Top-down educators insist that edicts from on high keep people from making bad decisions. They say that schools cannot be trusted to set their own curricula, so we must set them; that teachers cannot be trusted to teach well, so we must monitor them constantly; and that parents cannot be trusted to find the right school, so we must pick one for them. As evidence, they cite the current system's shortcomings.

But follow this road to its logical conclusion. We can infantilize teachers by monitoring their every move in the classroom, until we ultimately replace them with software. We can tell people where they must go to school, until we get rid of choice altogether in K–12 and higher education. We can align every student's learning experience with one non-evidence-based set of standards, until we finally have nothing but one national curriculum.

In every other part of your life, you have more options than you once did and more control in making a choice from among them. But in education, a significant cohort, though acting from well-meaning motives, has gone the other way. You may not be surprised to learn that your voice-activated, Internet-connected Samsung television can transmit anything said in your living room to a third party; such is the logical next step of the Internet of Things.[22] Similarly, software that spits out the micro-details of a classroom is a logical development. But it's unclear if it will attract highly qualified teachers to the profession. Just because we can do something does not necessarily mean we should. In a top-down system, no one has to educate consumers; we simply tell them what to do or where to go. In a marketplace, every provider has a strong incentive to tell its story to consumers, and find and convince those who are the best fit.

One problem left to be solved about marketplaces is marketing. Many, like the lead generators, will lie or stretch the truth. That means there is a regulatory cost of keeping potential bad actors in line, plus an additional cost in helping consumers understand what to look for.

Marketing isn't necessarily a bad thing; it helps the right schools and students find each other. But many industries spend 15 percent or more of revenues on marketing and sales. If education broadly adopts that model, we would see almost $100 billion a year in additional recruiting spend. Today in higher education, only the for-profit schools and online program managers spend that kind of money. As we approach the idea of marketplaces, we must decide how to best spend largely public dollars on recruiting and how to limit that spending while still ensuring an adequate flow of accurate information.

Markets are powerful places, and hold their players intensely accountable. Short of building a marketplace for education, any reforms we introduce will end as all the others have. As long as we remain fixated on rigid accountability systems, we will stay on the test-exalting, school-closing, teacher-firing hamster wheel. When Common Core does nothing to raise our ranking on international assessments or prepare more students for jobs in high-growth sectors or pull low-income children out of poverty, who among us will stand up and say "We were wrong" or offer to refund the billions of dollars we've spent? No one; they'll just say we all implemented it wrong.

If we tossed our entire education system out and rebuilt it from scratch with the present and future in mind, the result would likely bear no resemblance to what we have today. Our public K–12 system was founded with an Industrial Revolution–era mind-set, and we should never have expected it to prepare an increasingly diverse student population for college. The only surprise is that anyone would continue proposing further top-down, one-size-fits-all processes to improve on it. When it comes to shutting down weaker schools or lowering debt levels, government need not act unilaterally; it can follow the civil code, and allow people and organizations to hold each other accountable.

10

Ten for the Next Ten

Lessons for the Next Decade

Ross Baird and Daniel Lautzenheiser

Entrepreneurs have changed how we think about education reform in the past decade—dramatically transforming what and how instructors teach, students learn, and parents engage.[1] Ten years is a long time. Consider this:

- In 2015, Khan Academy has become a household name by reaching more than ten million students in forty languages every month with its pithy YouTube videos. In 2005, YouTube had just launched.
- In 2015, New Orleans is a hotbed for education innovation, a 100 percent charter school district home to some of the most groundbreaking innovations in charter schooling, teacher staffing, and entrepreneurship—ranging from Kickboard to Enriched Schools to 4.0 Schools. A decade ago, Hurricane Katrina devastated New Orleans—yet the disaster enabled a decade of wholesale systems transformation.
- A decade ago, titans such as Pearson, Kaplan, and McGraw-Hill held a near-oligopoly over educational resources. Today, McGraw-Hill no longer calls itself a "publisher," and EdSurge's ed tech index lists over fifteen hundred products across an array of areas including teacher support, curriculum, and school operations—many of them just a few years old.[2]

Despite this transformation, we think education entrepreneurship is only in the first inning of its potential. This essay discusses what we have learned from the last decade—and what trends will transform the next ten years.

We bring a diverse set of experiences to the table that have informed our thinking on education entrepreneurship. Ross has seen companies start and grow from the ground level as the founder and executive director of Village Capital, a venture capital firm that sources, trains, and invests in entrepreneurs solving major global challenges. Over the past five years, Village Capital has supported more than 450 entrepreneurs across an array of industries including agriculture, finance, and education. In education alone, Village Capital has helped launch fifty companies through its programs, with graduates raising over $30 million in follow-on capital.

Daniel is ideally positioned to see macro trends in education. He is a core member of the education practice at the Boston Consulting Group, a leading management consulting firm, where he works on an array of strategy and organizational problems facing schools, districts, and education companies. Before that, he spent five years observing the education policy landscape at the American Enterprise Institute. Many of the lessons we discuss below stem from Village Capital's experiences in funding early-stage education entrepreneurs, and the policy and strategic decisions necessary for education entrepreneurship to succeed.

Below are ten lessons we have learned from the past decade of education entrepreneurship that we believe will inform the next ten years. For the purposes of this chapter, when we discuss *education entrepreneurship*, we are talking about for-profit new businesses that are solving problems in education, rather than innovative policy and nonprofit innovations. While we believe that education reform requires the private sector, the public sector, and the nonprofit sector to work together, this chapter will focus on trends within for-profit start-up companies that impact the education sector.

Broadly speaking, the ten lessons we identify fit within three major trends:

Education entrepreneurship has moved from the margins to the mainstream. We are seeing a growing willingness from educators and policymakers to experiment with charter schools, different school district structures, and a wide number of education technology start-ups. At the same time, we are also seeing an increasing number of firms and investors willing to invest in education, and increasingly looking outside of Silicon Valley to do so. This does not mean that education entrepreneurship is universally acclaimed; the thorny—and at times divisive—world of education politics is as relevant for entrepreneurs as ever before. But we believe there is a real trend here, and this growth, despite some potential risks, is ultimately good news.

The successful education entrepreneurs are not "disrupting"—they're partnering. Education entrepreneurs need to be mindful of the particular potholes in the education landscape and work within systems to gain the credibility needed to grow. Partnering is critical to gain the support of those who are wary of attempts to "privatize" public education, school districts that have been burned in the past and are skeptical of the next education fad, and parents and teachers who don't want their students to be guinea pigs for over-hyped products. Education entrepreneurs are best served by: (1) solving a single problem within the education industry rather than trying to "disrupt" education; (2) paying careful attention to policy; and (3) working together with educators, parents, and students, rather than outside the system.

Improved learning outcomes will be the most important metric. One final trend we observe is that, increasingly, the most important metric of success in education entrepreneurship is improved learning outcomes, rather than metrics such as engagement, or even revenue, that are effective at measuring success in other industries. The past decade or so of education reform has seen a massive push to measure student learning and close the achievement gap between students of different racial and economic backgrounds. Despite some recent public pushback on Common Core and standardizing testing, we don't see this trend abating. At the same time, our understanding of what constitutes successful learning outcomes is broadening from just basic math and reading scores toward a more holistic understanding of the emotional and social skills like creativity and grit students need to succeed after school. Schools, parents, and policymakers will increasingly rely on improved learning outcomes in designing partnerships, and will reward the entrepreneurs who get it right.

With that in mind, let's look at our "ten for the next ten."

EDUCATION ENTREPRENEURSHIP HAS MOVED FROM THE MARGINS TO THE MAINSTREAM

Lesson 1: The Days of "We Don't Invest in Education . . . Sales Cycles Are Too Long" Are Over

The decision making in education technology purchasing is rapidly becoming more democratic. A decade ago, Pearson, McGraw-Hill, and others had near-monopolies on content purchasing decisions, and cost-prohibitive hardware was a core barrier to entry. Today, teachers nearly everywhere have broadband, which enables direct-to-teacher communications with new companies and much more rapid product improvement in response to teachers' needs. The federal E-Rate program has allocated nearly $8 billion to ensure that 99 percent of students will have broadband in the next five years, and adoption is accelerating.

This more open market comes with some potential risks. It is more difficult, say, for schools to implement a logically coherent curriculum if individual teachers are each using their own products. But it also comes with a massive opportunity. Now, more than ever, funders are willing to invest in education products and expect a return on their investment. In the past five years alone, ed tech financing has nearly quintupled, from $385 million in 2009 to almost $2 billion in 2014.[3] And it continues to grow: the second quarter of 2015 set a new record for both the number of ed tech deals (eighty) and financing ($765 million) across all sectors of education.[4] Nor is it just volume. Major corporations and mainstream Silicon Valley investors are engaging more than ever before with education entrepreneurs, and not merely as a corporate social responsibility. To cite several examples:

- In 2010, News Corp. acquired Wireless Generation, a Brooklyn-based assessments and analytics company, for $390 million; launched a new company, Amplify, which creates tablets and high-quality learning games; and hired Joel Klein, New York City's schools chancellor, to run it. By 2015, News Corp. had invested over $1 billion in Amplify.[5] Results have been mixed: a poor tablet launch in Guilford County (North Carolina) Schools (home to Greensboro) caused the company to reevaluate, and by mid-2015 News Corp. was quietly winding down tablet sales in favor of its learning management system. And yet the sheer scope of the foray from a major media player into education shows the belief that investors are willing to bet big in K–12.
- Andreesen-Horowitz, one of the largest and most successful venture firms in Silicon Valley, has actively started investing in industries with a strong regulatory presence, including education. The firm recently brought on former DC mayor Adrian Fenty, a notable figure in the education reform world for his work with Michelle Rhee in DC Public Schools, as special adviser for education, and has made several big investments in schools, most notably raising $100

million for AltSchool, a San Francisco-based network of microschools founded by a former Google exec.

- The largest education firms are now looking to entrepreneurs for innovation: Kaplan partnered with global technology accelerator Techstars to launch the Kaplan EdTech Accelerator supporting ten–fifteen start-ups a year with financial and corporate resources, while Pearson recently launched the $50 million Pearson Affordable Learning Fund to invest in education entrepreneurs globally improving learning for underserved populations. In July 2015, Pearson announced plans to sell FT Group, which includes the *Financial Times*, for $1.3 billion in order to be, in the words of Pearson CEO John Fallon, "100 percent focused on our global education strategy."[6]

There are many reasons for this growth. US K–12 and higher education is a $1 trillion industry. This is, to put it mildly, big business. And there are signs that this highly regulated business is cracking: charter schools have grown from a single school in 1991 to educating almost three million students (5 percent of the total) today, while districts like New Orleans and Washington, DC, have become hotbeds for entrepreneurship. These schools and districts serve as laboratories willing to prototype new education technologies and find new ways to teach students. If you're a venture capitalist who thinks "sales cycles are too long," you likely haven't looked at the major flow of resources going into the market in about five years, and we predict the investors who look again will be more successful.

Lesson 2: More Funds, Accelerators, and Seed Capital Mean More Swings at the Plate

Nowhere is the democratization of education technology better seen than the myriad funds and accelerators that have popped up to provide seed funding and training to education entrepreneurs. Over the past decade, we have seen a rapid growth of education accelerators—training programs that help education start-ups develop their venture and prepare to take on investment—as LearnLaunch, Penn GSE Kaplan Accelerator, Jefferson Education Accelerator, ImagineK12, and Ross's own firm, Village Capital, have launched programs. At the same time, investment funds are either launching new funds or growing their existing resources significantly: Owl Ventures, Learn Capital, NewSchools Venture Fund, Reach Capital, Rethink

Education, and New Markets have all launched new funds in the past five years. With the exception of NewSchools, each of these organizations was started within the past decade. And the investment strategy is shifting too, away from funding a small number of proven concepts and toward placing many small bets on a larger number of entrepreneurs. Elsewhere in this volume, for example, 4.0 Schools CEO Matt Candler discusses 4.0's "tiny schools" initiative that pilots, on a very small scale and with limited funding, new education techniques—say, a new approach to teaching reading as an afterschool program with a small group of students in a local district school. If it works, it can be scaled; if not, the investment is minimal.

Despite this growth, we are still far from making conclusions about how effective these ventures are. As a report published by the Aspen Institute's Network for Development Entrepreneurs and Village Capital states, "In order to better assess accelerator performance, we need more and better longitudinal data on the enterprises that receive support, as well as the enterprises that apply, but do not receive support."[7] Similarly, the Kauffman Foundation has cautioned, "The currently available data on accelerators are lacking and we should not base conclusions on preliminary efforts. As much as we want to support entrepreneurs and accelerators, we should not claim the economic benefits of accelerators with exaggerated numbers."[8] It is important to remember that the growth of accelerators is new and there is not enough data to unequivocally predict positive or negative conclusions about their performance.

That said, entrepreneurs in any industry historically have yielded a small number of firms that make dramatic changes, and the more firms that get an opportunity to succeed, the higher the likelihood of a dramatic change may be. So while we would be wise to exercise caution before declaring that all this activity in the education start-up space has "worked," we predict that because of sheer increase in volume, in the next decade we are far more likely to see one or two education entrepreneurs who truly transform the education industry. More swings at the plate mean some strike-outs; they also mean some home runs.

Lesson 3: Investors Should Look Outside Silicon Valley for Solutions

In the same way that presidential campaigns that are run from outside of DC can be more effective because they eschew Beltway wisdom, many of the most exciting growing education technology companies are launching from outside Silicon Valley, building on local assets. Cities are taking advantage of unique assets to empower start-up communities, rather than trying to become the "next Silicon Valley. Kickboard, for example, has an outstanding user experience honed in New Orleans' 100 percent charter school environment.

Pear Deck has done the same in testing hotbed Iowa City, Iowa. The city's unique advantage is in the education sector. The city's largest non-public employer is Pearson, the world's biggest education company and book publisher, and ACT, the organization that runs the ACT college entry test, is also headquartered there. Each year, the majority of elementary school students around the country take the Iowa Tests of Basic Skills. If you want to learn how to develop assessments that improve learning outcomes, there may well be no better place that Iowa City.

Pear Deck, launched in 2014, attacks a problem faced by educators worldwide: how do we engage all students with a single lesson? Pear Deck has created a new live presentation tool that connects to students' devices to make student assessment real time. It lets teachers ask students questions (preplanned or impromptu) during a lesson. Students respond through their computer or mobile device and teachers can display the results anonymously immediately, to quickly gauge understanding and ensure that none of their students are falling behind. The Pear Deck platform is shaped by learning science developed in Iowa City, which the founders say is made possible because of the quick access to experts in the field.

In Pear Deck's first year, 500,000 students are on the platform. And the future is bright. AOL founder Steve Case invested $250,000 in Pear Deck at South by Southwest as the national winner of Case's 2014 Rise of the Rest tours. Village Capital also recently invested in Pear Deck's latest investment round after it was selected by a peer group comprising the best education technology start-ups in the country. By taking advantage of local assets, Pear Deck has grown from its community to reaching national scale.

Even Silicon Valley recognizes the promise of start-ups using local resources: Owl Ventures, a Silicon Valley fund founded by venture capitalist Tory Patterson, has made one of its first investments in a Salt Lake-based assessment company, MasteryConnect. Steve Case calls the growth of non–Silicon Valley start-ups the "Rise of the Rest"—and we predict the Rest will rise exponentially.

Much can be done by cities and communities to enable education entrepreneurs to succeed. The Kauffman Foundation has done significant work measuring the health of entrepreneurial ecosystems across the United States and illustrates how entrepreneurs can make significant progress when enabled by four factors:[9]

Density. Density is the simple volume of both old and new firms in an area, and has been shown to have a significant relationship with the success of future entrepreneurs. Think Silicon Valley or Route 128 in Boston; entrepreneurship begets more entrepreneurship. In K–12 education, with its emphasis on local control, we see especially good opportunity in ecosystems where there have been a couple of commercial successes that can lead to new companies. For example, the growth and success of Blackboard and AOL in Washington, DC, have led their alumni to fast-growing education start-ups such as LearnZillion, which recruits expert teachers from across the country to create digital resources for math and English language arts. Education entrepreneurship in DC is further enabled by its robust charter school network; LearnZillion was founded by a former charter school principal.

Fluidity. Fluidity, or population flux, is the rate at which people are able to start and leave new firms. New Orleans's burgeoning economic ecosystem has a significant amount to do with a fluid talent base entering and exiting via Teach For America, AmeriCorps, teachNOLA, and the vibrant charter school network in the city. Jen Medbery started Kickboard in New Orleans not because she was from the city, but because Teach For America brought her there.

Connectivity. Connectivity is how connected entrepreneurs are to resources and to each other. Part of the Pear Deck origin story is Iowa City's assessment expertise. Another part is Iowa City's own history. After the tragic Iowa floods of 2008, economic development dollars to rebuild the city were channeled heavily into entrepreneurship. The outcome: a thriving community anchored by the Iowa Startup Accelerator, cofounded by two University of Iowa grads, and the EntreFest conference, one of the biggest start-up conferences in the country. Pear Deck's cofounders cite the connectivity and instant access to resources in Iowa as a competitive advantage that helped them test their product and build their company.

Diversity. Diversity, in Kauffman's terminology, speaks to both economic diversification (recognizing that a city is not overly reliant on a particular industry) and immigration (how effectively the city attracts immigrants). Perhaps the best example of an education start-up taking advantage of the diversity of two ecosystems is MPOWER Financing, which seeks to transform student lending through peer-to-peer loans, made possible by valuing students' ability to repay over traditional credit scores. MPOWER's founders are uniquely qualified to solve problems faced by immigrants from disadvantaged backgrounds—because they have lived the experience themselves.

Manu Smadja and Mike Davis came to the United States as immigrants with limitless potential, but thin credit histories. For "thin file" students (who come from families with little formal credit history, or bad FICO scores), obtaining access to higher education financing is difficult; according to a 2012 Harvard study, nearly half of students who drop out of college annually leave due to lack of financing.

MPOWER provides financing through an alternative credit metric that assesses students' future ability to repay, not their families' background or current credit history. The company looks at a student's educational achievement, extracurricular activities, and student profile and algorithmically determines how likely that student is to repay a loan. And unlike some other innovations in financing and lending in education, MPOWER seeks to democratize student lending by intentionally targeting students who are undervalued by the current market.

Lesson 4: The Business of Higher Education Is Changing

It's not just in the world of K–12 that entrepreneurship has hit mainstream; it's been making inroads in higher education, as well, where student debt and a changing job landscape are throwing the value of higher education into confusion. We see disproportionate opportunity for entrepreneurs in three areas:

Platforms that provide personalized, skills-based education for students and educators. Groups such as General Assembly are changing what higher education means: instead of paying for a four-year degree, you can pay for a four-month course that teaches you how to code—and land a job. Some of these companies, too, are creating new employee pools to take on existing industries. The new start-up Andela, for instance, is teaching African students to code and competing on both price and quality with traditional outsourcing shops. Based in Nigeria, Andela recruits students to learn the basics of computer coding over four months, then places them in a partner company—including Microsoft and Udacity—where they work remotely for four years while receiving continual training. Founded in 2014, Andela has already received $10 million in venture funding, including from Boston-based Spark Capital, who previously funded Twitter and Tumblr.

Financial tools that enable new students to access existing opportunities. Companies such as MPOWER are helping students from underrepresented backgrounds finance higher education. While better access to four-year colleges is great, it's hardly a transformation. But MPOWER and companies like it are also helping accelerate the growth of the skills-based platforms mentioned above; MPOWER is financing small loans for short training courses such as General Assembly, which changes how students think through the value proposition of attending school.

Better information for higher education. Part of the disparity in opportunity in US higher education has been information asymmetry—a problem entrepreneurs can solve. The start-up College Abacus, for example, took advantage of a change in policy to create a "net price calculator" where any college-going student could see his or her financial aid eligibility in a Kayak-like model that displays the cost of college after factoring in grants and student aid at up to three different colleges. Students are thus be able to compare the true cost of different colleges rather than being scared away by a high sticker price. The student loan lender and guarantor ECMC recently acquired College Abacus and is making the service available to a range of students.

Yet for-profit entrepreneurs who tackle higher education without an eye toward closing the opportunity gap face moral hazard and reputational risk: the public perception and poor outcomes from the current for-profit higher education industry create a negative backlash that help neither students nor entrepreneurs.

We predict that entrepreneurs who understand how higher education is transforming—and especially those who focus on improving student opportunity, rather than monetizing butts-in-seats—will build the best businesses of the next decade.

THE SUCCESSFUL EDUCATION ENTREPRENEURS ARE NOT "DISRUPTING," THEY'RE PARTNERING

Lesson 5: "If You Want to Go Far, Go Together"

The four lessons above paint a rosy picture of the state of education entrepreneurship. There is more money, from more funders, flowing to more entrepreneurs, in more diverse locations, and with much stronger system of support than a decade ago. But there remain real challenges that the next decade's entrepreneurs need to be mindful of, both relating to the nature of public education and to risks inherent in the edgy start-up culture seeking to "disrupt" rather than partner.

First of all, education entrepreneurs need to be mindful of the thorny politics of education. K–12 schooling, in particular, is seen as a public good funded by public dollars. There is a strong undercurrent that resists any attempts at "privatization" or profiting off the backs of students—whether that means actual for-profit companies or even nonprofit organizations that operate outside the traditional structure. And public viewpoints matter. In New York State, for example, parental concerns over student privacy shut down the nascent attempts of inBloom to track student data, while Amplify faced public pushback after a botched launch in Guilford County, North Carolina. In higher education, for-profit colleges and universities are grappling with plummeting enrollment in the face of poor public perception and US Department of Education investigations over high student debt and low graduation rates. The University of Phoenix, for example, the nation's largest for-profit college, recently announced plans to cut most of its associate degree programs and institute more rigorous admissions requirements. The changes are slated to bring enrollment down to 150,000 students by 2016—down from 460,000 in 2010.[10]

Even if an education start-up wins a district contract, prosaic technological concerns—having sufficient bandwidth to support a classroom of devices, remembering passwords to log onto tablets—can keep an otherwise promising tool from working. Entrepreneurs should recognize that schools are first and foremost in the business of education and have been burned in the past with expensive outlays on products and tools that looked pretty but failed to deliver.

For entrepreneurs to truly succeed, they will need to make sure that the education community feels it is part of the change. This means listening to concerns of teachers and principals, having patience in navigating the clunky bureaucracies of school districts versus rushing to implement, being tenacious on customer service, and, above all, making sure their products work for students and teachers (see lessons 8 through 10 below).

"Going far together" is one of the primary values Village Capital seeks in the ed tech start-ups we work with, and it actively informs our investment decisions. A recent Village Capital investment, Homework Unlocked, for example, aims to improve academic success in schools by fundamentally transforming how children learn at home. Homework Unlocked helps parents become better teachers by providing free math lessons for parents to brush up on basic math as well as new approaches to teaching math. Another Village Capital investment, Enriched Schools, brings the entire community into the local school by placing top-notch professionals in schools as substitute teachers—say, a local poet as an English sub—enabling schools to maintain high-quality instruction even on days when the regular teacher is absent.

Kickboard is an outstanding example of a company that is built not by a lone hero entrepreneur, but an ecosystem. In 2009 Jen Medbery, a former Teach For America teacher in New Orleans, had grown frustrated at the lack of reliable data for teachers to make informed decisions on classroom management and instruction. A software engineer by trade, Medbery developed Kickboard originally as a classroom management tool to help her and her fellow teachers manage student data and school culture and better link learning interventions to improved performance.

Based on demand from other charter schools in New Orleans, who had the ability to make speedy purchasing decisions and with flexible technology budgets, Medbery was able to gain enough initial traction to warrant the founding of the company. Kickboard set up shop at the Idea Village, an organization helping spur the post-Katrina entrepreneurship renaissance in New Orleans, and was an early partner of 4.0 Schools. Medbery left teaching to launch Kickboard full-time and raised her first $100,000 from Village Capital. Today, Kickboard has raised over $7 million and is in use nationwide, with over 500,000 students on the platform.

Jen Medbery is an exceptional leader, but forward-thinking principals in New Orleans provided the risk capital as early customers; leading entrepreneur supporters and investors such as the Idea Village and 4.0 Schools helped scale the business; and it all started when Teach For America put Medbery, a talented entrepreneur, in classrooms to begin with.

For the next decade, we believe the entrepreneurs who will be successful will follow the African proverb: "If you want to go fast, go alone; if you want to go far, go together."

Lesson 6: Entrepreneurs Need to Integrate, Not Disrupt (in Other Words—Pick a Single Problem to Solve, Rather Than "Fixing Education")

Entrepreneurs have the potential to transform education, yet entrepreneurs—particularly those coming from the "disruptive world" of Silicon Valley—all too often seek to completely turn education upside-down. The poster child of disruptive education, Sal Khan, says in his TED talk that Khan Academy is using video to "reinvent education."[11] Reinventing the system? Probably not—Khan Academy still uses the same teacher-student pedagogical relationship that has defined education for centuries. Delivering better instruction more conveniently? Quite possibly. And if so, that's a major win.

It's entrepreneurship 101 to first and foremost know the problem you are trying to solve. At Village Capital, this is the first thing we look for in bringing new ventures in, and the lesson we preach above all else. Kickboard identified a problem: a lack of reliable student data. MPOWER did too: the lack of financing for students without a credit score. As did Pear Deck: trying to engage all students in a single lesson. By focusing on the actual problem the company is trying to solve, an education entrepreneur can build quality partnerships and avoid some of the politics and infighting in the process that has marred "transformational reform" such as Apple's semi-failed attempts to sell iPads to the Los Angeles school district. Yes, your solution might not "fix K–12 schools" but if you can make teaching eighth-grade math just a little easier, that improves the lives of millions of students.

Lesson 7: Policy Matters More Than Ever

Most entrepreneurs have an agnostic, or even negative, approach to the government, but an understanding of policy and government partnerships in education is essential. This is because, for better or for worse, education is a heavily politicized and regulated field. Upward of 90 percent of K–12 students attend public schools, and a raft of regulations flow forth at the local, state, and federal levels that govern both K–12 and higher education. A 2015 report by the US Senate Heath, Education, Labor, and Pensions Committee, for example, estimated that new federal directives were issued to colleges and universities at a rate of one per day.[12] Nor does government involvement show any signs of abating. After all, as one of the editors of this volume has written, "public schools spend public dollars and hire public employees to serve the public's children. For better or worse, they're going to be governed by public officials."[13]

This manifests itself in countless ways when it comes to education entrepreneurship. Take StraighterLine, a company founded in 2008 that provides low-cost, online courses that students can transfer to a number of accredited colleges and universities. Despite being approved by the American Council on Education, StraighterLine can't receive formal accreditation because it offers only individual courses, not full degree programs, and under the arcane rules of accreditation, only institutions that offer degrees can be accredited. And because StraighterLine can't receive accreditation, its students can't use federal student loan dollars to pay for classes, since federal laws prohibit loans from going to unaccredited schools. Of course, the law makes some sense: accreditation is meant to protect consumers from unscrupulous institutions and to stop taxpayer dollars (in the form of student loans) from going to low-quality schools. But StraighterLine, as an online course provider, doesn't fit the mold of the traditional institutions accreditation is meant to govern. In other words, despite offering a flexible product at a low price—directly combating the soaring costs of college—and having received quality approval from a reputable third-party organization, StraighterLine faces an uphill battle for students. Burck Smith, StraighterLine's founder, is a good example of an entrepreneur engaging with policy, having written widely in policy forums and testifying before Congress on higher education innovation.[14] Education entrepreneurs would do well to follow his example; those who ignore policy do so at their own risk.

Policymakers themselves are recognizing this, and several changes provide pragmatic improvements to entrepreneurs. For example, the US Department of Education recently classified education technology as a legitimate use of Title 1 funding and released its first EdTech Developers' Guide, which provides a roadmap for key policy and implementation challenges that entrepreneurs are able to solve, with a specific focus on increasing opportunity for underserved students.[15]

Policymakers are making much more of a long-term bet on education technology—and while certainly for the better, this shift increases the burden of proof on new technologies to meaningfully help students, and especially disadvantaged students. With nearly all revenue going to education technology companies (at least those who sell to public schools) ultimately originating as public dollars, what the public is willing to buy matters most.

We predict that the entrepreneurs who approach government collaboratively when building their companies, with a focus on the underserved, rather than seeking to "disrupt" government, will ultimately take longer, but be more successful.

IMPROVED LEARNING OUTCOMES WILL BE THE MOST IMPORTANT METRIC

Lesson 8: Learning Outcomes Will Matter Above All, and Entrepreneurs Should Invest Early in Learning Outcomes Assessment

What happens in the classroom matters most of all, and learning outcomes are paramount. Schools and districts, the leading customers of education technology, are increasingly valuing measurable learning outcomes—and we predict that evidence of student learning will be necessary for a technology contract with a district in a decade.

In contrast, the defining goal over the past decade in education technology seems to have been "engagement." Companies have taken lessons from Silicon Valley to the classroom. For example, Facebook has created a vibrant online community, so funding flowed to a raft of education social networks or online class marketplaces. Household examples include Edmodo, a social network where teachers and students can collaborate and which has raised over $87 million in venture funding; BetterLesson, an online portal for teachers to share lesson plans; and Udemy or Coursera, which boast thousands of online courses and millions of users.

Engagement has been key because it's easy to measure. If you are a venture capitalist in Silicon Valley and you have a platform like Edmodo—described as the "Facebook for schools"[16]—and your background is in starting and investing in companies like Facebook, you can use the same core metrics: How many kids are using the platform? What is user retention like? What is engagement like? But there is not necessarily a correlation between students using a technology and that technology having a positive impact on learning outcomes. We're not saying that Edmodo doesn't improve outcomes; we are saying that we don't know either way.

Successful education companies that do not improve learning have caused parents and policymakers to keep a close eye on how well schools are preparing students for college and career. These fears are exacerbated by a growing sense that the United States is stagnant relative to international peers in student learning. We do not see outcomes assessment going away anytime soon. Indeed, recent blowback over the Common Core State Standards and standardized testing seems to be more about *over*-testing and perceived overreach from the federal government, not against the idea that learning outcomes matter. At the time of this writing, Congress has passed two bills reauthorizing NCLB, bills that keep regular end-of-year tests in place.

As a higher value is placed on learning outcomes, content that has evidence of promise in yielding higher learning outcomes will become more valuable than "platforms"—places where students and teachers can go to engage, but may not necessarily have quality content linked to better outcomes. The largest players in education have recognized this: Pearson and Kaplan, for example, have recently established Efficacy and Learning Science units, respectively. And start-ups are catching up. One recent alum of Village Capital's program is Texas-based Mathalicious, which creates outstanding math lessons based on real-world situations for middle and high school teachers and actively measures the results.

Assessing learning outcomes is not easy, and is expensive for a young company. In the next decade, however, we see an opportunity for entrepreneurs to start systematically measuring learning outcomes. Entrepreneurs can partner with large groups such as the Concord Consortium to help navigate this sometimes opaque world, and incubators can also play a role. The newly created Jefferson Education Accelerator, for example, is housed at the Curry School of Education at the University of Virginia, and is explicit that part of their mission is to study the impact and effectiveness of the growth-stage ed tech companies that join them.

Helping new education companies learn how to measure learning outcomes, and the value in doing so, is key to Village Capital's model. In spring 2015, Village Capital operated a national program for the top twelve education start-ups in the country, focused on developing a venture that could attract mainstream investment as well as measuring and improving learning outcomes. Many of the leading figures in education were involved in the program, from public officials Jim Shelton, outgoing deputy secretary of education at the US Department of Education, and John King, acting secretary of education at the department, to school leaders, including the heads of curriculum and learning from Washington, DC, and Baltimore. Each of these school leaders was adamant that measuring learning outcomes is crucial when making purchasing decisions.

We think that in the next ten years, entrepreneurs who understand and identify their place in the classroom—say, with curriculum, classroom management, and professional development products and services—and who start assessing outcomes early will be disproportionately successful.

Lesson 9: What Counts as Learning Outcomes Will Move Beyond Traditional Reading and Math

At the same time, what is meant by learning outcomes is broadening from traditional subjects like math and reading. Parents are now eager for schools to teach skills like creativity, critical thinking, analytic reasoning, and perseverance, which are necessary for college and career success. And entrepreneurs are listening.

In particular, there is a wide array of tools, games, and products that are teaching students how to collaborate with each other, solve problems, and think critically. For example:

- GlassLab has partnered with well-known gaming companies like Electronic Arts (EA) to design high-quality educational games that teach both core competencies like math and reading and skills such as critical thinking, and works with ETS and Pearson to assess the results. For example, GlassLab redesigned the popular EA SimCity game to create SimCityEDU. An early study found students who played the game made positive gains in systems thinking.
- Bright Bot, a Village Capital investment, uses technology to make creative thinking a key tool for self-driven learning. With apps to help kids write stories, draw, record songs, and make movies, the company's goal is to expand children's imaginations, and its story-authoring tool is linked to primary reading and language arts standards.
- Tynker is an online platform helping teach kids the basics of computer coding, with an emphasis on creativity, problem solving, and perseverance. The program has received strong reviews from students and parents, and boasts over a million users each month across the world.

Charter schools and innovative districts are leading the way in experimenting with these kinds of games and project-based learning approaches. Summit Public Schools, for example, is a network of nine charter schools in California and Washington State that utilizes a project-based learning approach that is heavy on technology to personalize instruction. Summit's approach focuses on four elements of college readiness, including "habits of success" (such as self-directed learning) and "cognitive skills" (such as critical thinking and communication), and its graduates are earning college degrees at higher rates than peers and the national average.

It's important to emphasize that many of these tools and resources are extraordinarily young, and despite some preliminary positive findings for the ones we have discussed above, we are in no way able to declare that these companies have fully figured out how to teach noncognitive skills, or that they would work in every school and for every student. The important takeaways for us are (1) that ed tech companies are responding to consumer demand to teach more than just reading and math and (2) that the best ones are engaged in a robust process of measuring their results and refining their model. We predict that more companies will follow suit in the decade ahead.

Lesson 10: Don't Forget About the People (in Front of the Classroom)

If the first rule of entrepreneurship is knowing the problem you're trying to solve, the next one might be you're only as good as your people—in this case, the teachers who are actually using the product. Indeed, any new product or service is just a tool, and will only be as successful as the teachers who use it. Education entrepreneurs should be mindful that teachers have established classroom practices, and entrepreneurs cannot simply expect to develop a new intervention that a teacher will adopt on day one, changing decades of pedagogical behavior. "Will teachers use this intervention the way they are supposed to?" ought to be the mantra of every education technologist.

Discussing how teachers will use technology gives potential investors fits. Investors want "strategies" and "engagement," not the dirty word of "professional development." As a consequence, PD, that large and confusing industry around how to improve teachers' effectiveness, is something entrepreneurs have largely left untouched. And yet the PD of the past hundred years has tended to be a few days at a conference over the summer—and it has been found wanting. A recent study by the Gates Foundation and the Boston Consulting Group found that very few teachers (fewer than 30 percent) are highly satisfied with the PD they receive, especially when it comes to teaching them how to read student data and use digital tools.[17] Another study of ten thousand teachers by TNTP confirmed these results, finding that districts spend an average of $18,000 per teacher per year on professional development with less than one-third of teachers seeing substantial improvement in their evaluations as a result.[18]

Yet professional development is critical for realizing the promise of ed tech products, not to mention a tremendous market opportunity. The Gates-BCG study estimated that more than $18 billion is spent annually on PD. We see entrepreneurs such as Richmond-based EdConnective changing professional development through real-time teacher feedback. EdConnective takes each teacher through a dynamic coaching process grounded in lessons from the highest-performing schools across the country. By using video lessons, EdConnective can provide eleven observations and twelve feedback sessions over a six-week period; in contrast, the average teacher receives only three such observations during an entire school year. We predict, as a sector that technology has barely touched, entrepreneurs have more opportunity to make real progress in PD than most sectors.

CONCLUSION

The ten trends we've outlined are what we see from our perch talking with hundreds of education entrepreneurs a year, investing in and backing companies, rigorously analyzing policy, and advising large companies and school systems on how to better make sense of the fast-changing landscape. As noted at the beginning of this chapter, we ultimately see three overarching trends:

- Education entrepreneurship is no longer marginal, but mainstream, and the best solutions are coming from everywhere, not just Silicon Valley.
- The most successful education entrepreneurs aren't "disrupting," they're partnering.
- Measuring learning outcomes, broadly defined, will soon be the most important metric for success.

Ultimately, building an education enterprise takes longer, and is almost certainly more frustrating, than a Silicon Valley consumer technology company, but the great companies will have loyal, long-lasting customers whose lives are transformed. The single biggest advice we have for education entrepreneurs: be patient, expect that change will take the entire decade, but the payoff will be worth the risk.

Conclusion

Entrepreneurship and American Education

Frederick M. Hess and Michael Q. McShane

W hen ridesharing pioneer Uber launched in 2010, it set out to solve a simple problem: it can be an enormous headache to rely on taxi-cabs. Cabs may or may not be around when you need them. To hail one, you stand on the street corner waving your arms, hoping an empty cab will appear. If you're not in a place where you can hail a cab, you call a taxi company and the dispatcher promises to have a cab there in a little while. Sometimes cabs are late, and occasionally they don't show up at all. All you can do to keep on top of things is call the dispatcher back—and ask for another generic update. Taxicab commissions limit the number of cabs allowed to operate and impose any number of outdated and byzantine regulations. Customer satisfaction is often an afterthought in a transaction that is, by design, a one-time thing.

Uber changed all that. By linking the GPS software in phones with an automated dispatch service, it made it quick and easy for riders to find drivers. This was as true from a home or a doctor's office as from the side of a city street. The software also allowed riders to track precisely how many minutes it would be until their ride arrived. By collecting ratings from users and drivers, Uber could police the interactions and enable riders to avoid problem drivers. Automatic billing and time-and-distance charges meant drivers no longer had to worry about riders refusing to pay and riders no longer had to worry about overcharges.

As a result of this small, simple innovation, Uber grew rapidly. By 2014, Uber was providing nearly one million rides a day.[1] By 2015, it reported employing more than one million drivers, more than four-fifths of whom reported driving for Uber because it allowed them to be their own bosses and set their own schedules.[2] Suggesting that Uber could be especially relevant for those without other transport in low-income communities, a study in Los Angeles found that UberX rides in low-income neighborhoods were less than half the price of taxis and arrived more than twice as quickly.[3]

Uber is a classic illustration of disruptive innovation at work. It's a case of entrepreneurs identifying a practical problem, leveraging knowledge or technology to devise a better solution, and then providing it in a way that upends old routines and assumptions. Uber didn't "fix" urban transportation problems, but it's had a profound effect on mobility, access, and quality of life. And it did all of this without tax dollars or government planning. That decentralized, dynamic problem-solving is the spirit that imbues the chapters of this volume—and, as we noted in the introduction, is the antithesis of the "systems" approach to problem-solving that can feel more familiar in the world of K–12 schooling.

This volume is animated by the presumption that it would be good for K–12 schooling if Uber-like approaches were more common when it came to taking on the taxing challenges that plague education: How can we better use school facilities? How can we help children find schools that are a good match for them? How can we help teachers identify the best strategies to address specific learning challenges? And so many more. But what does it take for entrepreneurial problem-solving to actually help, and how do we think about the obstacles it faces and the problems it may create? Those are the questions that the contributors have focused upon.

Too often, the K–12 model is far more reminiscent of a big-city taxicab commission than of Uber. The emphasis on systemwide behaviors (like making sure all of the cabs are painted the same color, have a uniform light on top, have the same credit card machine, or charge the same rates) can leave little room for new actors or the rethinking of fundamental assumptions. This is not to say that the solutions that they advocate for wouldn't make cabs better, it is just that game-changing innovations like Uber don't come out of taxicab commissions.

Again, it's worth noting that Uber did not "fix" urban transportation. In many cities, it is impractical. In others, there is not a large enough supply of drivers to meet the demands of riders. For many people, it is still too expensive. What it did do was help to solve a particular problem in an important way for a lot of people, while opening up the door to newer and better solutions. This is what entrepreneurial activity can do.

BIG IDEAS

Some key themes appear throughout the chapters here. One is the sense that the past decade or more has been a dynamic time in the world of educational entrepreneurship but that entrepreneurship's influence has nonetheless been muted by policy and circumstance. A second is that entrepreneurial activity requires a belief that failure is an essential component of problem-solving. A third is an understanding that what gets measured is what gets valued, and a fourth is the recognition that the entrepreneurial community has been too insular and isolated.

Entrepreneurs Are Frustrated but Have Experienced Increasing Influence

Many chapters touch on the frustration that entrepreneurs experience in American education today. School procurement systems are stifling and outdated. Teachers and principals have limited flexibility to redesign schools or put new tools to work in ambitious ways. Charter schooling and school voucher programs have not yet produced a robust supply of new schools. As Dmitri Mehlhorn, partner at venture investment network Vidinovo, argues in chapter 4, venture capitalists have substantially underinvested in education relative to what one might expect.

Yet, for all this, NewSchools Venture Fund CEO Stacey Childress notes in chapter 1 that entrepreneurs have made enormous strides since the year 2000. Enrollment in charter schools doubled, and then doubled again. Venture capital investments grew from almost nothing into the hundreds of millions. Companies like Wireless Generation and SchoolNet thrived and then their founders successfully sold those ventures at a handsome rate of return, emboldening more entrepreneurs and investors to seek to emulate their efforts. The contributors also suggest that it's safe to say that entrepreneurial activity is poised to keep growing. Matt Candler, CEO of 4.0 Schools and author of chapter 8, discusses the Tiny Schools approach as one way to accelerate reengineering, reduce risk and cost, and facilitate this kind of dynamism. In short, it's been an era of unprecedented entrepreneurial activity and that appears set to continue.

Failure Is an Inseparable Part of Entrepreneurship

It's easy for the casual observer to imagine that all the expertise and money involved in the world of venture capital and startups must deliver a high rate of success. The truth is quite different. As Dmitri Mehlhorn observes, 90 percent of all new enterprises fail. Failure is most of what new ventures actually do. That Darwinian process of figuring things out or learning from the mistakes of others is essential to the vitality of entrepreneurial activity.

While talk of "failure" raises a disquieting specter of disruption and uncertainty when it comes to children and schools, the value of failure has a familiar place when it comes to classrooms and learning. Harvard's Elizabeth City discusses in chapter 7 the notion that both teachers and students benefit by "failing forward"—that is, feeling free enough to try something new and to learn from the experience if it doesn't work out. In American education today, however, there is little tolerance for this kind of talk—in classrooms, schools, or the larger landscape.

What Gets Measured Gets Valued

As research analyst at Center for Reinventing Public Education Ashley Jochim observes in chapter 2, the No Child Left Behind era has been marked by a heavy emphasis on how students perform on state tests in reading and math. Teachers are increasingly evaluated based on those metrics, district schools are at risk of being sanctioned if their students don't perform adequately, and charter schools know their existence depends in large part on those same measures. The mantra of test-based accountability is that the tests are "a floor, not a ceiling." After all, nobody thinks reading and math are all that matter. The point is only to ensure that students are mastering basic skills. After that, even diehard testing advocates think schools should feel free to customize and instruct as they see fit. This construct, however, tends to work much better in theory than in practice.

For one thing, those simple "floor" metrics usually define the ways in which schools are judged and compared, but they also mean that new providers can really *only* demonstrate their mettle in terms of reading and math. This poses grave challenges for those inclined to focus on rethinking instruction in world languages or civics. When policy and philanthropy treat reading and math tests as the coin of the realm, it creates problems for entrepreneurs who aren't offering "whole school" models, focusing on tested grades or subjects, or tackling ELA and math in ways that don't map onto the tests. In the modern era, there's also been far less appetite or room for entrepreneurs who aren't focused on closing reading and math "gaps" for low-income, African American, or Latino youth. The metrics used to measure success shape the types of solutions that will be offered.

The Entrepreneurial Community Has Suffered for Its Insularity

In chapter 1, Stacey Childress highlights a 2011 study that found that Teach For America alumni accounted for key founders at nearly one in five of the new education ventures launched in the previous twenty years. That data point reflects a larger reality, which is that education entrepreneurs are likely to share common formative experiences and worldviews. This has produced a community that has tended to share certain assumptions (like the importance of reading and math tests), embrace certain policies (like teacher evaluation and charter schooling), and enter new locales with its own national network.

This insularity has contributed to a simmering tension in several cities where entrepreneurial activity and new school formation has been particularly in evidence—like New Orleans, Newark, and Detroit. Activists, politicians, and community members charge that these ventures are being done *to* marginalized communities, not *with* them. Part of this hostility emerges from the conflation between entrepreneurship and "education reform" more generally (a phenomenon we will tackle momentarily), but another comes from a genuine fear of snake-oil salesmen and carpetbaggers with agendas of their own.

TENSIONS

While the authors mostly sounded similar notes when it came to the preceding, there was more disagreement in some other areas. These particularly tended to deal with the "how" of educational improvement, the larger debates about reform, and the role of school choice.

Small Bets Versus Scaling What Works

Matt Candler's chapter makes a strong case for going small when it comes to entrepreneurship and innovation. Because new ventures are uncertain, he argues that it makes sense to make a large number of small bets and winnow them over time. This reduces risk for everyone involved and accelerates the rate at which new models can be tried. Adding a dash of irony is Candler's previous status as one of the pioneers of the KIPP Academies national growth strategy. Today, though, Candler is convinced that a top-down expansion strategy is inferior to a bottom-up strategy that encourages an organic bubbling up of new providers from the local community.

Candler's approach flies in the face of much of the thinking that has characterized educational innovation and entrepreneurship during the past decade. Philanthropists and investors have been eager to find what works and to invest in scaling it up. Proponents of the "scale up" approach point to the need across the country, the slow pace of change, and the uncertainty of Candler's recipe.

This tension highlights the competing visions of educational improvement noted in the introduction to this volume. Some see experimentation as eventually converging on a single or small number of "best" models, practices, or programs that should ultimately be adopted everywhere. Others see a far more fluid world, with "best" answers being highly contingent and context-dependent. This isn't a simple story of entrepreneurs versus bureaucrats, but of good-faith disagreements on the approaches most likely to serve the needs of schools and schooling.

Are Entrepreneurs "Education Reformers"?

Entrepreneurs have routinely been lumped into the broader "education reform" movement. This is reasonable enough, as many entrepreneurs are proud members of that movement, sharing the general enthusiasm for charter schooling, test-based accountability, the Common Core, and teacher evaluation. At the same time, not all entrepreneurs share these views—and more than a few reject them. Yet entrepreneurs have generally been saddled with the resulting baggage. Teacher concerns about over-testing, parental fears of data mining, conservative pushback against the Common Core, liberal pushback against school choice—these have all become part of the world that entrepreneurs must navigate.

Whereas entrepreneurs in other sectors are often seen as the heroic little guys battling entrenched giants, in education they are often depicted as part of a dark alliance bent on subverting a beloved public institution. What's more, many entrepreneurs enthusiastically embrace the heated rhetoric so familiar to those close to the education debates. As John Bailey, executive director of Digital Learning Now!, wryly observes, unlike entrepreneurs in most other dynamic sectors, it is not always clear that educational entrepreneurs actually *like* education. All of this combines into a huge obstacle for potential entrepreneurs to overcome.

In one sense, entrepreneurs have to be "reformers." The traditional shape of public schooling doesn't do much to create the space entrepreneurial ventures need to sprout or grow. So they have no choice but to pursue change. But how they articulate and approach all this need not mimic the agenda of policy-oriented reformers. How entrepreneurs and policy reformers coexist and complement one another is a dance that neither party has yet figured out.

How Important Is School Choice as a Driver of Entrepreneurial Activity?

School choice has played a significant role in fostering educational entrepreneurship. Charter schooling has made it possible for entrepreneurs to more easily launch new school models and rethink staffing, and for charter management organizations to create from scratch what are effectively small (or even midsized) school districts. Private schools have even more flexibility to experiment or to determine their approach to school models, staffing, and much else. In these schools, the barriers to entrepreneurial rethinking are correspondingly lower.

At the same time, it's not clear just how pervasive the entrepreneurial spirit is in charter schooling and the private school sector. Indeed, private schools often seem hidebound. The elite schools hold fast to tradition and routine, while parochial schools show little taste for entrepreneurial reinvention. Meanwhile, the vast majority of charter schools look and act remarkably like local district schools (and generally produce similar results), even as the larger charter community has shown itself far more interested in "scaling up" effective schools than in what it will take to nurture a supply of promising new models.

This tension is coming to a head because school choice is at an inflection point. In a number of cities, charter schools will soon be educating half or more of all public school students. This creates new opportunities and burdens for parents, educators, and local officials. Yet many of the mechanisms to help parents make informed decisions do not exist yet. As Harvard's Jon Fullerton notes in chapter 6, it is currently extraordinarily difficult to tell parents if a particular school will work for their child. There exist a plethora of crude outcome measures, but few that focus on *fit*. More generally, in the world of apps, online tutors, educational games, and the like, parents are having to choose among technologies and approaches with which they have little familiarity and for which quality measures are largely nonexistent.

WE WANT EXPERIMENTATION . . . THAT'S SURE TO DELIVER

A number of authors in this book pointed to what may be the central tension of entrepreneurship in American education: There are plenty of calls for experimentation—the need to "think outside the box," and a need to "fundamentally change" American schools—yet in the next breath, the same advocates who preach the Innovation Gospel insist on "no excuses" accountability systems aiming for 100 percent proficiency and authorize systems that require all schools and offerings to prioritize performance on state tests. While it's hypothetically possible to square this circle, the reality is that educational entrepreneurs are whipsawed between an appetite for risk-taking— and a strong aversion to risk-taking.

This tension is particularly evident in the inclination to support large, established "entrepreneurial" ventures like Teach For America or the KIPP Academies. These ventures have track records of success, have proven leaders, and constitute a well-known quantity. At the same time, these are the very things that tend to produce rigidity and routine in any organization. Organizations like TFA and KIPP, with more than two decades of experience, records of accomplishment, alumni networks, and many stakeholders are no longer agile newcomers or positioned to pioneer wholly new approaches. Rather, they become attractive to funders, policymakers, and education officials as they become less and less entrepreneurial upstarts and more and more a familiar piece of the new education establishment. Rather than think about new ways of preparing teachers, people keep supporting Teach For America. The consequence is that these organizations are asked to do more and more, stretching their ability to excel while potentially crowding out interest in unproven ventures.

Questions about the importance of entrepreneurship and our tolerance for uncertainty are also central to policy debates over entrepreneur-friendly reforms like education savings accounts, online learning, and expanded school choice programs. After all, such programs are, by their very nature, unproven.

A FEW TAKEAWAYS

As we observed in the introduction, reasonable people can disagree about the merits of educational entrepreneurship. Indeed, in chapter 5, Marc Tucker, president of the National Center on Education and the Economy, does a terrific job of articulating the relevant questions and qualms. From our perspective, though, the merits of the entrepreneurial impulse—especially in the American system—are clear. For those who share our take, we here offer a few suggestions regarding measures that can help facilitate entrepreneurship and orient it in the most socially useful ways.

For Funders

Make small bets as well as large.   Funders should seek to diversify their investment strategies, especially by boosting the share of small bets they make. This can help both to address the fear of "failing big" and the sense that so much of education reform today is imposed by outsiders on local communities. Insofar as the groups receiving the majority of funding are outsiders that come to town with their already-baked models, well-intentioned philanthropy can unwittingly exacerbate this divide. By consciously creating room for Matt Candler's Tiny Schools approach, funders both support potentially promising new ventures while democratizing involvement in "reform." An easy rule of thumb here is for funders to be sure they are devoting some modest percentage of their investment giving—whether that's 5 percent or 20 percent—to new ventures. One upside here is that the resources to support the development, prototyping, and testing process tends to be only a fraction of what it costs to make a meaningful contribution to an established operation.

Be ecumenical about metrics of success.   For both practical and political reasons, overreliance on reading and math scores as the barometer of school or product success suffers from manifold limitations. Practically speaking, it narrows the universe of products and leaves whole swathes of things we want schools to do for kids (such as teach art, music, world languages, the sciences, technical skills, and civics) out in the cold. Politically, it conflates ventures with standardized testing, which is an increasingly unpopular bedfellow. The point is not that funders should reduce their attention to metrics, but that they should focus on identifying and developing the most appropriate metrics—rather than settling for the most convenient ones.

For Entrepreneurs

Put the same effort into disrupting measurement as into disrupting pedagogy or education management.   Many of the promising entrepreneurial ventures of the past decade have sought to improve instruction or school operation. Less evident has been the same level of disruption in measurement. There are plenty of calls for new and better metrics to gauge the success of schools and instructional tools. Some measure mastery of content that is often short-changed. Others fall under the vague label of "non-cognitive" skills (like grit and perseverance). Still others seek better ways to track longer-term outcomes. These are areas where new approaches, unencumbered by familiar routines and established needs, offer vast potential. It would be great to see ventures trying to crack this nut as hard as they have tried to improve instruction and management, especially as it promises to open doors for a diverse array of other important efforts.

Start with Tiny Schools. Given varying tolerance for risk and limited resources for experimentation, Matt Candler's Tiny Schools model offers a compelling path forward. The creation of a new charter school typically entails a dozen or more employees, scores or even hundreds of students, and a budget north of $1 million—meaning that failure is slow, expensive, and enormously disruptive. As Candler explains, Tiny Schools mean that educators with a promising idea can start with five to ten kids on Saturday mornings in a public library or school cafeteria. Such a model allows entrepreneurs to experiment, fail, improve, and iterate over the course of several sessions at very low cost and at next to zero risk to students. Just as evolutionary change accelerates when new generations are born more often, so entrepreneurial invention benefits from shortened time horizons and more rapid iteration. If the idea bears fruit, it can be ramped up. Tiny Schools accomplish two central tasks. First, they lower the risk of starting a new school. If the teaching methods don't connect with students, at worst, they've lost a couple of Saturdays. Even if the transition can't be made to a whole-year model, only a few students are affected. Second, they lower the cost of experimentation. In starting an entire charter school, a large number of philanthropic dollars and then public dollars are spent on an experiment. It might work out, it might not. While over time there is reason to believe that this will lead to better schools, it is an expensive way to get there. By bridging the gap between nothing and a whole school, Tiny Schools create space for rapid iteration and improvement.

For States

Allow for E Corps and Limited-Profit LLCs. John Katzman, founder and CEO of the Noodle Companies, proposes the creation of a new corporate governance model, the E Corp. This would be a classification for for-profit education ventures that have a dual bottom line—a commitment to both making profit and improving education. Like the B Corp in which they are based, founders forgo the need to maximize profit and instead are held accountable by shareholders by a combination of profit and social benefit. This promises to especially aid education ventures that anticipate modest profit margins or long runways before profitability. Another measure that can assist mission-oriented for-profits is to allow for the creation of "low-profit limited liability" ventures. Currently ten states allow corporations to state that while they are for-profit, their goal is not to maximize income. This status allows foundations to score any contributions they make to these organizations toward their mandatory disbursements each year—even as the funders get a return on their investments. Rather than rely on foundation support in perpetuity, the idea is that the grantee organizations will eventually become self-sustaining.

Conduct a comprehensive regulatory review. Though mundane, rules regarding subjects like procurement, teacher preparation, new school creation, reporting, facilities, special education, online provision, staff development, and charter school authorization can create huge, counterproductive hurdles to new providers and new models of provision. While many of these regulations may have made sense at one time, many no longer do. State leaders would do well to put together a blue-ribbon panel of experts to scour the state education code to seek outdated and ill-suited statutes and regulations that may be stymieing entrepreneurial solutions without doing much to protect students. They can also encourage districts, charter authorizers, and schools of education to conduct like-minded surveys of their own operations, and to publicly report on where and what they're streamlining.

It's About Entrepreneurialism, Not Entrepreneurs

We began with the story of Uber, the plucky start-up turned tech leviathan that drastically improved the way we get ourselves across town. But Uber is a cautionary tale as well. Just ask Lyft. Lyft, also a ridesharing app, started two years after Uber. It's in only a third as many cities as Uber and it's valued at a fraction of Uber's worth. That has not stopped Uber from trying to stamp it out (and it may well be, in many ways, a consequence of Uber's aggressive moves).

Uber has paid bounties to Lyft drivers to become Uber drivers. Uber has overwhelmed Lyft's technology by purposely hailing and canceling thousands of rides during busy times. What's worse, as happened in New York City, Uber has worked with regulators to squeeze out Lyft. By pushing for regulations that give it an advantage in the marketplace, Uber can create what a representative of Lyft told the Taxicab and Limousine commission was "drastic and predictable—a monopoly."[4]

It took less than five years for Uber to go from upstart to budding monopolist. Indeed, Uber is both at once—it is still a plucky newcomer battling taxi commissions and regulators as well as an established operation eager to fend off new rivals. And from that we can draw perhaps the most important lesson for educators, policymakers, reformers, and would-be entrepreneurs: the source of dynamism here is *entrepreneurialism*, not any particular entrepreneur or entrepreneurial venture. Exciting new entrants age, grow, and evolve. Some succeed and some fail. Those that succeed, with time and success, tend to become members in good standing of the stodgy old establishment. That's the cycle of entrepreneurial life.

Entrepreneurship does not guarantee success. If anything, it ensures that there will be failure. (Of course, in a half-century of school reform has taught us anything, it's that system reform is also sure to produce failure—except that it will do so on a much larger scale and without the dynamism, inventiveness, and self-correction that characterizes vibrant entrepreneurial sectors.) For all its imperfections, though, educational entrepreneurship offers a degree of imagination and natural winnowing that seems especially well suited to the sprawling, diverse, and pluralistic nation that we live in and creates an opportunity for truly world changing products to emerge. Those who believe in the power of the entrepreneurial impulse do well to never cling to one or another venture. The social good is best served by creating the conditions for entrepreneurs (Uber and Lyft alike) to thrive if—and only if—they're serving the best interests of students.

Notes

Introduction

1. Michael Noer, "One Man, One Computer, 10 Million Students: How Khan Academy is Reinventing Education," *Forbes*, November 19, 2012, www.forbes.com/sites/michaelnoer/2012/11/02/one-man-one-computer-10-million-students-how-khan-academy-is-reinventing-education.
2. Dude Solutions, "Dude Solutions, Parent Company of SchoolDude and FacilityDude, Announces Growth Investment from Warburg Pincus of up to $100 Million," February 3, 2014, www.dudesolutions.com/press/dude-solutions-announces-growth.
3. Enriched, "About Us," http://enrichedschools.com/welcome/about_us.
4. Tim Hindle, "Entrepreneurship," *The Economist*, April 27, 2009, www.economist.com/node/13565718.
5. James Guthrie and Elizabeth A. Ettema, "Public Schools and Money," *Education Next* 12, no. 4 (Fall 2012), educationnext.org/public-schools-and-money.

Chapter 1

1. "Our History," Teach For America, https://www.teachforamerica.org/about-us/our-story/our-history.
2. Monica Higgins, Frederick M. Hess, et al, "Creating a Corps of Change Agents: What Explains the Success of Teach For America?" *Education Next* 11, no. 3 (Summer 2011): 18–25. Higgins and Hess identified fifty organizations, including Teach For America. Because of the nature of the study, TFA data was excluded from analysis, leaving forty-nine education reform organizations in the sample.
3. Aspire, New Leaders, TNTP, and Khan Academy all received grant funding from NewSchools. Newsela, eSpark, BrightBytes, eSpark and Schoolzilla received seed-stage equity investments.
4. Claudia Kalb, "9/11's Children Grow Up," *Newsweek*, September 7, 2009, http://www.newsweek.com/911s-children-grow-79477.
5. For more recent instances, see KPCB tweet from Vanity Fair Summit, October 9, 2014, https://twitter.com/kpcb/status/520252855832567808; and Scott Howard, "Things John Doerr Says," *Medium*, September 28, 2014, https://medium.com/tech-times/things-john-doerr-says-b30d52b65d98.
6. Thomas R Eisenmann, "Entrepreneurship: A Working Definition," *Harvard Business Review*, January 10, 2013.

7. J. Gregory Dees, "The Meaning of Social Entrepreneurship" (working paper, May 30, 2001), https://centers.fuqua.duke.edu/case/wp-content/uploads/sites/7/20fifteen/03/Article_Dees_MeaningofSocialEntrepreneurship_2001.pdf.

8. Kim Smith and Julie Landry Peterson, "What Is Educational Entrepreneurship?" *Educational Entrepreneurship: Realities, Challenges, Possibilities*, ed. Frederick M. Hess (Cambridge, MA: Harvard Education Press, 2006).

9. "Public Charter Schools Dashboard," National Association for Public Charter Schools http://www.publiccharters.org/dashboard/students/page/overview/year/2014.

10. "Mapping the Landscape of Charter Management Organizations: Issues to Consider in Supporting Replication," National Resource Center on Charter School Finance and Governance, 2005, https://www.usc.edu/dept/education/cegov/focus/charter-schools/publications/policy/MappingTheLandscape-SupportingReplication.pdf; "Schools by Management Organization," The Public Charter Schools Dashboard, National Association for Public Charter Schools, http://dashboard.publiccharters.org/dashboard/students/page/mgmt/year/2008.

11. "Schools by Management Organization," The Public Charter Schools Dashboard, National Association for Public Charter Schools, http://dashboard.publiccharters.org/dashboard/schools/page/mgmt/year/2011.

12. "Urban Charter School Study Report on 41 Regions," Center for Research on Education Outcomes, Stanford University, 2015, https://urbancharters.stanford.edu/download/Urban%20Charter%20School%20Study%20Report%20on%2041%20Regions.pdf.

13. In fall 2014, NewSchools engaged the Parthenon Group to, among other things, conduct analysis of charter sector performance and conditions in cities where market share was at or above 20 percent. The output of their analysis forms the basis of my assertions about the conditions necessary for charter market share to translate into improved citywide performance. The insights would not have been possible without their contributions, but the observations and any leaps of logic are solely my own.

14. I owe my insights about the factors that supported human capital entrepreneurship to a number of excellent analyses of the related policy and practice during the 2000s, chief among them: Andrew J. Rotherham and Ashley LiBetti Mitchel, *Genuine Progress, Greater Challenges: A Decade of Teacher Effectiveness Reforms*, Bellwether Education Partners, November 2014; Arthur Levine, *Educating School Teachers*, The Education Schools Project, September 2006; Daniel Weisberg et al., *The Widget Effect* The New Teacher Project, 2009.

15. Eric A. Hanushek, John F. Kain, and Steven G. Rivkin, "Teachers, Schools, and Academic Achievement," National Bureau of Economic Research Working Paper 6691, August 1998.

16. Eric A. Hanushek and Steven G. Rivkin, *How to Increase the Supply of High Quality Teachers* (Washington, DC: The Brookings Institution, 2004).

17. Robert Gordon, Thomas Kane, and Douglas Staiger, *Identifying Effective Teachers Using their Performance on the Job* (Washington, DC: The Brookings Institution, April 2006).

18. "Useful Stats: Venture Capital Investment Dollars, Deals by State, 2009–2014, *SSTI*, January 22, 2015, http://ssti.org/blog/useful-stats-venture-capital-investment-dollars-deals-state-2009-2014.

19. "News Corp Acquires Education Technology Provider," *Bloomberg Business News*, November 23, 2010, http://www.bloomberg.com/news/articles/2010-11-23/news-corp-acquires-wireless-for-360-million-to-expand-into-education; "Pearson Agrees to Acquire US Based Schoolnet for $230 Million," *Bloomberg Business News*, April 26, 2011, http://

www.bloomberg.com/news/articles/2011-04-26/pearson-agrees-to-acquire-new-york-based-schoolnet-for-230-million-cash.

20. Larry Berger and David Stevenson, "K–12 Entrepreneurship: Slow Entry, Distant Exit" (presented at the American Enterprise Institute, Washington, DC, September 2007), paper available at http://stanford.io/1CMSNTF.

21. Jenny Nagaoka, et al., "Foundations for Young Adult Success: A Developmental Framework." Consortium on Chicago School Research, University of Chicago, June 2015.

22. Nagaoka, et al., 2015.

Chapter 2

1. Anne Schneider and Helen Ingram, "Behavioral Assumptions of Policy Tools," *Journal of Politics* 52, no. 2 (1990): 510–529.

2. For a review of definitions, see Thomas A. Birkland, *An Introduction to the Policy Process: Theories, Concepts, and Models of Public Policy Making* (New York: M.E. Sharpe, 2011).

3. *Entrepreneurship* in this sense is not the same as *innovation*. Innovation is more disruptive; entrepreneurship can disrupt but may also simply improve an existing practice.

4. Digital Promise and IDEO, *Evolving Ed-Tech Procurement in School Districts* (Washington, DC: Digital Promise, 2013). See also Tricia Maas and Robin Lake, *A Blueprint for Effective and Adaptable School District Procurement* (Seattle: Center on Reinventing Public Education, 2015).

5. Common Core State Standards Initiative, 2015.

6. In a posthumous biography, CEO Steve Jobs is quoted as having described the textbook industry "ripe for destruction." Quoted in Steven R. Strahler, "Textbook Case of a Dying Biz," *Chicago Business*, March 3, 2012.

7. Strahler, March 3, 2012.

8. Diane Stark Rentner and Nancy Kober, *Common Core State Standards in 2014: Curriculum and Professional Development at the District Level* (Washington, DC: Center for Education Policy, 2014).

9. Ibid.

10. Sarah Garland, "Common Core Standards Shake Up the Education Business," *Hechinger Report*, October 15, 2013.

11. Robert Pondiscio, "Common Core's First Breakout Hit?" *Education Next*, June 10, 2015.

12. Garland, "Common Core Standards."

13. Sean Cavanagh, "Common-Common Core Testing Contracts Favor Big Vendors," *Education Week*, September 30, 2014.

14. Sean Cavanagh, "Amplify Insight Wins Contract From Common-Core Testing Consortium," *Education Week*, March 14, 2013.

15. Catherine Gewertz, "A Map of States' 2015 Testing Plans: The Dust Has Finally Settled," *Education Week*, February 4, 2015.

16. Robin Lake and Tricia Maas, "Will Charter Schools Lead or Lag?" in *Common Core Meets Education Reform: What It All Means for Politics, Policy, and the Future of Schooling*, ed. Frederick M. Hess and Michael Q. McShane (New York: Teachers College, Columbia University, 2014), 76.

17. Frederick M. Hess and Michael Q. McShane, *Common Core Meets Education Reform: What It All Means for Politics, Policy, and the Future of Schooling* (Cambridge, MA: Harvard Education Press, 2013).

18. Larry Cuban, "Buying iPads, Common Core Standards, and Computer-Based Testing," *Larry Cuban on School Reform and Classroom Practice* (blog), July 29, 2013, https://larrycuban.wordpress.com/2013/07/29/buying-ipads-common-core-standards-and-computer-based-testing/.

19. Michele Molnar, "Evaluating the Outlook for the Ed-Tech Industry in 2015," *Education Week*, January 16, 2015.

20. Just ten states (Alabama, California, Idaho, Iowa, Montana, Nebraska, New Hampshire, North Dakota, Texas, and Vermont) have no formal policy requiring teacher evaluations to take student achievement into account. See National Council on Teacher Quality, *State of the States 2013, Connect the Dots: Using Evaluations of Teacher Effectiveness to Inform Policy and Practice* (Washington, DC: NCTQ, 2014).

21. "Measures of Teacher Performance (Observation)," Center for Great Teachers and Leaders, American Institutes for Research, Databases on State Teacher and Principal Evaluation Policies, http://resource.tqsource.org/stateevaldb/.

22. Frederick M. Hess and Michael Q. McShane, *Teacher Quality 2.0: Toward a New Era of Education Reform* (Cambridge, MA: Harvard Education Press, 2014).

23. TNTP, *Reimagining Teaching in a Blended Classroom* (Washington, DC: TNTP, 2014).

24. "Traversing the Teacher Evaluation Terrain," (Washington, DC: Thomas B. Fordham Institute, November 18, 2013).

25. Maas and Lake, *A Blueprint*.

26. Jay Chambers et al., *How Much Are Districts Spending to Implement Teacher Evaluation Systems? Case Studies of Hillsborough County Public Schools, Memphis City Schools, and Pittsburg Public Schools* (Washington, DC: RAND and American Institutes for Research, 2013).

27. Sarah Garland, "Companies, Nonprofits Making Millions off Teacher Effectiveness Push," *Hechinger Report*, October 25, 2011.

28. Ibid.

29. Ibid.

30. National Council on Teacher Quality, *Teacher Preparation Program Student Performance Data Models: Six Core Design Principles* (Washington, DC: NCTQ, 2013).

31. National Alliance for Public Charter Schools, *Estimated Number of Public Charter Schools and Students, 2014–2015* (Washington, DC: NAPCS, 2014), http://www.publiccharters.org/wp-content/uploads/2015/02/open_closed_FINAL.pdf.

32. National Alliance for Public Charter Schools, *A Growing Movement: America's Largest Charter School Communities* (Washington, DC: NAPCS, 2013), http://www.publiccharters.org/wp-content/uploads/2014/01/2013-Market-Share-Report-Report_20131210T133315.pdf.

33. The Public Charter Schools Dashboard, National Alliance for Public Charter Schools, 2009–2010, http://dashboard.publiccharters.org/dashboard/policy/page/cap/year/2010.

34. National Association of Charter School Authorizers, *The State of Charter School Authorizing: A Report on NACSA's Authorizer Survey* (Washington, DC: NACSA, 2013).

35. Meagan Batdorff et al., *Charter School Funding: Inequity Expands* (Fayetteville, AR: School Choice Demonstration Project, Department of Education Reform, University of Arkansas, 2014).

36. Charter School Facilities Initiative, *Initial Findings From Ten States*, 2013, http://www.facilitiesinitiative.org/media/3080/csfnationalsummary-fnl_april2013_.pdf.

37. Office of Innovation and Improvement, US Department of Education, "Charter Schools Program," https://www2.ed.gov/about/offices/list/oii/csp/index.html?exp=7.

38. Ariana Prothero, "Obama's Budget Aims to Boost Charter School Funding," *Education Week*, February 2, 2015, http://blogs.edweek.org/edweek/charterschoice/2015/02/obamas_budget_proposes_boosts_charter_school_funding.html.

39. Education Commission of the States, *Charter Schools—What Rules Are Waived for Charter Schools?* (Washington, DC: ECS, 2014), http://ecs.force.com/mbdata/mbquestNB2?rep=CS1419.

40. National Alliance for Public Charter Schools, *Measuring Up: Automatic Exemption from Many State and District Laws and Regulation*, http://www.publiccharters.org/law-database/automatic-exemptions-state-district-laws-regulations/.

41. National Association for Charter School Authorizers, *One Million Lives in Action*, http://www.qualitycharters.org/one-million-lives/one-million-lives-in-action.html.

42. For Ohio, see Catherine Candisky and Jim Siegel, "GOP Plan Would Increase Accountability for Ohio Charter Schools," *Columbus Dispatch*, January 29, 2015. For Michigan, see Kyle Feldscher, "Democrats Announce Charter School Reforms That Would Increase Transparency," *MLive.com*, October 21, 2014, http://www.mlive.com/lansing-news/index.ssf/2014/10/democrats_announce_proposed_ch.html.

43. See, for example, Center for Research on Education Outcomes, *National Charter School Study* (Stanford, CA: CREDO, 2013).

44. Michael Q. McShane, Jenn Hatfield, and Elizabeth English, *The Paperwork Pile-Up: Measuring the Burden of Charter School Applications* (Washington, DC: American Enterprise Institute, 2015), http://www.aei.org/publication/the-paperwork-pile-up-measuring-the-burden-of-charter-school-applications.

45. Some critics allege that the laser-like focus on quality in New Orleans has led to uniformity in the sector. See Cowen Institute, *The State of Public Education in New Orleans* (New Orleans: Tulane University, 2014).

46. Ted Regarber and Alison Consoletti Zgainer, eds., *The Essential Guide to Charter School Operations: Survey of America's Charter Schools* (Washington, DC: Center for Education Policy, 2014).

47. Jennifer Booher-Jennings, "Below the Bubble: 'Educational Triage' and the Texas Accountability System," *American Education Research Journal* 42, no. 2 (2205): 231–268.

48. Center for Education Policy, *States' Perspectives on Waivers: Relief from NCLB, Concern About Long-term Solutions* (Washington, DC: Center on Education Policy, 2013).

49. Jennifer Brown, "Cost Doesn't Spell Success for Colorado Schools Using Consultants to Improve Achievement," *Denver Post*, February 19, 2012.

50. Ibid.

51. Ibid.

52. Government Accountability Office, *School Improvement Grants: Education Should Take Additional Steps to Enhance Accountability for Schools and Contractors* (Washington, DC: GAO, 2012).

53. Alyson Klein, "School Improvement Grant Program Gets Mixed Grades in Ed. Dept. Analysis," *Education Week*, November 21, 2013.

54. GAO, *School Improvement Grants*.

55. Office of School Turnaround Monitoring, Department of Education, http://www2.ed.gov/programs/sif/monitoring/index.html.

56. National Center for Educational Evaluation and Regional Assistance, *A Focused Look at Rural Schools Receiving School Improvement Grants* (Washington, DC: Institute for Education Sciences, 2014).

57. Tricia Maas and Robin Lake, *A Blueprint*.

58. Frederick M. Hess, *Cage-Busting Leadership* (Cambridge, MA: Harvard Education Press, 2013).

59. Martin R. West, *Preserving the Federal Role in Encouraging and Evaluating Education Innovation* (Washington, DC: Brookings Institution, 2015).

Chapter 3

1. Joel Rose, "How to Break Free of Our 19th-Century Factory-Model Education System," *The Atlantic*, May 9, 2012, http://www.theatlantic.com/business/archive/2012/05/how-to-break-free-of-our-19th-century-factory-model-education-system/256881.

2. Julie L. Peterson, "For Education Entrepreneurs, Innovation Yields High Returns," *Education Next* 14 (Spring 2014), http://educationnext.org/for-education-entrepreneurs-innovation-yields-high-returns.

3. William D. Eggers and Anna Muoio, "Wicked Opportunities," *Deloitte University Press*, April 15, 2015, http://dupress.com/articles/wicked-problems-wicked-opportunities-business-trends.

4. "Technology Industry Leaders Like Mark Zuckerberg, Pierre Omidyar Raise $100 Million for Startup AltSchool," *Economic Times*, May 6, 2015, http://economictimes.indiatimes.com/small-biz/small-biz-usa/technology-industry-leaders-like-mark-zuckerberg-pierre-omidyar-raise-100-million-for-startup-altschool/articleshow/47173964.cms.

5. Michael Winters and Tyler McNally, "2014 US Tech Edtech Funding Hits $1.36B," *edSurge*, December 23, 2014, https://www.edsurge.com/n/2014-12-23-2014-us-edtech-funding-hits-1-36b.

6. "Ed Tech Investment & Exit Report—2014 on Track for New Funding Record," *CB Insights* (blog), September 8, 2014, https://www.cbinsights.com/blog/ed-tech-investment-report-2014/.

7. "2015 Startup Funding on Pace to Reach Highest Levels Since 2000," *MatterMark* (blog), June 12, 2015, http://foundationcenter.org/gainknowledge/research/keyfacts2014/foundation-focus.html.

8. "Why Direct-to-Consumer Models Matter in Education," *New Schools Venture Fund Blog*, April 25, 2014, http://www.newschools.org/blog/dtoc.

9. Why Direct-to-Consumer Models Matter in Education," *New Schools Venture Fund Blog*, April 25, 2014, http://www.newschools.org/blog/dtoc.

10. "EdSurge Exclusives View from the Top," September 14, 2011, https://www.edsurge.com/n/edsurge-exclusives-view-from-the-top.

11. George Anders, "How to Launch a Billion Dollar Startup on a Shoestring," *Forbes*, May 2, 2012, http://www.forbes.com/sites/georgeanders/2012/05/02/thrifty-startup; Mark Suster, "Why It's Morning in Venture Capital," *Slideshare*, June 29, 2014, http://www.slideshare.net/msuster/why-its-morning-in-venture-capital.

12. Marc Andreessen, "Why Software Is Eating the World," *Wall Street Journal*, August 20, 2011, http://www.wsj.com/articles/SB10001424053111903480904576512250915629460.

13. Eric Schmidt and Jonathan Rosenberg, *How Google Works* (Grand Central Publishing, 2014), Google E-book, https://books.google.com/books?id=fEJ0AwAAQBAJ&.

14. International Business Innovation Association, "Business Incubation FAQs," http://www.nbia.org/resources/business-incubation-faq.

15. Foundation for Excellence in Education, "Education Savings Accounts (ESA): Innovation and Customization," http://excelined.org/downloads/policy-summary-education-savings-accounts-esa-innovation-customization.

16. Arianna Prothero, "Some States Put Parents in Charge of Student Spending," *Education Week*, February 24, 2015, http://www.edweek.org/ew/articles/2015/02/25/some-states-put-parents-in-charge-of.html.

17. Hamish McKenzie, "Say What? Duolingo Points to Data's Important Role in Online Education," *PandoDaily*, May 30, 2013, https://pando.com/2013/05/30/say-what-duolingo-points-to-datas-important-role-in-online-education.

18. Michael Moe and Ben Wallerstein, "The New Innovator's Dilemma," *Huff Post Business*, October 29, 2013, http://www.huffingtonpost.com/michael-moe/the-new-innovators-dilemm_b_4173283.html.

19. Frederick M. Hess and Andrew P. Kelly, "A Federal Education Agenda," *National Affairs*, No. 13, Fall 2012, http://www.nationalaffairs.com/publications/detail/a-federal-education-agenda.

20. Robin L. Flanigan, "State Laws Lift Virtual Ed. Enrollment Caps," *Education Week*, August 27, 2012, http://www.edweek.org/ew/articles/2012/08/29/02el-enrollment.h32.html.

21. Andrew P. Kelly, "Tomorrow's Online Schools: Let's Get Them Here Today," American Enterprise Institute, October 15, 2013, http://www.aei.org/publication/tomorrows-online-schools-lets-get-them-here-today/.

22. Michael Horn, "No Surprise: Accrediting Agency Opts to Stunt Innovation," *Forbes*, August 8, 2013, http://www.forbes.com/sites/michaelhorn/2013/08/08/no-surprise-accrediting-agency-opts-to-stunt-innovation.

23. Frederick M. Hess and Chester E. Finn, Jr., "What Innovators Can, and Cannot, Do," *Education Next*, Spring 2007, No. 2, http://educationnext.org/what-innovators-can-and-cannot-do.

24. EdSurge, "Marc Andreessen on the Potential Promises of EdTech Investments," December 2, 2011, http://www.fastcoexist.com/1678918/marc-andreessen-on-the-potential-promises-of-edtech-investments.

25. Deborah H. Quazzo et al., "Fall of the Wall: Capital Flows to Education Innovation," GSV Advisors, July 2012, http://gsvadvisors.com/wordpress/wp-content/themes/gsvadvisors/GSV%20Advisors_Fall%20of%20the%20Wall_2012-06-28.pdf.

26. Alpine Task Force on Learning and the Internet, *Learner at the Center of a Networked World*, The Aspen Institute, 2014, http://csreports.aspeninstitute.org/Task-Force-on-Learning-and-the-Internet/2014/report/details/0046/Task-Force-Introduction-and-Challenges.

27. "RegData," Mercatus Center, George Mason University, http://regdata.org/.

28. "Regulation Rodeo," American Action Forum, http://regrodeo.com/.

29. Tricia Maas and Robin Lake, *A Blueprint for Effective and Adaptable School District Procurement*, Center on Reinventing Public Education, January 2015, http://www.crpe.org/publications/blueprint-effective-and-adaptable-school-district-procurement.

30. Phil Martin and Steve Pines, "Improving Ed-Tech Purchasing," *Digital Promise* (blog), http://www.digitalpromise.org/blog/entry/improving-ed-tech-purchasing.

31. Michael Q. McShane, Jenn Hatfield, and Elizabeth English, *The Paperwork Pile-Up: Measuring the Burden of Charter School Applications*, American Enterprise Institute, May 19, 2015, http://www.aei.org/publication/the-paperwork-pile-up-measuring-the-burden-of-charter-school-applications.

32. Christopher B. Swanson, *Cities in Crisis 2009: Closing the Graduation Gap*, America's Promise Alliance, April 2009, http://www.aei.org/publication/the-paperwork-pile-up-measuring-the-burden-of-charter-school-applications.

33. Charles Hugh Smith, "Is Fee-for-Service What Ails America's Health Care System?" *Daily Finance*, January 18, 2010, http://www.dailyfinance.com/2010/01/18/ is-fee-for-service-what-ails-americas-health-care-system.

34. US Department of Energy, "Energy Department Makes Additional $4 Billion in Loan Guarantees Available for Innovative Renewable Energy and Efficient Energy Projects," press release, July 3, 2014, http://energy.gov/articles/ energy-department-makes-additional-4-billion-loan-guarantees-available-innovative-renewable.

35. "Residential Renewable Energy Tax Credit Program," US Department of Energy, http:// energy.gov/savings/residential-renewable-energy-tax-credit.

36. "Commercializing Space," National Aeronautics and Space Association (NASA), http:// www.nasa.gov/externalflash/commercializingspace/.

37. US Senators Thune, Alexander, Roberts, Burr, Coburn, and Enzi, "Reboot: Re-Examining the Strategies Needed to Successfully Adopt Health IT," United States Senate, April 16, 2013, http://www.thune.senate.gov/public/index.cfm/files/ serve?File_id=0cf0490e-76af-4934-b534-83f5613c7370.

38. Arne Duncan, "The Link Between Standards and Innovation," speech at Innovate to Educate Symposium, Richmond, VA, October 27, 2010, http://www.ed.gov/news/ speeches/link-between-standards-and-innovation-secretary-arne-duncans-remarks-innovate-educate-symposium-richmond-va.

39. Frederick M. Hess, "No Room for For-Profits in i3," *Rick Hess Straight Up* (blog), April 6, 2010, http://blogs.edweek.org/edweek/rick_hess_straight_up/2010/04/no_room_for_ for-profits_in_i3.html; Frederick M. Hess, "The Irrational Fear of For-Profit Education," *Wall Street Journal*, December 17, 2012, http://www.wsj.com/articles/SB10001424127887 3237511045781468933442238424; "Investing in Innovation Fund (i3) Eligibility," US Department of Education, http://www2.ed.gov/programs/innovation/eligibility.html.

40. Valerie Strauss, "AFT's Weingarten on Why She Got Arrested, 'the Gall' of Reformers, Etc.," *The Washington Post*, March 12, 2013, http://www.washingtonpost.com/blogs/ answer-sheet/wp/2013/03/12/ afts-weingarten-on-why-she-got-arrested-the-gall-of-reformers-etc/.

41. David Sirota, "Getting Rich Off of Schoolchildren," *Salon*, March 11, 2013, http://www. salon.com/2013/03/11/getting_rich_off_of_schoolchildren/.

42. Betsy Isaacson, "Tesla's Model S Sedan Named Safest Car in the History of Cars," *Huffington Post*, August 8, 2013, http://www.huffingtonpost.com/2013/08/20/tesla-model-s-safest-car_n_3786294.html.

43. Maya Kosoff, "Elon Musk Didn't Like His Kids' School, So He Made His Own Small, Secretive School Without Grade Levels," *Business Insider*, May 22, 2015, http://www. businessinsider.com/elon-musk-creates-a-grade-school-2015-5.

44. Michael Trucano, "Lessons from the Drafting of National Educational Technology Policies," *World Bank EduTech Blog*, June 12, 2015, http://blogs.worldbank.org/edutech/ lessons-drafting-national-educational-technology-policies.

45. Kim Smith and Julie Petersen, *Pull and Push: Strengthening Demand for Innovation in Education*, Bellwether Education Partners, 2011, http://bellwethereducation.org/sites/ default/files/pull-and-push.pdf.

46. Arthur C. Brooks, "Start Helping the Helpers," *New York Times*, October 17, 2014, http:// www.nytimes.com/2014/10/18/opinion/arthur-c-brooks-start-helping-the-helpers. html?_r=0&assetType=opinion.

47. Hess and Kelly, "A Federal Education Agenda."
48. *10 Elements of High-Quality Digital Learning*, Foundation for Excellence in Education, http://digitallearningnow.com/policy/10-elements/.
49. Timothy B. Clark, Marvin H. Kosters, and James C. Miller III, eds., "Reforming Regulation," conference sponsored by the American Enterprise Institute for Public Policy Research and the National Journal, 1980, http://www.aei.org/wp-content/uploads/2014/03/-reforming-regulation_162552508012.pdf.
50. Ohio Department of Education, "Ohio Department of Education Rates Community School Authorizers," press release, June 9, 2015, http://education.ohio.gov/Media/Media-Releases/Ohio-Department-of-Education-Rates-Community-Schoo#.VbkS5vlVikr.
51. "About the National Council for State Authorization Reciprocity Agreements (NC-SARA)," NC-SARA, http://nc-sara.org/about.
52. Foundation for Excellence in Education, *Leading in an Era of Change, Making the Most of State Course Access Opportunities*, July 2014, http://excelined.org/2014/07/21/leading-era-change-course-access-whitepaper/.
53. *Learner at the Center of a Networked World.*
54. Ibid; and "Student Privacy Pledge," Future of Privacy Forum & Software & Information Industry Association, 2014, http://studentprivacypledge.org/.
55. *Student Data Privacy: Building a Trusted Environment*, Foundation for Excellence in Education, http://excelined.org/student-data-privacy/.
56. John Bailey, Carri Schneider, Tom Vander Ark, "Using Prizes and Pull Mechanisms to Boost Learning," Getting Smart and Digital Learning Now, June 2014, http://gettingsmart.com/publication/using-prize-pull-mechanisms-boost-learning/.
57. The Center for American Progress, the American Enterprise Institute, and New Profit, *Stimulating Excellence: Unleashing the Power of Innovation in Education*, May 2009, https://www.americanprogress.org/issues/education/report/2009/05/05/6097/stimulating-excellence/; and John Bailey, Carri Schneider, and Tom Vander Ark, "Funding Students, Options, and Achievement," Foundation for Excellence in Education, 2013, http://digitallearningnow.com/site/uploads/2013/04/Funding-Paper-Final.pdf.
58. "Stanford University & Digital Learning Now Focus on Online Education," *Digital Learning Now Blog*, May 2014, http://digitallearningnow.com/news/blog/stanford-university-digital-learning-now-focus-on-online-education/.
59. John Bailey, et al., "Leading in an Era of Change: Making the Most of State Course Access Programs," Foundation for Excellence in Education and EducationCounsel LLC, 2014, http://digitallearningnow.com/site/uploads/2014/07/DLN-CourseAccess-FINAL_14July2014b.pdf; and Digital Learning Now, "Digital Learning Report Card 2014," 2015, http://excelined.org/2014DLNReportCard/.
60. The Center for American Progress, the American Enterprise Institute, and New Profit, "Stimulating Excellence: Unleashing the Power of Innovation in Education," May 2009, https://www.americanprogress.org/issues/education/report/2009/05/05/6097/stimulating-excellence/.
61. "NASA Technology Transfer Program: Bringing NASA Technology Down to Earth," NASA, http://technology.nasa.gov/.
62. Led Mirani, "Why Eton, Britain's 574-Year-Old High School, Is Embracing Ed Tech," *The Atlantic*, January 16, 2014, http://www.theatlantic.com/education/archive/2014/01/why-eton-britains-574-year-old-high-school-is-embracing-ed-tech/283123/.

63. Andrew J. Rotherham, "Why One Innovator Is Leaving the Public Sector," *TIME*, March 23, 2011, http://content.time.com/time/nation/article/0,8599,2061024,00.html.
64. Stimulating Excellence.

Chapter 4

1. Larry Cuban, "Educational Entrepreneurs Redux" in *Educational Entrepreneurship*, ed. Frederick M. Hess (Cambridge, MA: Harvard Education Press, 2006).
2. Peter H. Diamandis, "Why Billion-Dollar, 100-Year-Old Companies DIE," *Huffington Post*, February19, 2013, http://www.huffingtonpost.com/peter-diamandis/why-billion-dollar-100-ye_b_2718262.html.
3. "Education Spending: History and Charts for US Governments," www.usgovernmentspending.com/education_spending; http://nces.ed.gov/pubs93/93442.pdf.
4. Karen Lee, *Venture Capital: A Business of Failing* (Stanford, CA: Stanford Graduate School of Business, 2014), http://stanfordbusiness.tumblr.com/post/63832781211/venture-capital-a-business-of-failing.
5. Richard Branson, *Losing My Virginity: How I Survived, Had Fun, and Made a Fortune Doing Business My Way* (New York: Crown Publishing Group, 2011).
6. James Q. Wilson, *Bureaucracy: What Government Agencies Do and Why They Do It* (New York: Basic Books, 1989).
7. Eric Liu and Nick Hanauer, "The 'More What, Less How' Government," *Democracy: A Journal of Ideas* 19 (2011), www.democracyjournal.org/19/6786.php?page=all.
8. Henry Levin, "Why Is This So Difficult?" in *Educational Entrepreneurship*, ed. Frederick M. Hess (Cambridge, MA: Harvard Education Press, 2008); David Tyack and Larry Cuban, *Tinkering Toward Utopia: A Century of Public School Reform* (Cambridge, MA: Harvard University Press, 1995).
9. Dmitri Mehlhorn, "How to Make Teachers More Like Doctors," *The Atlantic*, September 23, 2014, www.theatlantic.com/education/archive/2014/09/how-to-make-teachers-more-like-doctors/380643/.
10. Thomas Kuhn, *The Structure of Scientific Revolutions* (Chicago: University of Chicago Press, 1962).
11. Jared Diamond, *Guns, Germs, and Steel: The Fates of Human Societies* (New York: W.W. Norton & Company, 1997).
12. See, for example, Diane Ravitch, *The Death and Life of the Great American School System* (New York: Basic Books, 2010). One chapter title refers to private-sector ideas as coming from the "The Billionaire Boys Club," a reference to an investment and social club who explicitly celebrated lying, cheating, stealing, and murder as acceptable means to pursue personal and professional goals. For a list of other examples of rhetoric hostile to outside ideas, see *The Progressive*'s website, www.publicschoolshakedown.org.
13. Anthony Cody and Wendy Lecker, *Charter Schools: An Experiment Gone Awry* (Washington, DC: National Education Policy Center, October 21, 2014), http://nepc.colorado.edu/blog/charter-schools-experiment.
14. Larry Cuban, "Are School Reforms More Like a Pendulum or a Hurricane?" *Larry Cuban on School Reform and Classroom Practice* (blog), September 7, 2010, https://larrycuban.wordpress.com/2010/09/07/are-school-reforms-more-like-a-pendulum-or-a-hurricane/.
15. See, for example, Lora Cohen-Vogel et al., "Implementing Educational Innovations at Scale: Transforming Researchers Into Continuous Improvement Scientists," *Educational Policy* 29, no. 1 (2015): 1–21.

16. John Kenneth Galbraith, *The Great Crash, 1929* (New York: Houghton Mifflin Harcourt Publishing Company, 1954).

17. Hyman Minsky, "Schumpeter and Finance," in *Market and Institutions in Economic Development: Essays in Honour of Paulo Sylos Labini*, ed. Salvatore Biasco, Alessandro Roncaglia, and Michele Salvati (New York: St. Martin's Press, 1993).

18. *See generally* Ross Levine, "Financial Development and Economic Growth: Views and Agenda," *Journal of Economic Literature* 35, no. 2 (1997): 688–726; Jeremy Stein, "Efficient Capital Markets, Inefficient Firms: A Model of Myopic Corporate Behavior," *Quarterly Journal of Economics* 104, no. 4 (1989): 655–669.

19. Reid Hoffman, "LinkedIn's Series B Pitch to Greylock," http://reidhoffman.org/linkedin-pitch-to-greylock.

20. John Graham and Scott Smart, *Introduction to Corporate Finance*, 3rd ed. (Independence, KY: South-Western Cengage Learning, 2012): "Though it is somewhat counterintuitive, companies growing that rapidly usually consume more cash than they generate because growth required ongoing investments in fixed assets and working capital."

21. William Megginson, "Toward a Global Model of Venture Capital?" *Journal of Applied Corporate Finance* 16, no. 1 (2004): 89–107. This article notes the superior sophistication and depth of the United States venture capital sector versus others around the world.

22. National Venture Capital Association, "Frequently Asked Questions about Venture Capital," 2012; National Venture Capital Association, "Venture Impact: The Economic Importance of Venture Capital-Backed Companies to the US Economy," 2011; Stuart Fraser et al., "What Do We Know About Entrepreneurial Finance and Its Relationship with Growth?" *International Small Business Journal* 33, no. 1 (2015): 70–88.

23. Graham and Smart, *Introduction to Corporate Finance*; Eric Hippeau, "Why Venture Capital Is Key to Our Economic Recovery," *Huffington Post*, February 25, 2009, http://www.huffingtonpost.com/eric-hippeau/why-venture-capital-is-ke_b_160511.html.

24. Deborah Gage, "The Venture Capital Secret: 3 out of 4 Start-Ups Fail," *Wall Street Journal*, September 20, 2012, www.wsj.com/articles/SB10000872396390443720204578004980476429190.

25. Mahendra Ramsinghani, *The Business of Venture Capital: Insights from Leading Practitioners on the Art of Raising a Fund, Deal Structuring, Value Creation, and Exit Strategies* (New York: Wiley & Sons, 2011).

26. Aileen Lee, "Welcome to the Unicorn Club: Learning from Billion-Dollar Startups," *TechCrunch*, November 2, 2013, http://techcrunch.com/2013/11/02/welcome-to-the-unicorn-club/.

27. See, for example, Tamera Elias, "LPs and the Venture Capital Asset Class: A Candid Conversation," *Venture Capital Review*, 2010, no. 26, www.ewhv.com/news/detail/lps_and_the_venture_capital_asset_class_a_candid_conversation.

28. Dileep Rao, "Why 99.95% Of Entrepreneurs Should Stop Wasting Time Seeking Venture Capital," *Forbes*, July 22, 2013, www.forbes.com/sites/dileeprao/2013/07/22/why-99-95-of-entrepreneurs-should-stop-wasting-time-seeking-venture-capital/.

29. Jeffrey Sohl, *The Angel Investor Market in 2013: A Return To Seed Investing* (Durham, NH: Center for Venture Research, April 30, 2014), https://paulcollege.unh.edu/sites/paulcollege.unh.edu/files/2013%20Analysis%20Report%20FINAL.pdf.

30. PitchBook, "4Q 2014 US Venture Industry Report," http://pitchbook.com/4Q2014_US_Venture_Industry_Report.html.

31. See, for example, CB Insights, "The Series B Venture Capital Firms," www.cbinsights.

com/blog/series-b-crunch-tech-investors/; Danielle Morrill, "While the Pace of Series B Investment Stabilized in 2014, Capital Concentration (and Valuations) Are Still Going Up," Mattermark, January 27, 2015, https://mattermark.com/while-the-pace-of-series-b-investment-remains-steady-capital-concentration-and-valuations-are-going-up/; Nick Frost, "Q1 2015 US Startup Funding Analysis" Mattermark, April 13, 2015, https://mattermark.com/q1-2015-u-s-startup-funding-analysis-mattermark-daily-monday-april-13th-2015/.

32. Paul Gompers and Josh Lerner, *The Venture Capital Cycle* (Cambridge, MA: MIT Press, 2004).

33. Melissa A. Clark et al., *The Effectiveness of Secondary Math Teachers from Teach For America and the Teaching Fellows Programs* (Washington, DC: Institute of Education Sciences, 2013), http://ies.ed.gov/ncee/pubs/20134015/pdf/20134015.pdf; Center for Research on Education Outcomes, *Urban Charter Schools Report* (Stanford, CA: Stanford University, March 18, 2015), http://credo.stanford.edu/research-reports.html; Stanford University's Center for Research on Education Outcomes, *Urban Charter Schools Report*, March 18, 2015.

34. Center for Research on Education Outcomes, *National Charter School Study* (Stanford, CA: Stanford University, March 18, 2015), http://credo.stanford.edu/research-reports.html.(in reading, 25% of charters had stronger learning gains than traditional public schools, while 56% showed no significant difference and 19% had weaker learning gains).

35. Kim Smith and Julie Petersen, *Social Purpose Capital Markets: Financial Capital for Social Entrepreneurs in Education* (Washington, DC: NewSchools Venture Fund, October 25, 2007), www.newschools.org/wp/wp-content/uploads/social-purpose-capital-markets.pdf.

36. Karl Zinsmeister et al., *Major Achievements of American Philanthropy (1636 to 2014)* (Washington, DC: Philanthropy Roundtable, forthcoming), www.philanthropyroundtable.org/almanac.

37. Richard L. Colvin, "The New Philanthropists," *Education Next* 5, no. 4 (2005): 34–41.

38. Tom Vander Ark, "Private Capital & Public Education: Toward Quality at Scale" (working paper, American Enterprise Institute, Washington, DC, 2009).

39. Katie Ash, "K–12 Marketplace Sees Major Flow of Venture Capital," *Education Week*, January 31, 2012, www.edweek.org/ew/articles/2012/02/01/19venture_ep.h31.html.

40. See, for example, Andrew Flowers, "The Science Of Grading Teachers Gets High Marks," FiveThirtyEight, July 20, 2015, http://fivethirtyeight.com/features/the-science-of-grading-teachers-gets-high-marks/.

41. See, for example, Sarah Reckhow and Jeffrey Snyder, "The Expanding Role of Philanthropy in Education Politics," *Educational Researcher* 43, no. 4 (2014): 186–195.

42. Richard L. Colvin, "The New Philanthropists," *Education Next* 5, no. 4 (2005): 34–41.

43. Walt Gardner, "Stop the Education Reform Pendulum," *Education Week*, June 7, 2010, http://blogs.edweek.org/edweek/walt_gardners_reality_check/2010/06/stop_the_education_reform_pendulum.html.

44. The recent failure of data-storage nonprofit InBloom illustrates the risk. As Ariel Bogle of New America wrote, "InBloom's failure is a teachable moment in trust-building and accountability for the next company in this space." Ariel Bogle, "What the Failure of inBloom Means for the Student-Data Industry," *Slate*, April 24, 2014, www.slate.com/blogs/future_tense/2014/04/24/what_the_failure_of_inbloom_means_for_the_student_data_industry.html.

45. See, for example, Brian Feinstein and Trevor Oelschig, *The Industry Software Revolution* (New York: Bessemer Venture Partners, April 1, 2015), https://bvp.app.box.com/ TheIndustrySoftwareRevolution.

46. Public-sector promotion of innovation, such as the Department of Education's Investing in Innovation (i3) program, relies on results-based metrics to identify best practices.

47. John Bailey, *Odd Man Out: How Government Supports Private-Sector Innovation, Except in Education* (Washington, DC: American Enterprise Institute, 2011), www.aei.org/ wp-content/uploads/2011/10/03-Private-Enterprise-Bailey.pdf.

48. See David Osborne and Ted Gaebler, *Reinventing Government: How the Entrepreneurial Spirit Is Transforming the Public Sector* (London: Penguin Books Ltd, 1992). Chapter 5 reviews many developments in this area.

49. Aram Roston, "Smart Money: The Venture Capitalists Who Stake Intelligence Technology," *DefenseNews*, May 24, 2013, http://archive.defensenews.com/ article/20130524/C4ISR02/305240013/ Smart-Money-Venture-Capitalists-Who-Stake-Intelligence-Technology.

50. Jay P. Greene, *Small Change? Foundations Are Turning to Education-Reform Advocacy. How's It Going?* (Washington, DC: Philanthropy Roundtable, 2013), www. philanthropyroundtable.org/topic/k_12_education/small_change.

51. Paul Graham, "A Unified Theory of VC Suckage," March 2005, www.paulgraham.com; "Valley of the Dudes," *The Economist*, April 4, 2015, www.economist.com/news/ business/21647611-tech-firms-can-banish-sexism-without-sacrificing-culture-made-them-successful-valley.

52. Alison B. Wagonfeld, "Venture Capitalist Vinod Khosla on Reasons for Long-Term Optimism About Technology and the Economy," *Harvard Business Review*, December 2008, https://hbr.org/2008/12/venture-capitalist-vinod-khosla-on-reasons-for-long-term-optimism-about-technology-and-the-economy.

53. Kim Smith and Julie Petersen, *Pull and Push: Strengthening Demand for Innovation in Education* (Washington, DC: Bellwether Education Partners, 2011), http:// bellwethereducation.org/sites/default/files/pull-and-push.pdf.

54. EdSurge, "TeachersPayTeachers Gets VC Funding," May 22, 2014, www.edsurge. com/n/2014-05-22-teacherspayteachers-gets-vc-funding.

55. Jonathan Shieber, "Following Its May Financing, Teachers Pay Teachers Names Former Etsy Exec as CEO," *TechCrunch*, Aug 7, 2014, http://techcrunch.com/2014/08/07/ following-its-may-financing-teachers-pay-teachers-names-former-etsy-exec-as-ceo/.

56. Teach For America, "Social Entrepreneurship & Innovation," www.teachforamerica.org/ alumni/career-leadership/leading-education/social-entrepreneurship-innovation.

57. Barnett Berry, *Teacherpreneurs: Innovative Teachers Who Lead but Don't Leave* (New York: Wiley & Sons, 2013).

58. Dmitri Melhorn, "Why Teachers Have No Voice," October 7, 2014, http://dropoutnation .net/2014/10/07/why-teachers-have-no-voice/.

59. Harvard Graduate School of Education, "A User's Guide to Peer Assistance and Review," www.gse.harvard.edu/~ngt/par/parinfo/.

60. US Department of Education, "Hillsborough County Public Schools," www.ed.gov/labor-management-collaboration/conference/hillsborough-county-public-schools.

61. Kim-Mai Cutler, "Altschool Raises $100M From Founders Fund, Zuckerberg To Scale A Massive Network of Schools Around Personalized Learning," *TechCrunch*, May 4, 2015, http://techcrunch.com/2015/05/04/

altschool-raises-100m-from-founders-fund-zuckerberg-to-scale-a-massive-network-of-schools-around-personalized-learning/.

Chapter 5

1. Eric A. Hanushek, Paul E. Peterson, and Ludger Woessmann, *Education Next* 12, no. 4 (2012), http://educationnext.org/is-the-us-catching-up/.

Chapter 6

1. Barbara Means et al., *Evaluation of Evidence-Based Practices in Online Learning: A Meta-Analysis and Review of Online Learning Studies* (Washington, DC: US Department of Education Office of Planning, Evaluation, and Policy Development Policy and Program Studies Service, Revised September 2010).
2. Janice M. Beyer, "Research Utilization: Bridging the Gap Between Communities," *Journal of Management Inquiry* 6 (1997): 17–22; see also Martha S. Feldman and James G. March, "Information in Organizations as Signal and Symbol," *Administrative Science Quarterly* 26 (1981): 171–186; and Nabil Amara, Mathieu Ouimet, and Réjean Landry, "New Evidence on Instrumental, Conceptual, and Symbolic Utilization of University Research in Government Agencies," *Science Communication* 26 (2004): 75–106.
3. Cynthia E. Coburn, Judith Toure, and Mika Yamashita, "Evidence, Interpretation, and Persuasion: Instructional Decision Making at the District Central Office," *Teachers College Record* 111 (2009): 1115–1161.
4. There are exceptions—some charters and CMOs have had rigorous evaluations performed (for instance, Joshua D. Angrist et al., "Inputs and Impacts in Charter Schools: KIPP Lynn," *American Economic Review: Papers & Proceedings* 100 (May 2010); Christina Clark Tuttle et al., "KIPP Middle Schools: Impacts on Achievement and Other Outcomes," *Mathematica Policy Research* [2013]; Will Dobbie and Roland G. Fryer, "Are High-Quality Schools Enough to Increase Achievement Among the Poor? Evidence from the Harlem Children's Zone," *American Economic Journal: Applied Economics* 3, no. 3, 2011), though they are still in the minority. States that report median student growth percentiles also allow parents at least some (fairly crude) insight into the effectiveness of different schools by controlling for prior student achievement.
5. Mark Dynarski et al., *Effectiveness of Reading and Mathematics Software Products: Findings from the First Student Cohort* (Washington, DC: U.S. Department of Education, Institute of Education Sciences, 2007).
6. "Urban School Superintendents: Characteristics, Tenure, and Salary Eighth Survey and Report," Council of the Great City Schools (2014).
7. "NCEE—Contracts and Grants Awarded in Fiscal Years 2011 and 2012," Institute of Education Sciences, http://ies.ed.gov/pdf/NCEEFY20112012.pdf.
8. In fact, a recent survey of IES commissioned RCTs determined that 90 percent of these evaluations found no effect. "Randomized Controlled Trials Commissioned by the Institute of Education Sciences Since 2002: How Many Found Positive Versus Weak or No Effects," Coalition for Evidenced-Based Policy (July 2013).
9. Liana Heitin, "Common-Core Textbooks to Receive Online Ratings," *Education Week*, August 20, 2014, http://www.edweek.org/ew/articles/2014/08/15/01curriculum.h34.html.
10. Jon Fullerton, "The Data Challenge," in *Customized Schooling*, ed. Frederick Hess and Bruno V. Manno (Cambridge, MA: Harvard Education Press, February 2011): 153–172.
11. Liana Heitin, "Review of Math Programs Comes Under Fire," *Education Week*, March 17,

2015, http://www.edweek.org/ew/articles/2015/03/18/review-of-math-programs-comes-under-fire.html.

12. "About the WWC," Institute of Education Sciences, http://ies.ed.gov/ncee/wwc/aboutus. aspx.

13. In fact, designs that do not have a randomized assignment into treatment and control groups can at most meet group design standards "with reservations." Institute of Education Science, *What Works Clearinghouse: Procedures and Standards Handbook, Version 3.0*, March 2014, ies.ed.gov/ncee/wwc/pdf/reference_resources/wwc_ procedures_v3_0_draft_standards_handbook.pdf.

14. Robert Murphy et al., *Blended Learning Report*, Michael and Susan Dell Foundation, 2014, http://5a03f68e230384a218e0-938ec019df699e606c950a5614b999bd.r33.cf2. rackcdn.com/MSDF-Blended-Learning-Report-May-2014.pdf.

15. Note that the WWC does produce "Practice Guides" aimed at providing educators with recommended strategies from the research base. These guides have a somewhat lower standard of evidence than other WWC reports; however, they focus on instructional strategies and not products. Thus, these reports are useful for product and service design, but provide little information on whether any particular product actually works.

16. For one account of the rise of A/B testing in web-based businesses see Brian Christian, "The A/B Test: Inside the Technology that Is Changing the Rules of Business," *Wired*, April 25, 2012, http://www.wired.com/2012/04/ff_abtesting/.

17. Office of Educational Technology, *Ed Tech Developer's Guide* (Washington, DC: US Department of Education, April 2015), 27, http://tech.ed.gov/files/2015/04/Developer-Toolkit.pdf; for a discussion of Khan Academy's approach, see Lynn Wang, "How Khan Academy Uses A/B Testing to Improve Student Learning," *Apptimize*, http://apptimize. com/blog/2014/07/how-khan-academy-uses-ab-testing-to-improve-student-learning/.

18. Tom Vander Ark, "Short Cycle Efficacy Trials Key to Personalized Learning," *Getting Smart*, December 24, 2013, http://gettingsmart.com/2013/12/ short-cycle-efficacy-trials-key-personalized-learning.

19. Note that this is different from the private sector, where impacts can be measured in dollars and profits or in user behaviors that the business values.

20. Martin West, unpublished presentation, 2010.

21. See, for instance, Thomas J. Kane, "Frustrated with the Pace of Progress in Education? Invest in Better Evidence," *The Brown Center Chalkboard*, March 5, 2015, http://www. brookings.edu/research/papers/2015/03/05-education-evidence-kane.

22. See, for instance, Jim Manzi, "The Experimental Revolution in Business," in *Uncontrolled: The Surprising Payoff to Trial-and-Error for Business, Politics, and Society* (New York: Basic Books, 2012): 143–168.

23. Donald Fagen, "I.G.Y. (What a Beautiful World)," on *The Nightfly*, Warner Bros. Records, 1982, compact disc.

Chapter 7

1. David Tyack and Larry Cuban, *Tinkering Toward Utopia: A Century of Public School Reform* (Cambridge, MA: Harvard University Press, 1995).

2. Elizabeth A. City, Richard F. Elmore, and Doug Lynch, "Redefining Education: The Future of Learning Is Not the Future of Schooling," in *The Futures of School Reform*, ed. Jal Mehta, Frederick M. Hess, and Robert B. Schwartz (Cambridge, MA: Harvard Education Press, 2012), 151–176.

3. Ted Kolderie, *The Split Screen Strategy: Improvement + Innovation* (Edina, MN: Beaver's Pond Press, Inc., 2014), http://www.educationevolving.org/pdf/Book-Innovation-Plus-Improvement.pdf.
4. Scott Murphy, "Future Protocol a.k.a. Back to the Future," School Reform Initiative, June 2008, http://schoolreforminitiative.org/doc/future.pdf.

Chapter 8

1. Carol Dweck, *Mindset: The New Psychology of Success* (New York: Ballantine Books, 2006).
2. Ibid.
3. Bahiy Watson, "1881 Institute," http://www.the1881school.org.
4. Kim Gibson, "NOLA Micro Schools," http://nolamicroschools.org.
5. Jonathan Johnson, "Rooted School," http://www.rootedschool.org.
6. Vera Triplett, "Noble Minds | Institute for Whole Child Learning," http://www.nobleminds.org.
7. 4.0 Schools, "4.0 Schools' Launch Program," http://4pt0.org/programs/launch.

Chapter 9

1. *Talking 'Bout Lead Generation: Selling Students to the Highest Bidders*, Noodle special report, January 13, 2015, https://www.noodle.com/articles/talking-bout-lead-generation-selling-students-to-the-highest-bidders.
2. C. A. E. Goodhart, "Money, Information, and Uncertainty" *AGRIS*, EBSCO*host* (accessed October 19, 2015).
3. Anya Kamenetz, *The Test: Why Our Schools Are Obsessed with Standardized Testing—But You Don't Have to Be* (New York: PublicAffairs, 2015), Kindle edition.
4. James Loewen, *Lies My Teacher Told Me: Everything Your American History Textbook Got Wrong* (New York: The New Press, 1995), Kindle edition.
5. Ibid.
6. Named in honor of Obi-Wan Kenobi's sage advice in *Star Wars IV*: "Your eyes can deceive you; don't trust them."
7. College Completion Report," KIPP, http://www.kipp.org/results/college-completion-report.
8. Ry Rivard, "Gauging Graduates' Well-Being," *Inside Higher Ed*, May 6, 2014, https://www.insidehighered.com/news/2014/05/06/gallup-surveys-graduates-gauge-whether-and-why-college-good-well-being.
9. "ASA Statement on Using Value-Added Models for Educational Assessment," April 8, 2014, http://www.scribd.com/doc/217916454/ASA-VAM-Statement-1.
10. Wayne Au, "High-Stakes Testing and Curricular Control: A Qualitative Metasynthesis," *Educational Researcher* 36 (2007): 258–267, doi:10.3102/0013189X07306523; Laura S. Hamilton, Brian M. Stecher, Julie A. Marsh et al., *Standards-Based Accountability Under No Child Left Behind: Experiences of Teachers and Administrators in Three States* (Santa Monica, CA: RAND, 2007), http://www.rand.org/content/dam/rand/pubs/monographs/2007/RAND_MG589.pdf.
11. Tom Loveless, *How Well Are American Students Learning?* (Washington, DC: Brookings Institution, February 2012), http://www.brookings.edu/~/media/research/files/reports/2012/2/brown-center/0216_brown_education_loveless.pdf.
12. Alden S. Blodget, "Brains and Schools: A Mismatch," *Education Week*, September 10, 2013, http://www.edweek.org/ew/articles/2013/09/11/03blodget.h33.html.

13. Nathaniel von der Embse and Ramzi Hasson, "Test Anxiety and High-Stakes Test Performance Between School Settings: Implications for Educators," *Preventing School Failure: Alternative Education for Children and Youth* 56 (2012): 180–187, doi:10.1080/10 45988X.2011.633285.

14. Joseph E. Stiglitz, "Asymmetries of Information and Economic Policy," *Project Syndicate*, December 4, 2001, http://www.project-syndicate.org/commentary/ asymmetries-of-information-and-economic-policy.

15. Michael Rothschild and Joseph Stiglitz, "Equilibrium in Competitive Insurance Markets: An Essay on the Economics of Imperfect Information," *Quarterly Journal of Economics* 90 (1976): 629–649, doi: 10.1007/978-94-015-7957-5_18.

16. "Report: What Do Parents Want From Colleges?" Noodle, January 9, 2015, https://www .noodle.com/articles/report-what-do-parents-want-from-colleges.

17. Steve Cohen, "A Perfect Storm Is Heading Toward Higher Education," *Time*, February 25, 2015, http://time.com/3720815/college-costs-parent-dissatisfaction/.

18. Kelly Andrews, "125 Influential People and Ideas," *Wharton Alumni Magazine*, March 2012, https://www.wharton.upenn.edu/125anniversaryissue/lynch.html.

19. "State by State Legislative Status," Benefit Corp Information Center, http://www .benefitcorp.net/state-by-state-legislative-status.

20. "Why B Corps Matter," https://www.bcorporation.net/what-are-b-corps/ why-b-corps-matter.

21. Clare McCann, "Transfer Students Are Losing Time and Money," *The Hill*, August 29, 2014, http://thehill.com/blogs/pundits-blog/ education/216210-transfer-students-are-losing-time-and-money.

22. Natasha Lomas, "Today in Creepy Privacy Policies," *TechCrunch*, February 8, 2015, http:// techcrunch.com/2015/02/08/telescreen/.

Chapter 10

1. The authors would like to thank Katrina Calixte, Nasir Qadree, and Edith Gummer for their invaluable contributions to this chapter.

2. Education Technology Industry Network, *2014 U.S. Education Technology Market: PreK–12 Report*, February 25, 2015, http://www.siia.net/Divisions/ETIN-Education-Technology-Industry-Network/Resources/ Webinars/2014-US-Education-Technology-Market-PreK–12-Report.

3. Ainsley O'Connell, "Edtech Funding Soars To Nearly $2 Billion," *Fast Company*, January 25, 2015, http://www.fastcompany.com/3040805/fast-feed/ edtech-funding-soars-to-nearly-2-billion.

4. Michele Molnar, "Ed-Tech Venture Capital Boom, and the K–12 Piece of the Pie: It's Complicated," *Education Week*, July 22, 2015.

5. Laura Colby, "News Corp. Is Winding Down School Tablet Sales," *Bloomberg*, June 26, 2015, http://www.bloomberg.com/news/articles/2015-06-26/ news-corp-said-to-wind-down-school-tablet-sales-as-buyers-balk.

6. Michele Molnar, "Pearson to Sell Financial Times and Focus Solely on 'Global Education Strategy,'" *Education Week*, July 23, 2015, http://blogs.edweek.org/edweek/ marketplacek12/2015/07/pearson_to_sell_financial_times_to_focus_solely_on_global_ education_strategy.html.

7. The Aspen Network of Development Entrepreneurs and Village Capital, *Bridging the 'Pioneer Gap': The Role of Accelerators in Launching High-Impact Enterprises*, June 3, 2013.

8. Jared Konczal, "Evaluating the Effects of Accelerators? Not So Fast," *Forbes*, August 8,

2012, http://www.forbes.com/sites/kauffman/2012/08/08/evaluating-the-effects-of-accelerators-not-so-fast/.

9. Dane Stangler and Jordan Bell-Masterson, *Four Indicators to Assess Local Ecosystem Vibrancy*, Ewing Marion Kauffman Foundation, March 2, 2015.

10. Goldie Blumenstyk, "U. of Phoenix Looks to Shrink Itself with New Admissions Requirements and Deep Cuts," *Chronicle of Higher Education*, June 30, 2015, http://chronicle.com/article/U-of-Phoenix-Looks-to-Shrink/231247/.

11. Salman Khan, "Let's Use Video to Reinvent Education," TED 2011, March 2011, http://www.ted.com/talks/salman_khan_let_s_use_video_to_reinvent_education?language=en.

12. Task Force on Federal Regulation of Higher Education, *Recalibrating Regulation of Colleges and Universities*, http://www.help.senate.gov/imo/media/Regulations_Task_Force_Report_2015_FINAL.pdf.

13. Frederick M. Hess, "Why Can't Politicians Get Out of Schooling?" *Rick Hess Straight Up* (blog), March 30, 2015.

14. See, e.g., Burck Smith, "Keeping College Within Reach: Improving Higher Education Through Innovation," testimony before the U.S. House of Representatives Education and the Workforce Committee, July 9, 2013, http://edworkforce.house.gov/uploadedfiles/smith_testimony_final.pdf.

15. US Department of Education, *Enhancing Education Through Technology (Ed-Tech) State Program*, http://www2.ed.gov/programs/edtech/index.html.

16. E.B. Boyd, "Edmodo, A 'Facebook for Schools,' Chalks Up API To Become Classroom Platform," *Fast Company*, March 6, 2012, http://www.fastcompany.com/1822900/edmodo-facebook-schools-chalks-api-become-classroom-platform.

17. Bill and Melinda Gates Foundation, "Teachers Know Best: Teachers' Views on Professional Development," April 2015, http://collegeready.gatesfoundation.org/wp-content/uploads/2015/04/Gates-PDMarketResearch-Dec5.pdf.

18. TNTP, "The Mirage: Confronting the Hard Truth About Our Quest for Teacher Development," August 4, 2015, http://tntp.org/publications/view/the-mirage-confronting-the-truth-about-our-quest-for-teacher-development.

Conclusion

1. Ellen Huet, "Uber Says It's Doing 1 Million Rides Per Day, 140 Million In Last Year," *Forbes*, December 17, 2014, http://www.forbes.com/sites/ellenhuet/2014/12/17/uber-says-its-doing-1-million-rides-per-day-140-million-in-last-year/.

2. Uber, "The Top 10 Facts You May Not Know About Uber Driver Partners," http://newsroom.uber.com/2015/08/the-top-10-facts-you-may-not-know-about-uber-driver-partners/.

3. Jonathan Hall, "New Study Finds Uber Cheaper, Faster, More Reliable For Lower-Income Neighborhoods in LA," Uber, http://newsroom.uber.com/2015/07/new-study-finds-uber-cheaper-faster-more-reliable-for-lower-income-neighborhoods-in-la/.

4. Joshua Brustein, "Uber and Lyft Fight Proposed NYC Rules—and Each Other," *Bloomberg Business*, May 28, 2015, http://www.bloomberg.com/news/articles/2015-05-28/uber-and-lyft-fight-proposed-nyc-rules-and-each-other.

Acknowledgments

For over ten years, we have been studying the role that entrepreneurship plays in education. At various times, we broached this topic with researchers, advocates, teachers, state education leaders, union representatives, and policymakers in private gatherings and at public events. In June 2015, we convened a public research conference at the American Enterprise Institute to discuss new papers we had commissioned on the subject. What resulted was a spirited dialogue that has raised as many important questions as it has answered.

The chapters collected here are the culmination of that discussion, each exploring an important component of the landscape of educational entrepreneurship. How does the K–12 system foster entrepreneurship? Where does it get in the way? The authors are researchers and practitioners who have been at the forefront of some of the most important entrepreneurial ventures of the past decade-plus.

We are indebted to all of those who have been involved in this project and pushed our thinking on these ideas, but we would like to especially thank the following discussants for providing outstanding and concentrated feedback during our June conference: Edith Gummer of the Kaufmann Foundation, Derrell Bradford of NYCAN, Deborah McGriff of the NewSchools Venture Fund, and Gerard Robinson of the American Enterprise Institute.

We are also indebted to the steadfast support provided by AEI and its president, Arthur Brooks. The Gates Foundation, the Templeton Foundation, and the Kaufmann Foundation generously provided financial support for this project, and we are deeply grateful for their involvement and encouragement throughout the process. We'd also like to thank the terrific staff at AEI, especially Sarah DuPre for her work managing and overseeing this project and coordinating the conference. Max Eden, Jenn Hatfield,

Elizabeth English, Rooney Columbus, and Isaac Woodward of AEI also provided key assistance during the conference and editing of the papers. Finally, we express our gratitude to the Harvard Education Press team, particularly our editor Caroline Chauncey, who offered skillful and timely guidance throughout the course of this project.

About the Editors

Frederick M. Hess is director of education policy studies at the American Enterprise Institute. An educator, political scientist, and author, he studies K–12 and higher education issues. His books include *The Cage-Busting Teacher* (Harvard Education Press, 2015), *Cage-Busting Leadership* (Harvard Education Press, 2013), *Breakthrough Leadership in the Digital Age* (Corwin, 2013), *The Same Thing Over and Over* (Harvard University Press, 2013), *Education Unbound* (ASCD, 2010), *Common Sense School Reform* (Palgrave Macmillan, 2006), *Revolution at the Margins* (Brookings Institution Press, 2002), and *Spinning Wheels* (Brookings Institution Press, 1998). He is also the author of the popular Education Week blog *Rick Hess Straight Up* and is a regular contributor to *The Hill* and *National Review Online*. Hess's work has appeared in scholarly and popular outlets such as *Teachers College Record, Harvard Education Review, Social Science Quarterly, Urban Affairs Review, American Politics Quarterly, Chronicle of Higher Education, Phi Delta Kappan, Educational Leadership, U.S. News & World Report, USA Today, Washington Post, New York Times, Wall Street Journal, The Atlantic,* and *National Affairs*. His edited volumes include *Educational Entrepreneurship: Realities, Challenges, Opportunities* (Harvard Education Press, 2006), *The Future of Educational Entrepreneurship: Possibilities for School Reform* (Harvard Education Press, 2008), and *Private Enterprise and Public Education* (Teachers College Press, 2013). Hess serves as executive editor of Education Next, as lead faculty member for the Rice Education Entrepreneurship Program, and on the review board for the Broad Prize for Public Charter Schools. He also serves on the boards of directors of the National Association of Charter School Authorizers and 4.0 Schools. A former high school social studies teacher, he teaches or has taught at the University of Virginia, University of Pennsylvania, Georgetown University, Rice University, and Harvard University.

Michael Q. McShane is director of education policy at the Show-Me Institute and an adjunct fellow in education policy studies at the American Enterprise Institute. He is the author of *Education and Opportunity* (AEI Press 2014). He edited *New and Better Schools* (Rowman and Littlefield, 2015) and coedited *Teacher Quality 2.0* (Harvard Education Press, 2014) and *Common Core Meets Education Reform* (Teachers College Press, 2013). His commentary has been published in outlets such as *USA Today, Washington Post,* and *Huffington Post.* He has also been featured in education-specific outlets including *Teachers College Commentary, Education Week, Phi Delta Kappan,* and *Education Next.* His academic and policy work has been published in *Education Finance and Policy, Journal of School Choice, National Affairs,* and numerous white papers. He is a former high school teacher.

About the Contributors

John Bailey is the vice president of policy and executive director of Digital Learning Now! He cofounded Whiteboard Advisors, which provides strategic consulting for investors, entrepreneurs, and philanthropies. Bailey previously served at the White House as special assistant to the president for domestic policy during the Bush administration, where he coordinated education and labor policy. He has also worked at the Bill and Melinda Gates Foundation and was a top technology and innovation adviser to the secretary of commerce. Bailey served as the nation's second director of educational technology, where he oversaw more than $1 billion in annual grants and research projects.

Ross Baird is the founder and executive director of Village Capital, which finds, trains, and funds entrepreneurs solving major global challenges. Over the past five years, Village Capital has supported more than five hundred entrepreneurs in health, education, energy, agriculture, and financial inclusion through programs worldwide and has invested in fifty entrepreneurs through an affiliated fund. Enterprises funded by Village Capital have created seven thousand jobs and raised more than $100 million. Before founding Village Capital, Baird worked with First Light Ventures, a seed-stage venture fund, and in the development of four education-related start-up ventures.

Matt Candler is the founder and CEO of 4.0 Schools (4pt0.org), an incubator of new schools, start-ups, and start-up communities. To date, 4.0 has created forty-three organizations by finding, coaching, and connecting aspiring founders across the United States. Candler began his career teaching at Casady School in Oklahoma City, Oklahoma. He then returned to his hometown, Atlanta, to help stage the 1996 Olympics as a member of the chief operations officer's office. Following the Games, Candler helped local groups start charter schools throughout the southeastern United States. He also served as founding co-principal of a K–8 school in North Carolina. In 2001, Candler joined KIPP Foundation, where his team established thirty-seven new schools across the United States. In 2004, he moved to New York City to help found the first citywide charter school incubator in the nation. Since inception, the NYC Charter Center has helped the charter sector grow from 24 schools to more than 197, serving more than eighty-three thousand students. In 2006, he moved to New Orleans to serve as the first CEO of New Schools for New Orleans, the nation's first school reform "harbormaster." He also served as chairman of the Louisiana Association of Public Charter Schools, helping it recover after Hurricane Katrina to become one of the most effective charter advocacy and policy shops in the United States.

Stacey Childress is the CEO of NewSchools Venture Fund. Before joining NewSchools, she led the K–12 Next Generation Learning team at the Bill and Melinda Gates Foundation, investing in schools and technologies that support personalized learning for US middle and high school students. Before that, she was on the faculty of the Harvard Business School, where she wrote and taught about entrepreneurial activity in public education in the United States. Early in her career, she taught in a Texas public high school.

Elizabeth City is lecturer on education and director of the Doctor of Education Leadership program at the Harvard Graduate School of Education. City has served as a teacher, instructional coach, principal, and consultant. She has authored or coauthored many publications, including *Meeting Wise: Making the Most of Collaborative Time for Educators* (Harvard Education Press, 2014), *Data Wise, Revised and Expanded Edition: A Step-by-Step Guide to Using Assessment Results to Improve Teaching and Learning* (Harvard Education Press, 2013), *Strategy in Action: How School Systems Can Support Powerful Learning and Teaching* (Harvard Education Press, 2009), *Instructional Rounds in Education: A Network Approach to Improving Teaching and Learning* (Harvard Education Press, 2009), and *Resourceful Leadership: Tradeoffs and Tough Decisions on the Road to School Improvement* (Harvard Education Press, 2008).

Jon Fullerton is the executive director of the Center for Educational Policy Research at Harvard University. He has extensive experience working with policymakers and executives in designing and implementing organizational change and improvements. Before coming to Harvard, Fullerton served as the Board of Education's director of budget and financial policy for the Los Angeles Unified School District. From 2002 to 2005, he was vice president of strategy, evaluation, research, and policy at the Urban Education Partnership in Los Angeles, where he worked with policymakers to ensure that they focused on high-impact educational strategies.

Ashley Jochim is a research analyst at the Center on Reinventing Public Education. Her work can be found in the *Policy Studies Journal, Politics and Governance,* and *Political Research Quarterly,* as well as numerous edited volumes, including *Handbook of Research on School Choice* (Routledge, 2009) and *The Oxford Handbook of American Bureaucracy* (Oxford University Press, 2010).

John Katzman is the founder and CEO of The Noodle Companies, an education enterprise focused on improving transparency and efficiency in education. Previously, Katzman founded 2U and served as its CEO and chairman until 2012. 2U works with major research universities to create high-quality online degree programs. Before founding 2U, Katzman founded The Princeton Review and served as its CEO and chairman until 2007. His writing has been featured in the *Washington Post, The Atlantic,* and MSNBC; he has authored or coauthored five books; and he is a frequent lecturer and panelist. He sits on the board of directors of several for- and nonprofit organizations, including the National Association of Independent Schools, the Woodrow Wilson Foundation, the National Alliance of Public Charter Schools, and Renaissance Learning. He has also advised or invested in dozens of education tech organizations.

Daniel Lautzenheiser is a senior analyst at the Boston Consulting Group, focusing on education. In this role, he works with education organizations ranging from K–12 school districts to universities on strategy and organizational issues. Previously, he was the program manager of AEI's education policy studies department. During that time, he worked closely with scholars on a range of pre-K through higher education issues, including editing research papers on diverse topics such as the rising cost of higher education and the federal role in K–12 schools. He also served as a researcher on two iterations of the US Chamber of Commerce's seminal *Leaders and Laggards* reports. He has written on a wide variety of subjects ranging from charter schooling to digital learning to higher education innovation, with his work appearing in *Education Week*, the *Huffington Post*, and *National Review*.

Dmitri Mehlhorn is a partner at Vidinovo. Previously, he served as president of Bloomberg BNA Legal, a Virginia-based division of Bloomberg LP. Before that, he spent seven years as the managing director at Gerson Lehrman Group, where his responsibilities included global research management, new market sales, and legal/regulatory affairs. He has also played a role in educational advocacy, helping found Hope Street Group, a 501(c)(3), a national nonprofit focused on centrist innovation in healthcare and education; StudentsFirst, a 501(c)(4) focused on K–12 educational performance; and the Great New England Public School Alliance, a group funded by Michael Bloomberg and focused on electoral advocacy in New England.

Marc S. Tucker is the president and chief executive officer of the National Center on Education and the Economy. Tucker served in the 1970s as the associate director of the National Institute of Education, in charge of the nation's government-funded research on education policy. He then created the Carnegie Forum on Education and the Economy at Carnegie Corporation of New York, and authored its report *A Nation Prepared: Teachers for the 21st Century*. He led the Carnegie Forum team as it created the National Board for Professional Teaching Standards and served as the board's first president. Tucker then founded the National Center on Education and the Economy and, in that role, created the Commission on the Skills of the American Workforce, the New Commission on the Skills of the American Workforce, the New Standards Consortium, America's Choice (a comprehensive school reform program), the National Institute for School Leadership, and Excellence for All (a high school reform program). He was appointed by President Clinton to the National Skills Standards Board. He has been author, coauthor, or editor of many articles and several books and reports, including, *America's Choice: High Skills or Low Wages!*, *Standards for Our Schools: How to Set Them, Measure Them, and Reach Them*, *Thinking for a Living: Education and the Wealth of Nations*, *The Principal Challenge*, and *Tough Choices or Tough Times*. He has also testified frequently before the US Congress and state legislatures.

Jillian Youngblood is the vice president of insights for Noodle, an education enterprise focused on improving transparency and efficiency in education. She has authored and coauthored a number of reports and white papers on topics such as predatory lead generation in higher education, trends in the college admissions landscape, and parent satisfaction with colleges. She is a frequent writer and speaker on all things education, with an emphasis on K–12 school choice, college admissions, and learning disabilities. Previously, she worked in the Bloomberg administration, where she managed New York City's federal and state legislative portfolios on public health, and on Capitol Hill, where she was a lead staffer for the 9/11 Health and Compensation Act.

Index

A/B testing, 116–118, 119
accountability for schools. *see also*
    NCLB; performance; testing
  for charter schools, 45
  evidence needed for, 106–107
  inauthentic measures for, 161–164
  policy affecting, 23, 46–48
  policy supporting, 67–68
  test-based, 46, 49, 200
Achievement First, 26, 33
administrators. *see* school leaders
Advantage Schools, 19
AltSchool, 59, 93–94
Aspire Public Schools, 20
assessment. *see* evaluation of
    entrepreneurial outcomes; testing
authorizers for charter schools, 21,
    44, 45, 67

B Corps (benefit corporations), 172
Blended Learning Report (Michael &
    Susan Dell Foundation), 115–116
Bridge the Gap, 148
Broad Residency, 25

capital. *see* financial considerations
carrots (incentives), 36, 37, 63–64
CCSS (Common Core State
    Standards), 23, 29,
    37–40, 165–166
Center for Research on Education
    Outcomes (CREDO), 21

Chancellor Beacon Academies, 19
charter management organization
    (CMO), 18–20, 115–116
Charter School Growth Fund
    (CSGF), 20
charter schools, 16–22. *see also*
    school (parent) choice; Tiny
    Schools Project
  authorizers for, 21, 44, 45, 67
  citywide performance
    influenced by, 21–22
  funding of, compared to district
    schools, 44
  history of, 16–17, 58
  market share of, 17–18
  multisite school networks for, 18–20
Charter Schools USA (CSUSA), 19
Class Wallet, 31
Clever, 30
CMO (charter management
    organization), 18–20, 115–116
Common Core State Standards
    (CCSS), 23, 29, 37–40, 165–166
Common Sense Media, 113–114
competition
  arguments for and against,
    95–99, 103
  compared to best fit, 157
  between district and charter
    schools, 44
ConnectEDU, 2
convenings, 141

costs for entrepreneurs. *see also*
    funding for entrepreneurs
  of evaluating products, 112
  Internet distribution and supply
    chains, 55–56
  launching start-ups, 56–57
  for multisite school networks, 18
costs for students. *see* funding
    for students
course access policies, 58–59
CREDO (Center for Research on
    Education Outcomes), 21
CSGF (Charter School
    Growth Fund), 20
CSUSA (Charter Schools USA), 19

digital learning, 53–54. *see also*
    technology
  funding policies for, 70–74
  lack of credit and recognition
    for, 61, 74
  limitations of, 100–101
  models for, supporting, 67–68
district leadership. *see* school leaders
district schools. *see also* school
    (parent) choice; school system
  funding of, compared to charter
    schools, 44
  performance of, 21–22, 32, 162
Duolingo, 59

E Corps (education corporations),
    172–174, 206–207
Edison Learning, 19
Edmodo, 30
EdReports, 113–114
educational entrepreneurship,
    3–4, 15–16, 36
  challenges of, 59–66, 199–200
  combining with system
    reform, 135–136
  compared to system reform, 5–6
  cultivating, 66–75
  equity in, 137–138

favorable conditions for, 53–59
  funding for, 7, 14, 77–94
  growth of, reasons for, 13–15
  history of, 1–2, 11–34, 177–179
  impact of, evaluating. *see* evaluation
    of entrepreneurial outcomes
  implementing in
    classroom, 125–142
  incentives for, 6
  integrating into the school system,
    179, 187–189
  policy affecting, 6–7, 35–51
  receptibility of school system
    to, 126–135
  scalability of, 14–15, 145–146
  social aspect of, 14, 15–16
  starting small, 145–156,
    201–202, 206
  trends in, 178–196
  value of, 4
education corporations (E Corps),
    172–174, 206–207
education management organization
    (EMO), 18–20
education savings account
    (ESA), 58–59, 72
education system. *see* school system
education technology. *see* technology
Education Trust, 24
efficacy, evaluating. *see* evaluation of
    entrepreneurial outcomes
1881 Institute, 153
Elementary and Secondary Education
    Act (ESEA), 40
EMO (education management
    organization), 18–20
EngageNY, 38
Enriched Schools, 2
entrepreneurs
  characteristics of, 3, 7–8, 12, 15,
    136, 143–144
  developing, 139–141, 146–148
  evaluating products, motivation for,
    107–108, 123–124

evaluating products, participation in, 122–123
examples of, 12–14
insularity of, 201
parents as, 139
recommendations for, 205–206
as reformers, 202–203
school leaders as, 139
students as, 138
teachers as, 138–139
entrepreneurship, educational. *see* educational entrepreneurship
equity, 137–138
ESA (education savings account), 58–59, 72
ESEA (Elementary and Secondary Education Act), 40
evaluation of entrepreneurial outcomes, 3, 10, 105–124. *see also* testing
benefits of, 123–124
A/B testing, 116–118, 119
importance of, 106–107
lacking, reasons for, 110–113
learning network, 118–124
limitations of, 124
negative metrics/criteria for, 160–164
reviews, 113–114, 119
stakeholders in, 107–110
success metrics/criteria for, 79, 82–83, 84–85, 86, 88–90, 159–160, 168–169, 179, 191–194, 200, 205
What Works Clearinghouse (WWC), 114–116, 119
Expeditionary Learning, 38

Family Educational Rights and Privacy Act (FERPA), 62
FERPA (Family Educational Rights and Privacy Act), 62
financial considerations. *see* costs for entrepreneurs; funding for entrepreneurs

for-profit entrepreneurs
B Corps (benefit corporations), 172
E Corps (education corporations), 172–174, 206–207
EMO (education management organization), 18–20
policies biased against, 64–66
priorities of, 171–172
success of, compared to nonprofits, 158–159
trends in, 178–196
for-profit schools, 93–94
4.0 Schools, 143, 145–155
Framework for Teaching (Danielson), 41
funding for entrepreneurs, 181–182. *see also* costs for entrepreneurs
for education technology, 28–29
performance-based, 70–72
philanthropists, 14, 54–55, 70, 84–86, 87
policies regarding, 70–74
procurement of, 7, 62–63, 67
R&D investments, 69–70
recommendations for, 205
venture capital, 77–94
funding for students
ESA (education savings account), 58–59, 72
MPOWER, 186

Gallup and Purdue, 162–163, 166, 171
General Assembly, 59
government policy. *see* policy

hybrid investment vehicles, 91

IIS (Instructional Improvement Systems), 29
InBloom, 2
incentives (carrots), 36, 37, 63–64
incubators, 57
incumbent protections, 59–60

innovation
  arguments against, 99–103
  arguments for, 95–98
  change-averse attitudes
    stifling, 78–81, 84
  cultivating, 66–75
  failure rate of, 79, 82, 199–200, 208
  integrating into the school system,
    100, 101–103, 167–169
  success metrics needed for, 79,
    82–83, 84–85
institutional-based systems, 61
Instructional Improvement
  Systems (IIS), 29
instructional materials, 38–39
international schools, performance of,
  96–98, 99–100, 102
Internet. *see also* digital learning
  distribution and supply chains
    using, 55–56
  start-up costs using, 56–57

K¹² virtual schooling company, 94
Khan Academy, 1, 30
KIPP (Knowledge Is Power Program)
  charter schools, 1, 13, 20, 26, 162

learning network, 118–124
LearnZillion, 30–31
Li'l Stories, 148–149
limited-profit LLC, 206–207
Los Angeles Unified School District, 2

marketplace, education system as,
  157–158, 166–176
Marzano Teacher
  Evaluation Model, 41
MPOWER, 186
multisite school networks, 18–20
Musk, Elon, 65–66

NAEP (National Assessment
  of Educational Progress),
  22, 165–166

National Association of Charter
  School Authorizers, 45
National Council on Teacher Quality
  (NCTQ), 40
National Heritage
  Academies (NHA), 19
NCLB (No Child Left Behind),
  13, 23, 46
NCTQ (National Council on Teacher
  Quality), 40
Nearpod, 31
NewSchools Venture Fund, 20, 28
News Corp, 28
New Teacher Center (NTC), 25–26
NHA (National Heritage
  Academies), 19
Noble Minds Institute, 153–154
No Child Left Behind (NCLB),
  13, 23, 46
NOLA Micro Schools, 153–154
nonprofit entrepreneurs
  CMO (charter management
    organization), 18–20, 115–116
  success of, compared to
    nonprofits, 158–159
NTC (New Teacher Center), 25–26

online learning. *see* digital learning
outcomes. *see* evaluation of
  entrepreneurial outcomes;
  performance
outside learning. *see* digital learning
Owl Ventures, 28–29

parents
  as entrepreneurs, 139
  evaluation of entrepreneurial
    outcomes needed by, 109–110
  school choice by, 58–59, 86, 89,
    98–99, 160–161, 169–171, 203
Partnership for Assessment of
  Readiness for College and
  Careers, 29
Pearson, 28

performance
of district schools, influenced by
charter schools, 21–22, 32
of education innovations, funding
based on, 70–72
as success metric, 86, 88–90, 168–
169, 179, 191–194, 200, 205
of teachers and school leaders,
22–26, 40–43
persuasion (sermons), 37
philanthropists, 14, 54–55, 70,
84–86, 87, 90–91
pipelines for teachers and school
leaders, 24–25
policy, 35–51
biases against for-profit
entrepreneurs, 64–66
CCSS (Common Core
State Standards), 23, 29,
37–40, 165–166
charter schools affected by, 43–46
course access policies, 58–59
Elementary and Secondary
Education Act (ESEA), 40
future goals and challenges of,
48–51, 190–191
incentives (carrots), 36, 37
incentives, misaligned, 63–64
incumbent protections
affecting, 59–60
innovation, supporting by, 66–75
NCLB (No Child Left Behind),
13, 23, 46
persuasion (sermons), 37
Race to the Top (RTTT), 23, 29, 40
regulations (sticks), 36, 61–63,
67–68, 207
school accountability
affected by, 46–48
teacher evaluation affected by, 40–43
technology growth
affected by, 29–30
working with, 189–191
policymakers

evaluation of entrepreneurial
outcomes needed by, 110
recommendations for, 49–51, 66–68,
70–74, 206–207
PRI (program-related investment), 70
principals. *see* school leaders
procurement system, 62–63, 67
professional development, 25–26, 42
program-related investment (PRI),
70
providers of education
blended learning, 115–116
digital learning, 53–54, 67–68,
70–74, 100–101
transferring learning credit
between, 74
public policy. *see* policy

R&D investments, 69–70
Race to the Top (RTTT), 23, 29, 40
RCT (randomized controlled trial),
116. *see also* A/B testing
reciprocity agreements, 67–68
regulations (sticks), 36, 61–63,
67–68, 207
Relay Graduate School of
Education, 25–26
Rethink fund, 28–29
reviews, as evaluation tool,
113–114, 119
Rooted School, 153–154
RTTT (Race to the Top), 23, 29, 40

SBAC (Smarter Balanced Assessment
Consortium), 29, 39
scalability, 14–15, 145–146. *see also*
multisite school networks
school (parent) choice
driving educational
entrepreneurship, 58–59, 203
as success metric, 86, 89, 98–99
transparency in, 160–161, 169–171
school boards, empowering, 21
SchoolDude, 2

School Improvement Grants
(SIGs), 46
school leaders
effectiveness of, 21–22
as entrepreneurs, 139
evaluation of entrepreneurial
outcomes needed by, 108–109
performance of, improving, 22–26
pipelines for, 24–25
Schoolnet, 28
school system. *see also* charter
schools; district schools
change-averse nature of, 78–81, 204
improvements to, combining with
entrepreneurship, 135–136
as marketplace, 157–158, 166–176
receptibility to
entrepreneurship, 126–135
reforming, compared to educational
entrepreneurship, 5–6
United States, compared to other
countries, 96–98
sermons (persuasion), 37
Share My Lesson, 39
SIGs (School Improvement
Grants), 46
Smarter Balanced Assessment
Consortium (SBAC), 29, 39
social entrepreneurship, 14, 15–16
sticks (regulations), 36, 61–63,
67–68, 207
students. *see also* school
(parent) choice
as entrepreneurs, 138
funding for, 58–59, 72, 186
performance of, evaluating, 23

teachers, 91–94
empowering, by investors, 92
as entrepreneurs, 92–93, 138–
139, 140–141
evaluation of entrepreneurial
outcomes needed by, 108–109

performance of, evaluating,
23–24, 40–43
performance of, improving, 22–26
pipelines for, 24–25
preparation for, 42–43
professional development for,
25–26, 42, 194–195
Teachers Pay Teachers, 31
teachers' unions, 93
Teach For America (TFA), 1,
12, 24, 57
technology, 2, 26–31. *see also*
digital learning
business models for, 30
educational market needs met
by, 28, 31
financial resources for, 28–29
policies affecting, 29–30
role in entrepreneurship, 136
spending on, 26–27
teacher evaluation tools, 40–42
teacher expertise used in, 30–31
transferring, 74
trends in, 27–28
*10 Elements of High Quality Digital
Learning* (Foundation for
Excellence in Education), 67
testing. *see also* evaluation of
entrepreneurial outcomes
assessment services, 39
A/B testing, 116–118, 119
limitations of, 160, 161, 168, 200
test-based accountability, 46, 49,
200
TFA (Teach For America), 1,
12, 24, 57
The New Teacher Project. *see* TNTP
Tiny Schools Project, 149–156
Title I School Improvement Grants
(SIGs), 46
TNTP (formerly The New Teacher
Project), 24
trusted learning environments, 68–69

Uber, 197–198, 207–208
unCommon Construction, 148
Uncommon Schools, 20, 26
U.S. News & World Report, 161, 171
UTRU (Urban Teacher Residencies
    United), 25

venture capital, 77–94
    challenges of, in school system,
        78–81, 84–86
    characteristics of, 81–82
    entrepreneurial talent needed for,
        87
    hybrid investment vehicles for, 91
    philanthropic sector of,
        84–86, 87, 90–91

political constituencies
    influencing, 87
positive developments in, 86–87
possible backlash in, 87–88
private sector of, 86, 87, 91–94
recommendations for, 88–94
specialization by, 82–83
success metrics needed for, 79,
    82–83, 84–85, 86, 88–90
virtual learning. *see* digital learning

WGen (Wireless Generation), 28
WWC (What Works Clearinghouse),
    114–116, 119, 167

Yang Camp, 149